YES
TO
LIFE

YES
TO
LIFE

MEMOIRS OF

CORLISS LAMONT

HORIZON PRESS

NEW YORK

ACKNOWLEDGMENTS

The author wishes to thank the following persons, publishers and institutions, holding copyright on the works or quotations specified, for permission to reprint:

Paul H. Beattie, for the excerpt from his essay "The Prospect for Humanism"; *The Churchman*, for the excerpt from Robert Johansen's essay in the February, 1981 issue; Mrs. Daniel Cory, for the quotations from the writings of George Santayana; The Center for Dewey Studies, University of Southern Illinois, and Rare Book and Manuscript Library of Columbia University for the two letters from John Dewey to the author; the Estate of Albert Einstein, for the use of Einstein's letter of May 16, 1953 to William Frauenglass; *Free Mind* (a publication of the American Humanist Association) and Edward Lamb, for his statement in the Jan.-Feb. 1976 issue; John Kenneth Galbraith, for the statements quoted in Chapter XVIII; Katharine Hepburn, for unpublished letters to the author; Gerald Larue, for the excerpt from an unpublished letter to the author; Anne Morrow Lindbergh, for unpublished letters to the author; McMaster University, The Bertrand Russell Archives, Res.-Lib. 1981, for the three unpublished Russell letters to the author; The Mercantile-Safe Deposit and Trust Company, Baltimore, Maryland, Trustee under the Will of Henry L. Mencken, for the unpublished letter to the author; *The New York Times Magazine*, for quotation from James Reston's article in the December 31, 1978 issue © 1978 by The New York Times Company; Pantheon Books, a Division of Random House, Inc., for the quotation from *Gift From the Sea* by Anne Morrow Lindbergh; Prometheus Books, for the excerpt from *Humanist Ethics*, Morris B. Storer (ed.); Norman Rosten, for the unpublished poem, "The Ballad of Mount Snow."

In addition, I want to thank heartily Marcia Bradley, my research assistant, Virginia Marberry and Joyce Rose, my secretary, for their valuable work on the manuscript. And I am especially grateful to Ben Raeburn, Editor of Horizon Press, for his careful and creative editing of the book.

—C. L.

Correction:

Page 103: In paragraph 3 the fifth and sixth lines were to have been corrected by the typesetters, to read as follows:

the capitalist system. The U.S. Customs seized these posters and held them as seditious. The National Council on Freedom from Censorship,

To My Beloved Children and Grandchildren

Contents

Photographs

following page 128

Foreword

Friends told me when I was in my late seventies that it was time for me to write my autobiography. I thought they were right. Instead, however, of offering the story of my life as it has unfolded from year to year, I have followed a method quite common these days, giving an account of my pursuits and experiences in key episodes and highlights that ought to show what kind of person I am. I have omitted descriptions of activities and interests that on reflection seemed minor.

I have had little recourse to my twenty four-drawer files containing hundreds of letters and important documents. My correspondence over sixty years, including love letters, would make another book, but I am not sure this would be really worthwhile.

In these *Memoirs* I have not dealt in detail with the intimacies of my family life, whether they have involved parents, wives or children, because of the wish for privacy. I have often been appalled at the extent to which the media "reveal" on the slightest pretext the sexual behavior not only of well-known people, but of anyone and everyone. However, in this volume I do give my views on sex relations and marriage.

In composing these *Memoirs*, I have drawn occasionally on my earlier books and articles, correcting serious errors and rewriting to bring out the full significance of events. Particularly helpful to me have been my *Basic Pamphlets*, a series of essays on fundamental national and international problems, started in the early Fifties and continuing through 1979. This volume of *Memoirs* concludes with events throughout 1980.

—C.L.

Chapter I FAMILY BACKGROUND

It is a wonder that I was ever born and so able to write this book. For in the bloodthirsty clan wars that ravaged Scotland century after century, the Clan Lamont, from which I am descended and which had its origin in the thirteenth century, came close to being exterminated. During the tumultuous seventeenth century the cruel and powerful Campbell Clan in 1636 swept down on the vastly outnumbered Lamonts, whose lands were situated on the west coast of Scotland, near Glasgow, and laid siege to their castles Toward and Ascog. The Campbells unloosed their artillery and at one point a cannon ball "crashed through the castle wall [of Toward] into the room where the principal people were dining, and knocked the joint out of the butler's hands as he was bringing it in" (*True Relation of Sir James Lamont of that Ilk, His Actings and Sufferings*, c. 1661).

Soon after this episode the Lamonts of both Toward and Ascog castles concluded that their situation was hopeless and surrendered under articles of honorable capitulation that promised them safe conduct and liberty to depart for another part of the country. The treacherous Campbells, however, immediately seized the Lamonts marching out of the castles, killed in cold blood a number of women and children and took the men in boats to the nearby city of Dunoon. According to *True Relation,* "There in the churchyard they most cruelly murthered, without assyse or order of law by shotts, by durks, by cutting their throats, as they doe with beasts, above one hundred, and lastly they hanged on one tree thirty and six at one tyme of the chiefs and speciall gentlemen of that name [Lamont], and before they were half hanged they cutt them downe and threw them in by dozens in pitts prepared for the same; and many of them striving to ryse upon their feet were violently holden downe until that by throwing the earth in great quantity upon them they were stifled to death."[1]

I have visited the city of Dunoon twice and, as a loyal member of today's Clan Lamont Society, have looked with sadness on the impressive memo-

rial stone of grey granite that bears testimony to the clan warfare and to the
Lamonts' unfortunate part in it. A bronze tablet at the base of the monu-
ment reads:

> To the memory of their loyal forefathers who perished near this
> spot, the Clan Lamont dedicate this monument September 1, 1906.
> During the civil wars of the 17th century the Lamonts espoused the
> Royalist cause, thereby incurring the hostility of the neighboring clans
> who laid siege to the castles of Toward and Ascog. Sir James Lamont of
> that ilk was forced to surrender at Toward on 3rd June, 1646, when in
> violation of the articles of capitulation and indemnity signed by the
> besiegers, over 200 of the Lamonts were bound and carried in boats to
> Dunoon and there murdered.

Musing over this shocking massacre, I have wondered how any Scottish
Lamonts survived and am happy that a number of them were able to
emigrate to Northern Ireland (Ulster). As the Lamonts were a sturdy folk
and migrated to many different countries, it is not surprising that some of
the more adventurous Scotch-Irish Lamonts in Northern Ireland decided
to cross the ocean to America. The widowed Mrs. John Lamont and her
three sons, Archibald, John and Robert, sailed across the Atlantic about
1750 and settled in North Hillsdale, New York. Robert Lamont (1726-89),
my great grandfather, had three sons and a daughter and was the American
progenitor of my branch of the Lamont family; his gravestone can still be
seen in the North Hillsdale cemetery. His son William (1756-1852) served
as an American soldier in the Revolutionary War.

On my mother's side of the family, I had an ancestor who also fought for
the cause of independence in the Revolutionary War. He was Elihu Corliss, who took part in the Battle of Bunker Hill. My mother, Florence
Corliss Lamont, had as a lineal ancestor William Bradford (1589-1657) who
sailed to America with the Pilgrims on the ship *Mayflower* in 1620 and later
became the able Governor of the Plymouth Colony for many years. He was
one of my grandfathers eight generations back. My mother's brother
Charles Corliss was married to the American novelist Anne Parrish.

I am not trying to trace the lives of my ancestors in any detail, but want to
give a brief picture of who they were, where they lived and what they did. I
have a feeling of profound piety towards my forebears and am proud that
the Lamonts had the strength of character and intelligence to survive
successfully seven centuries of grave vicissitudes and constant ordeals. The
Lamonts in colonial days and in the United States after the War of Independence were honest, average, hard-working and usually religious members
of society. They rated as good citizens. It was only at the beginning of the
twentieth century that a few of the Lamonts attained a measure of promi-
nence in the American community.

My uncle, Hammond Lamont (1864-1909), my father's elder brother,
was a brilliant teacher of English at Harvard and Brown Universities. Later

the Managing Editor of the *New York Evening Post* for six years and Editor
of *The Nation* for three, he was the first genuine liberal in the Lamont
family. At the height of his career, he died at forty-five after an operation
from which he never recovered consciousness. It was a prime example of
the tragedy of premature death.

My father, Thomas W. Lamont (1870-1948), son of a Methodist minister
of slender means in upper New York State, tells about his early youth in his
delightful book, *My Boyhood in a Parsonage.* After his graduation from
Phillips Exeter Academy in 1888 and Harvard College in 1892, he started
to work as a newspaper reporter on *The New York Tribune*, but soon turned
to business and finance. In 1911 Father became a partner in J. P. Morgan &
Co., the leading banking firm in the United States, and in 1943 Chairman
of the Board.

After the United States entered World War I in 1917, he went to
England and France in November of that year as an unofficial adviser to
President Wilson's Government Mission headed by Colonel E. M. House.
During this trip Father came to know a number of the British and French
leaders in the Allied war effort; and also consulted with his old friend and
Phillips Exeter classmate, Colonel William B. Thompson, head of the
American Red Cross Mission to Russia, about how to bring about better
relations between the new Soviet Government and the Allies. At a luncheon in London with Prime Minister Lloyd George, Thompson and Father
convinced him that limited cooperation with Lenin's regime might keep
the Soviets in the war against Germany.

Thompson and Father returned to New York on Christmas Day, 1917,
and a few days later went to Washington to persuade President Wilson to
take a more moderate attitude towards the Soviet Union. Wilson refused
even to see them and a few months later ordered an American expedition-
ary force along with the armies of Britain, France, Japan and lesser nations
to invade the U.S.S.R. But the Communist regime prevailed over all the
interventionist forces. Father later commented: "Of all the essays that
sober statesmen have ever been guilty of, that of attempting in the spring of
1918 to overturn the Soviet Government (which by that time had control
over vast millions of Russians and of the regions they occupied) was, as we
look back, the maddest." So it was that my father took a vital interest in
Soviet Russia long before I did and when I was still a schoolboy.

In January 1919 Father was back in Europe to serve for five months as a
representative of the United States Treasury at the Paris Peace Conference. He worked hard over the economic problems facing the Conference,
particularly those concerned with the controversial German reparations,
and came into close contact with most of the leading diplomats at the
Conference.

Father had wide cultural and educational interests, serving on the
governing boards of Phillips Exeter and Harvard, and becoming a trustee
of the Carnegie Foundation for the Advancement of Teaching, the Metro-

politan Museum of Art and the American School of Classical Studies. His
individual philanthropies were generous and innumerable. In 1918 he
bought the liberal *New York Evening Post,* but, unable to make a financial
success of it and finding that it took too much time from his business
interests, he sold it after a few years.

Father's friends and associates were not solely in the field of finance, but
came from many other spheres, notably those of literature and art. Both he
and my mother, a Smith graduate, were highly cultured and socially
sensitive. They were a good-looking couple, ever warm and lively compan-
ions, had hosts of friends, and were particularly fond of England and the
English. They made their house at 107 East 70th Street in New York City a
sort of "International Inn" where authors, poets and statesmen could find a
quiet homelike atmosphere. Visitors included England's Poet Laureate
John Masefield, poet Walter de la Mare, dramatists John Drinkwater and
Robert Nichols, and novelists John Galsworthy, Charles Morgan and H. G.
Wells. Lord Robert Cecil and Marshal Jan Christiaan Smuts of South Africa
were also occasional guests. I was often at dinner when such persons were
present and drank in the fascinating conversation, even daring to take part
in the table-talk myself.

One evening when we were going into dinner Mr. Nichols put his hand
on my shoulder in a friendly way and remarked, "I know how hard it is for
you, Corliss, to have such a famous father." My immediate response was,
"Why, I have never had any such feeling at all. I admire my father and am
proud of him."

In a letter to my mother in 1942 Marshal Smuts wrote: "There is no
doubt that your house is an international meeting place, and an influence
for good, for international understanding and conciliation, second to none
in the wide world." Of course, conversing with and listening to my parents'
stimulating visitors made a significant contribution to my education.

Outside of my immediate family, two relatives were of primary importance for my education—Uncle Jack (John Palmer Gavit) and his wife, Aunt
Lucy (my father's sister). A journalist and at one time Managing Editor of
the *New York Evening Post,* Uncle Jack was a jolly fellow, always telling
amusing stories and jokes. He and Aunt Lucy aroused in me a special
interest in science, and went on from there to intrigue me with the
pseudo-science of Spiritualism.

Their belief in an afterlife, in which the souls of the dead could communi-
cate with the living, was considerably stimulated by the early death, at
twenty-one, of their promising son Joe. Aunt Lucy thought that she herself
was a medium and in regular communication with the spirits of the dead.
For my twenty-first birthday in 1923 she presented me with a poem, "A
Man Thou Art Today," supposedly dictated to her by Joe from "the other
side." On another occasion, at Sunday lunch, she claimed she had an
important message for my father from J. Pierpont Morgan (the elder). We
all became deadly silent to hear the news from the beyond. When Aunt

Lucy announced solemnly that old J. P.'s message was, "Tom, you're doing a fine job!" my father was not impressed, my mother was scornful and brother Tommy let out a loud guffaw.

Despite these strange goings-on, there is no doubt that the Gavits, with their broad knowledge in science, journalism and international affairs, were important in the intellectual life of the Lamont family. Entirely apart from their Spiritualism, I had become much interested while at Harvard in the question of personal immortality, which for thousands of years had been one of the main issues in philosophy. Though Aunt Lucy was clearly an amateur as a medium, I felt that she and other Spiritualists warranted investigation by the so-called science of psychical research. Their continued stress on a future life was surely a factor in my own professional study of that subject.

I have been trying to give a picture of the informal home background that always affects and intermeshes with the formal education that one may receive at school or college. In my case, as with my two brothers—Thomas S. (1899-1967), Austin (1905-1969) and my sister Eleanor (1910-1961)—my family education was extraordinarily broad and profound. My parents, entering into the life of the mind with animation, giving and receiving constant intellectual stimulus, kindled in their children a zest for knowledge and a liking for the best in literature, music and the arts. Devoted to their children, they found that devotion wholeheartedly returned. It was a happy family.

One of our most rewarding customs was to gather after supper on a Sunday evening and for each member to read aloud a poem of his own choosing. To this day I remember my father reading in a tone of suspense two of his Kipling favorites, "Gunga Din" and "Danny Deever." ("O, they're hangin' Danny Deever in the mornin' ".)

The readings with my family were an important element in my growing love for poetry through the years, culminating in my editing in 1936 an anthology of poetry entitled *Man Answers Death*,[3] centered around the Humanist belief that this life is all. Much later I published a small book of my own poems, *Lover's Credo*.[4] I became active in two major poetry groups: the Academy of American Poets and The Poetry Society of America; of the latter I was for a few years a Vice-President and a member of its Executive Board.

As time went on, I entered more and more into the lively conversations that were a part of every family meal. And as I became more unorthodox, there was never the least tendency to silence me or to censor any of my offbeat ideas. The Lamont table was an open forum.

As part of our informal education, the Lamont children profited greatly from the voluminous letters that Father and Mother sent us both from home and their frequent travels abroad. They were always meeting with leading figures in government, public affairs and the literary world, and told us of fascinating conversations and the probable shape of things to come—the kind of letter-writing that seldom takes place today with communication made so easy by telephone and rapid travel.

For my twenty-first birthday on March 28, 1923, when I was still an undergraduate at Harvard, both my father and mother sent me most affectionate letters. Father wrote:

New York City
March 26, 1923

Dear Old Corliss:

Ten thousand congratulations on your twenty-first! Long life, prosperity and happiness attend you! Bless you. Keep young and brave and true.

Years ago there was a successful play here in N.Y. "When We Were Twenty-one." It was very reminiscent. So I have a right to be. When I was 21 it was just after the opening of my Senior Year at Harvard—September 30, 1891. I roomed in old Thayer Hall—on the third floor back, No. 16, looking out on Appleton Chapel. I used to dash up those three flights like a 120-yard hurdler. James G. King, '89, father of your Clubmate, roomed on the same floor. My roommate was Edward Livingston Hunt (now a specialist in neurology). In my Senior year he got rusticated for foolishly cribbing in laboratory work. Said he didn't realize the rule, and I guess he didn't. I used to go out to Lexington to see him in his rustication. I was alone for about six weeks. One afternoon (Sunday) I was writing in my room—a special Sunday article for the Boston Herald which paid me the then princely salary of $50 per month, a gentle tap came on the door and I gently murmured "come in." Nothing happened but another and louder tap. Then I yelled: "Come in, you old fool!"

In stalked President Eliot. He was Ned Hunt's Father's classmate of 1855 or '56 and came to talk over Ned with me.

. . . I can remember those days very vividly and yet they are really long ago. If—on the day I was 21—I had looked forward to thirty years, I would have said that the end of that period would have meant that life was almost over. Yet when that time has gone, life seems more full than ever of interst and even excitement. There are more problems than ever waiting to be solved; there are more real things to be done. Every day the world is a more vital place to live in. Every day there offer more chances to help along. Much of my life for two years past has been devoted to helping poor Mexico to her feet, to improving the relations between Mexico and America. The accomplishment of that task is one of my daily prayers.

Well, isn't this the darndest birthday letter—three lines about you and the rest about myself! I meant to have spent all the time telling you how excellent I think your theme on the Negro Question is; how interesting your letter that described so vividly your daily life and works.

Your mother is better of her neuritis but still not perfect. Lord Robert Cecil arrives tomorrow.

Goodbye, Cor dear. I only hope that when you are my age you will be blessed with a son half so fine and loyal and half the comfort that you have always been to us.

Your Loving Father

March 28, 1923

My own darling Cor:

This is to wish you all the happiness in the world, and all the blessings in heaven on your 21st birthday. I never knew a boy better fitted for manhood than you are. I can not tell you how fond and proud I am of you, how I admire and trust you, and how deeply happy it makes me that you have grown to be just the kind of man I most wanted you to be. I think you really care intensely for all the things in life that are the most worthwhile and most beautiful—and when I think of you tonight my heart grows warm and happy and thankful.

You have always been lovely to me, and especially dear to me, and I look forward with real happiness to seeing you grow, and develop all the gifts that seem to be yours. You have made a wonderful start, dearest Cor, and I feel that you are going to be a real blessing to your day and generation, and to stand for all that is high minded and courageous and fine.

Goodnight and God bless you my darling precious boy,

from your loving
Mother

I meant to send you some present beside the watch, but I have been in bed with neuritis for nearly a week.

One of the most amusing letters Father ever wrote came during the spring of 1931 when he took a group of eight friends, including Walter Lippmann and Professor Gilbert Murray, on a trip to Greece:

Le Petit Palais
Athens, Greece

April 17, 1931

Dearest Tommy and Ellie, and Young Tommy and Teddy and Lansing, and Corliss and Margaret and Little Margaret and my darling Ellie—

. . . The landing at Patras last Wednesday evening was like an Anthony Hope novel, or a light opera—better than the one that Kit Morley wrote and produced. The Governor of the Province, the Captain of the Port in full gold braid, a representative of the Greek Cabinet, the American Consul and Vice Consul—all came dashing out to the steamer in a special tender, lined themselves up in formal array in the saloon and tendered us the welcome of Greece. They insisted

upon sabotaging all the steamer's landing arrangements—despite our
earnest entreaties—and in landing us and our 42 pieces of luggage
before anything could happen. It was a struggle between the Governor and Metcalfe as to who should carry your mother's bottle bag and
hat box (Eleanor knows more about these two great factors in our
European travels than the rest of you do.) The whole performance
would have made Tommy and Corliss shrink worse even than the rest
of us. The Governor marched us up the quay to the hotel, where they
gave us a very decent and entirely informal dinner. They proposed
toasts to us—"The descendants of the ancient ACHAEANS TO THE
MODERN ULYSSES, Etc."

After dinner it was discovered that two trunks were missing. Metcalfe was invisible. So I sneaked away from the Government officials
and had myself rowed out in the midnight darkness to a lighter out in
Patras Harbor. It was loaded with a thousand trunks and loose bed
springs, which acted as traps to catch you as you searched with
matches through the swaying trunks. But I located the missing ones
and got back undiscovered.

The Cabinet representative assured me next morning that they had
taken extraordinary precautions for our comfort and that, under Government orders, he had himself personally inspected all the W.C.'s in
the hotel on our floor! Quel Devouement! . . .

I received a typical travel letter from Mother in England in the summer
of 1936:

Dear Cor:

I have had a most interesting time here, and feel that I have more
insight into foreign affairs, particularly as they touch the League of
Nations and war and peace. I have talked with every shade of opinion.
I started with Gilbert Murray and Lord Cecil. Then, feeling very
highminded and full of Peace, went to the Astor's at Cliveden for
Sunday where I felt like a dove among hawks. They were all *terribly*
down on sanctions. Among them were Geoffrey Dawson, editor of the
Times and a very powerful man over here. They almost tore me to
shreds.

Then I went to luncheon and sat next Winston Churchill, who
strange to say, was very pro-League, but against Article 16 in its
present form. He, and most people here, want to have a series of
regional pacts, a series of Locarnos, very definite but not affecting
every nation equally. The countries right around an aggressor would
go to war to prevent her action, if no other way were possible. The
countries farther removed, would start economic sanctions, and the
countries farthest removed, would send their blessings. I also sat next
to Grandi at a luncheon. Father had told me on no account to mention
sanctions or the war, and Neville Chamberlain, on my other side, said
"Be very careful what you say to him." But just then the maid filled my
glass with white wine for the second time, and I drank it, turned to Mr.

Grandi and said "Now *do* tell me how sanctions are working in Italy?" He was really delighted, instead of slaying me, and said that everyone but me avoided the subject, and he was so glad I had brought it up, etc. etc. and then proceeded to talk most interestingly on the whole subject. Viva Vivo! I didn't help matters, though, by insisting on calling him "Mr. Gandhi."

Last night we went to a dinner given for the King, a small one. It was very good fun, and I will give you a lurid account of it when I return. . . .

My parents greatly enjoyed giving big family parties at Thanksgiving, Christmas, New Year's, Easter and other special occasions. They included not only their children and their grandchildren, who came to sixteen in number, but various relatives, and sometimes close friends. I often made a jovial toast, such as "Here's champagne to our real friends and real pain to our sham friends!" Or I would give a definition, for example, of Platonic love as "Play for her and tonic for him." Occasionally I also read what I called "Humanist Invocations." Here is one of my Christmas dinner invocations:

We are celebrating today the birth of one who expressed magnificiently in word and deed the beauty of human love and the ideal of human brotherhood. Jesus gave up his life to bring peace on earth and good-will among men. A selfless martyr for the cause of humanity, he displayed in his teachings and actions a radically democratic spirit and a deep sense for the fundamental equality of man; a fearless fighter for his vision of the true and the good, he died on the cross in moral challenge to the established institutions and social iniquities of his time.

In this era of crisis and the crumbling of moral ideals under the impact of recurring economic tension and war, we find wisdom and inspiration in the ethical teachings of Jesus. Thinking of his great and radiant personality, we rededicate ourselves this day to the struggle for international peace and understanding; for equality and freedom among all countries and races; for a living democracy that penetrates every sphere of human existence.

Christmas is a time for happiness and love and generosity—among families, among neighbors, among nations, among all peoples of the earth. On this day, however dark the state of the world may seem, we say: let all those who can feel joy and give joy fling out their banners, flaunt them amid the grim crises of these times, and defy with singing hearts the evils of this era. And let us recall the poet Lunacharsky's lines:[5]

"O happy earth! Out of the blood of generations
Life yet will blossom innocent and wise;
And thou, my Planet, shalt be cleansed of lamentations
A jade-green star in the moon-silvered skies."

My typical invocation for Thanksgiving Dinner read:

> On this Thanksgiving Day we express deepest gratitude for the many good things of life that our fortunate families share:
> For this plentiful food and drink;
> For the beautiful children and grandchildren who grace our lives;
> For our dear friends and relatives wherever they may be;
> For this beloved home with its treasured associations;
> For the health and joy and laughter we have known within these walls;
> For the happy memories we hold in common, of loving parents and grandparents, of brothers and sisters, of beautiful places where we have gone together.
>
> And we are grateful, too:
> For earth and sky and sun;
> For shimmering waves and flowing waters, for singing bird and billowing cloud;
> For autumn's pageant of radiant colors;
> For the splendor of sunsets and the glow of turquoise dusk;
> For church spires rising in the distance:
> For our fellow-men who help to sustain us with their work and who surround us with their warmth;
> For good books, good music and good company.
> In all these things and many more we rejoice today, and with the hope that all families everywhere may enjoy an abundant and happy life.

Although my father was a successful banker, and a Republican in politics, he was in essence a liberal, particularly in international affairs. For instance, he broke away from the Republican presidential ticket in 1920 when he voted for the Democratic candidate, Governor James M. Cox, against the lugubrious Republican Senator Warren G. Harding on the issue of the United States entering the League of Nations. As for my mother, she joined with Father in supporting the League of Nations and the American League of Nations Association; and they were pleased when at Harvard I worked to establish a special college section of the League of Nations Association.

Mother also actively supported birth control, civil liberties, the Womens Trade Union League of New York and various poetry societies, and took an M.A. degree in philosophy at Columbia University. After World War II, both Father and Mother continued their international liberalism, backing the United Nations and the United Nations Association of the U.S.A. In general, my parents effectively contradicted the widely accepted stereotype of rich people and Republicans as conservative or reactionary plutocrats opposed to all forms of progress and liberalism.

They gave most generously of their time to the care and upbringing of their four children and to shared pleasures with them. Naturally, my parents had their shortcomings and inconsistencies. But in the large their lives built up into an outstanding achievement that heartened all who knew them. Their children were truly blessed in having such affectionate, considerate and intelligent parents.

Chapter II   SCHOOL, COLLEGE AND MARRIAGE

I was born in Englewood, New Jersey on March 28, 1902, a Good Friday as it happened. My mother hoped that this was an omen for my becoming deeply religious, but it did not turn out that way. An attractive suburban town across the Hudson River a few miles up from New York City, Englewood sprawls in a hodge-podge of houses from the top of the Palisades down into the valley. Many Manhattan businessmen, like my father, maintained their residences there.

I have most happy boyhood memories of Englewood. We lived in a spacious house with wide lawns, big trees and a tennis court; my parents kept a couple of riding horses for a few years and I did a good deal of riding on nearby roads on a white horse called "Cream of Wheat." In the first part of the twentieth century Englewood had not succumbed to the automobile age. During the winters the downtown stores still made deliveries in horse-drawn sleighs; and my friends and I took vast delight in hooking rides on the runners of these sleighs; in one afternoon we would cover a large part of the town in that way.

The boys in my age group organized the Junior Sportsmen Club for playing football, in which I was not outstanding but survived the rough-and-tumble cheerfully. In fact, I seemed to thrive on it so much that my fellow players gave me the nickname "Toughie," which stuck to me for several years.

I also belonged to a Boy Scout troop, with George Baker as Scoutmaster, and liked their slogan, "Do a Good Turn Daily." On Saturdays we hiked and picnicked on the Palisades. Between the cliffs and Highway 9W there were two or three hundred yards of empty land on which, early one spring, Scoutmaster Baker assigned to each boy the task of building a small log cabin—a pretty tough assignment, for we had to find fallen trees and then chop or saw them. It looked almost impossible to me. I found many big branches on the ground with their leaves still on them and proceeded to construct a sort of Indian wigwam by leaning the branches against the wide crotch of a bifurcated tree. I worked on the wigwam for two Saturdays, decided it was in good enough condition for human habitation; and the next Saturday when it started to rain about half of the troop came at my invitation into the wigwam to eat their sandwich lunches. That wigwam was unquestionably my supreme achievement as a Boy Scout.

While growing up in Englewood, I was not oblivious to the existence of the fair sex. At Miss Florence's dancing school I met many of the most attractive girls in town. Our house on Beech Road was close to the home of the Dwight W. Morrows. Mr. Morrow—a partner with my father in J.P. Morgan & Co., who became Ambassador to Mexico and a U.S. Senator from New Jersey—had three lovely daughters, Elisabeth, Anne and Constance. Elisabeth (later Mrs. Aubrey Morgan) and Anne (later Mrs. Charles Lindbergh) were in my age group and I became very fond of them. They went to Smith College and occasionally I enjoyed a Smith prom as the guest of one or the other.

I had a lively correspondence with Elisabeth and Anne, who published one of her letters to me in her book, *Bring Me a Unicorn*.¹ I loved both of these wonderful sisters as friends. Unfortunately, Elisabeth had a weak heart and died at the tragically premature age of 30. Anne married Lindbergh a year after I married Margaret Irish. She and I remained good friends and for years met for lunch occasionally in New York City, when she would drive in for the day from her home in Darien, Connecticut. To talk with her was always exciting and refreshing, a joy to the spirit.

My wife and I spent a ski weekend with her now and then, especially at the Big Bromley ski hill near Manchester in southern Vermont. On one memorable weekend in February, 1967, when we took over a small house at another ski hill, Mt. Snow in West Dover, Vermont, there were three Lamonts and Anne with five close Morrow relatives. We had a very merry time; for me it was the high point of the skiing season that year.

Anne and I carried on an active correspondence starting when she was still a student at Smith, from which she graduated in 1928, and have continued it for more than fifty years down to the present, discussing literature for the most part. She wrote marvelous letters, warm, sensitive and deeply appreciative of writers and poets. Her letters to me were of the same distinctive calibre as those published in her various books. We disagreed considerably on politics and economics, but our friendship remained firm through all domestic and international crises; and she endured heart-rending crises with great fortitude and gallantry. Here is one of her typical letters to me, dated December 26th, 1946, and written from Scott's Cove in Darien, Connecticut:

Dear Corliss,

This was meant to be a Christmas note but I could not get to it, partly because I was in bed up to Christmas Eve. I have been meaning to write it for a long time. And since Christmas is a time of openness of heart one thinks of it as an excuse to write and thank people for nice things they have done.

I meant to write it at the end of the summer (not a time for openness of heart—particularly—but *you* were open). For you wrote me from North Haven so generously, spontaneously, said how sorry you were that we had not had our usual North Haven meeting and you sent me your lovely tribute to North Haven at the Centenary Celebration (that "Harbor of Refreshment" is a lovely phrase). I am glad you expressed it so well for all of us who love it.

And you wrote me encouraging me to write, which meant more to me than I can tell you. The whole letter did.

The last two years I have not been able to write at all, not because of any superhuman difficulties but just because of the ordinary wear and tear of living, of having children, of moving, of inadequate help, of not having anything "extra" to put into writing. Nothing in the realm of heroics, only the every day of life. Only weariness.

But you have had a difficult year, perhaps more than that. "You know," you said lightly the last time I saw you, I think, last Spring at Amey's tea, "You get tired of being smeared!" I *do* know! It is the most difficult thing on earth. Having one's words, one's deeds perhaps, misunderstood, misused. Calumny, Distrust, Hate, Isolation, I have tasted them all. The hardest part of it is not simply *standing* it. I think we are both still Puritan-Presbyterian enough to *stand* things pretty well.

The hardest part is remaining *open* while taking it. It is comparatively simple to be a Stoic, to shut the door and simply grit one's teeth and bear it. But it's only half the battle as you have found out. The difficult thing is to bear it without armor, so to speak, to carry it and still remain open-hearted, generous, believing, hopeful, loving, and of course still vulnerable. For all that means being vulnerable, being willing to be hurt again instead of closing oneself up in armor for good.

So you see I was touched by your letter, because it was so open and generous. And I am glad you are still writing (not that I might not disagree with it, I probably would, though I am not a political creature and don't want to fight in those realms. But I am on the side of the mystics and you don't believe in God! etc. etc.!) But I am glad you are still writing because I think one must go on giving, willy nilly, whether one is hurt or not.

And as for being hurt. I think George Sand was right about that. I think I read you once her famous letter to Flaubert. But perhaps you would like to see it again. I used to read it over and over, like an incantation, against the hurt of rejection.

"What do I care for this or that group of men, these names which have become standards, these personalities which have become catchwords? I know only wise and foolish, innocent and guilty. I do not have to ask myself where are my friends or my enemies. They are where torment has thrown them. Those who have deserved my love, and who do not see through my eyes, are none the less dear to me. The thoughtless blame of those who leave me does not make me consider them as enemies. All friendship unjustly withdrawn remains intact in the heart that has not merited the outrage. That heart is above self-love, it knows how to wait for the awakening of justice and affection . . . ."

I'm afraid this is going to be a century of smearing, so you'd better stick that in your files, or Margaret's! It's hard on the *wives* of the men who get smeared too! I feel for her.

Well, I am afraid this sounds like a Carl Elmore sermon instead of a Christmas note. And in spite of being on the side of the mystics, I did not mean to do that.

Anyway, Blessings to you all. (Do you object to blessings? You unbeliever?!) Well, love to you all then!

Anne

Did I tell you? I was so pleased you liked my "Elegy under the Stars."

When my father died after a long illness early in February, 1948, Anne Lindbergh wrote me:

Scott's Cove
Darien, Connecticut

February 4th, 1948

Dear Corliss,

I cannot somehow say anything conventional about grief. And yet I want to send some word to you. Perhaps you will be too busy even to read it. I am sure you are overwhelmed with the inevitable world's side of death which almost keeps one from feeling true sorrow, or the true value of the wonderful relationship and person that is gone. But I am sure it will come back, both the sorrow and the sense of value. They are, of course, interlocked and one cannot wish to separate them but only hope they come and open their doors. With your capacity for finding what is essential in life, I am sure you will find whatever this hard experience has to give.

I send my love and thoughts to you all. It is only this, perhaps, that one wants to say: "I am thinking of you." I know what a great help you must be to your mother.

Anne

It was back in 1915 that my father and mother transferred their head-quarters to New York City and transformed their Englewood residence into a weekend country house. In New York they rented for some eight years a comfortable house at 49 East 65th Street from Franklin D. Roosevelt when he was Assistant Secretary of the Navy in the Woodrow Wilson Administration. I used to browse in F.D.R.'s big library on the second floor. It was in that house that I became extremely ill one winter with a very bad throat and a high temperature. The doctor insisted that a culture from my throat be analyzed. The report came through the next day and showed, the doctor stated, that I had such an advanced case of diphtheria that there was little chance of my surviving. I still remember my mother weeping and praying at the side of my bed, although I was actually feeling better. The next morning the crisis came to a sudden end when the doctor telephoned to say that my culture had gotten mixed up with another boy's and that in fact I did not have diphtheria at all.

In 1921 my parents moved into a large residence of their own which they built at 107 East 70th Street in the city. During those years we did not desert Englewood; we drove out there to spend the weekends, and I continued to see all my old friends, meeting some of them Sunday mornings at the Sunday School of the Presbyterian Church of Englewood. The study of the New Testament in that school became important in my education. I was not religious in any orthodox sense, but felt a burning admiration for Jesus as a man and a fervent wish to live up to his ethical ideals. Our Sunday School had its amusing moments. One morning the teacher, a young lady in her twenties, came across an unfamiliar word in the Bible. Looking around helplessly, she asked, "Does anyone know what 'circumcision' means?" Well, I did and probably others, too, but there was complete silence, and the teacher passed on to other matters.

When my father and mother had settled down in New York in 1915, I took an important step in my education by becoming a pupil at St. Bernard's School, of which John C. Jenkins and F. H. Tabor were co-headmasters. It was there that I learned really to study, under the special guidance of Mr. Tabor. I eagerly read, not only all the assigned books, but many others. St. Bernard's students staged a play at the beginning of every Christmas vacation; and one year I took the part of Polonius in Hamlet. It awakened an enthusiasm for Shakespeare that has never left me. At the same time I learned to play soccer, became a member of the school team at center or right forward, and was captain during my last year at St. Bernard's. I played a vigorous and, I fear, rather rough game of soccer which, I always thought, was a better and safer sport than football. During my Senior year my name was engraved on a tablet, with a roll of earlier students, as St. Bernard's Scholar for 1916.

Graduating that same year, I went on in the Fall to four rewarding years at the Phillips Exeter Academy. Though I did fairly well in my studies there, I spent too much time on extra-curricular activities, becoming Editor-in-chief of The Exonian, the school bi-weekly; Secretary of The Phillips Exeter Monthly; President of the G. L. Soule Debating Society; a member of the Academy hockey team and Class Historian. Looking back as

I write these Memoirs, I realize that blessed—or cursed—with a super-abundance of energy, I initiated at Exeter the great mistake of my life, that of taking on too many interests and responsibilities.

I should have heeded Anne Lindbergh's warning in her *Gift from the Sea:* "Too many activities, and people, and things. Too many worthy activities, valuable things and interesting people. For it is not merely the trivial which clutters our lives, but the important as well. We can have a *surfeit of treasures*."[2]

One of the most dramatic and dangerous episodes in my life took place at Exeter towards the end of my Upper Middle year. In the spring of 1919 the Academy baseball team was doing well, winning a high percentage of its games, but there were underground rumors among the students that the coach, John Carney, was relying on some rather shady methods. It was said that the night before a game he would bake a number of baseballs in an oven to make them harder and then see to it that these balls were used by the opposing pitcher against the Exeter batters, who then knocked out two-baggers or home runs with frequency.

I became much disturbed by this rumor. It was plainly bad sportsmanship to have Exeter winning games in an underhanded way, so I persuaded a classmate to go with me to the Principal, Dr. Lewis Perry, and tell him about the situation. He agreed with our reactions completely and called in Coach Carney next day to confront him with the accusations. Surprisingly enough, Carney confessed immediately to the ball-baking. Principal Perry fired him within a week and a French teacher, Henry C. Blake, took over in his place.

Many students were convinced that Coach Carney had been treated unfairly. Knowing my leading role in the situation, about 150 boys assembled under my second-floor window in Peabody Hall one evening after supper and noisily called for me to come down; they wanted to throw me in the Exeter River. I was not afraid of the river—a rather small and tranquil stream, and I could swim—but I *was* nervous about possible physical injury if the excited crowd got hold of me. At this point, through the intervention of fate or luck, the Exeter track coach, George Connors, a popular figure on the campus, suddenly appeared, and was able to calm the crowd down and disperse it. I missed my night-time swim in the river. That baseball exposé was the first big civics battle of my life.

My four years at Phillips Exeter, until I graduated in 1920, were the happiest of my youth. It was a big school, with some 600 boys from every part of the United States and from many different strata, and the scholarship students came from families that were economically under-privileged. It was at Exeter that I learned for the first time the true meaning of democracy, becoming friends with boys of so many different backgrounds, temperaments and skills. That spirit of democracy enriched the first-rate intellectual training that the school offered.

From there I went on to Harvard College in the autumn of 1920 and spent four more valuable years of education. At first I made the same mistake as at Exeter of participating in too many extra-curricular activities. In my very first week I entered the competition to become Manager of the Freshman Football Team and won. A few months later I joined a hard-working group who were competing to become editors of the college daily, *The Harvard Crimson*, and was chosen for the board of that illustrious newspaper. In my first two years at Harvard I spent more time working for the *Crimson* than on my studies.

Then during my Junior year I had a great awakening due to the stimulating influence of "Copey," Professor C. T. Copeland, and his famous course, English 12, but even more to the impact of a less known English teacher, the author Willard Connely. Both "Copey" and Connely made me see that my main purpose in going to college should be to steep myself in the cultural values and history of the Western world and, as one who wanted to become a writer, to learn to express myself in clear and grammatical English. Without abandoning my extra-curricular interests entirely, I shifted my emphasis to my courses, and especially the reading required or recommended in them. So for my last two years at Harvard I was primarily a student, obtained high marks in my courses, was elected to the Phi Beta Kappa Society and graduated *magna cum laude*. My father and mother, indeed my entire family, were quite astonished at these results. So was I.

My field of concentration at Harvard was English Literature, not a subject that would naturally lead a student in the direction of political liberalism or radicalism. However, I found myself increasingly interested in political discussions at the Harvard Liberal Club; and also often argued in favor of the United States joining the League of Nations against my classmate in Harvard '24, Henry Cabot Lodge, Jr., who was strongly opposed to the move. Of course, his grandfather, Senator Henry Cabot Lodge, had been the single most effective opponent in the Senate against the United States entering the League.

In 1923, our Junior year, Lodge, Jr. wrote an article for *The Harvard Advocate* entitled "Political Sentimentalists," in which he termed people like myself "college visionaries" because of our support of the League and American participation in it. I responded three months later in the *Advocate* with a piece called "Ideas for Irreconcilables," in which I urged college students to join in the movement to reverse the Senate's rejection of the League and to join the college division of the League of Nations Non-Partisan Association which I had helped to form. I claimed that Lodge had "grown morbidly sentimental over sentimentalism."

It is worth noting that in this dispute my parents were wholeheartedly on my side. They had all along advocated the entry of the United States into the League and thought that Senator Lodge had done a signal disservice to America and the world at large by leading the all too successful opposition to the League in the Senate. After our graduation from Harvard in 1924 the younger Lodge and I carried on a controversial correspondence that has lasted most of our lives, he ever conservative and Republican; I always liberal, left and Democratic.

As a counterpart to Lodge, Harvard '24 had Charlie Poletti, the son of an immigrant Italian granite worker, who worked his way through college and the Harvard Law School, a bright, joyous, energetic, warm person who became my best friend in the Class. We were both Democrats and liberals. In the summer of 1926, stimulated by the ignorance of our classmates about civil rights, Poletti and I made a three-week trip through the South to study the Negro question. In 1934 I had the honor of being Poletti's best man at his marriage to Jean Ellis. When in 1938 Herbert Lehman was elected Governor of New York State, Poletti was elected Lieutenant Governor on the same Democratic ticket. From 1943 to 1946 he served in a military capacity for the Allies in Italy. Charlie Poletti and I have remained lifelong friends.

I maintained my special interest in the League of Nations after leaving Harvard and spent a large part of the summer of 1924 in Geneva as a member of an informal committee established by Professor Manley O. Hudson of the Harvard Law School to acquaint foreign visitors in Geneva, especially Americans, with the workings of the League. I also became associated with the Geneva School of International Studies, with Professor Alfred Zimmern as Director, which concentrated on studies of the League. That the League of Nations eventually failed to maintain international peace and to prevent World War II was a bitter disappointment.

As a Senior at Harvard in the Class of 1924, I was elected Vice-Chairman of the Harvard Union and Chairman of its Undergraduate Committee. Every year the Union scheduled a series of lectures for its student members and the general public, choosing such subjects as "The Conquest of the North Pole," "The Fauna and Flora of the Amazon," and "Wild Life in Darkest Africa." All mildly interesting, but not exactly thrilling.

At a meeting of the Union's Governing Board I proposed that we invite as speakers Eugene V. Debs, head of the Socialist Party and still in prison for opposing America's participation in World War I; William Z. Foster, organizer of the great steel strike of 1919 and later Secretary of the Communist Party; and Professor Scott Nearing, economics teacher who had then recently been dismissed from the University of Pennsylvania on account of his radical views. More than fifty years later in 1973, the University of Pennsylvania acknowledged its error and reinstated Nearing with the title of Professor Emeritus. Very much alive, he celebrated his 90th birthday in 1979, and is still firing away with his writing and lecturing.

The Governing Board of the Union decisively disapproved of my slate of speakers, as did Harvard President A. Lawrence Lowell. I considered the issue one of academic freedom, which includes the right of college and university students to hear outside lecturers of their choice. The incident produced a lot of publicity in the press and a great furor in Harvard circles. The Governing Board and I received numerous letters either denouncing or praising our positions. A college dean told me I had been untactful in stirring up such a matter when Harvard was about to launch a financial drive for $10,000,000, a campaign of which I had been unaware. The final result was that in a few months the Union's program became somewhat liberalized, with speakers now and then on controversial subjects.

When this episode took place, I was far from being a radical. I simply wanted, along with many of my fellow students, to hear a left-wing interpretation of domestic and international affairs. After the Harvard powers-that-be put up such a battle to prevent this, my suspicions became aroused and I started to study Socialism seriously for the first time.

After his graduation from Harvard, my elder brother, Tommy, had gone to Cambridge University, England, for a year of broadening post-graduate study. Since I was uncertain about my future course after receiving my A.B. degree, I followed my brother's example, except that I went to New College, Oxford, instead of to Cambridge. Founded more than 600 years ago in 1379, New College is bounded by part of the ancient Oxford city wall and has one of the most lovely gardens of the Oxford Colleges. My year at New College was most fruitful. I took the program PPE (Philosophy, Politics, Economics) and had as my tutor a profound philosopher, H.W.B. Joseph. I also studied with a well-known economist, Lionel Robbins, who was later elevated to the House of Lords. I had stimulating tutorial conferences with both Joseph and Robbins, but my main emphasis was on reading classics that I had neglected at Harvard. I did not neglect athletics and played on the New College soccer team.

That I had applied too late for entrance to New College to obtain a room in one of the regular dormitories was fortunate because I was assigned to quarters in the home of Julian and Juliette Huxley, just opposite the Hollywell Street entrance to the college. Julian Huxley, later knighted, was the elder brother of novelist Aldous Huxley, and an eminent biologist; in his maturer years a leading spokesman for the philosophy of naturalistic Humanism in Great Britain. The Huxleys and I soon became good friends; it was a friendship that lasted all our lives. Since I developed into a writer and speaker on behalf of the Humanist philosophy and movement in America, a strong intellectual kinship grew between me and Huxley, who was also for a few years Secretary General of the United Nations Educational, Scientific and Cultural Organization (UNESCO). During my year at Oxford I also came to know John Masefield and his family who lived about three miles outside of the city on Boar's Hill.*

While in England I managed to make good use of my letters of introduction my parents had given me. So it was that I went for a Sunday lunch to Lord and Lady Astor's at Cliveden, had tea with John Buchan, and spent a weekend with H. G. Wells and his wife. Lady Nancy Astor was pretty, vivacious, witty and an effective member of the Conservative Party in the

*See Chapter VIII.

House of Commons. On first contact, H. G. Wells seemed an unimpressive little man, but once he got talking he became a fascinating figure, discoursing extensively in his squeaky voice on politics, history and international relations.

I left New College in June of 1925 with genuine regret that I was not returning to this quiet center of study and reflection. I joined my parents for a month's trip to Europe, the high point of which was a week in incomparable Florence and a call on the art critic, Bernard Berenson, at his Villa I Tatti a few miles outside of the city of Settignano. He personally showed us his magnificent collection of paintings and gave us tea overlooking a large, beautiful garden with rows of flowers intertwined in graceful patterns. A Harvard graduate, Berenson left I Tatti and its treasures to Harvard University when he died at the age of ninety-four.

Soon after returning to the United States in the Fall of 1925, I started work on a Ph.D. thesis at Columbia University under the guidance of Professor Frederick J. E. Woodbridge, an outstanding Naturalist (or Humanist) philosopher. The subject of my thesis was the idea of immortality and the title "Issues of Immortality."[*] Professor Woodbridge had one of the keenest minds I have ever encountered and did much to develop my philosophic capabilities. I was also able to take a good course under Professor John Dewey, whom I regarded as America's greatest philosopher. He was in essence a Humanist, but preferred the word *Naturalist* to describe his position.

I was greatly pleased when in 1928 I was invited to become an Instructor in Philosophy at Columbia. In this position I taught not only philosophy, but also a full year's course called "Introduction to Contemporary Civilization," which began with the Middle Ages in the twelfth century and came down to the early nineteenth century, interlinking a history and analysis of politics, economics, philosophy and science. There were massive reading requirements, most of which I fulfilled. In giving the course, I discovered that I was really taking it myself. The assigned reading relied especially on Professor John H. Randall's great book, *The Making of the Modern Mind* (1926).[3]

As we approached the end of the course and animatedly discussed capitalist economics in the United States, I found that I was becoming more and more liberal in my opinions. And by the time the course had ended, I had become an out-and-out radical, believing in a planned and democratic Socialism. Thus it turned out that Columbia had probably taught me more than its own undergraduates.

It was also in 1928 that I married Margaret Hayes Irish, who had graduated from Barnard College in 1925, a beautiful and intelligent woman from Troy, New York. The daughter of a physician, she was on the staff of the magazine, *The Living Age*, and her literary style was better than mine.

---

*See Chapter VI.

She and I were in accord on most of the fundamental issues of the time; for many years she was an active member of the Socialist Party.

At 450 Riverside Drive in a building owned by Columbia University, we rented an apartment which had an open fireplace and a grand view to the west of the majestic Hudson and sunsets beyond. Across the street was Riverside Park, good for sledding in the winter and walking the whole year round. The length of the Park made up for its narrowness. Just north of it was historic Claremont Inn, an old landmark among restaurants where I enjoyed the food and river views. Riverside Park was a godsend to me during most of my life.

Margaret was a handsome woman, but made little attempt to display her feminine qualities. She drove me wild by always being late for everything. Extremely shy and self-conscious, she held back from publishing the fine poetry she had written. In a hundred different ways bound up with the intimacies of marriage we gradually became incompatible. I obtained a divorce in 1962 when I was sixty years of age and all our four children had graduated from college.

In 1929, during my second year of teaching at Columbia, I temporarily became involved with Harvard again when that University peremptorily dismissed twenty scrubwomen in order to avoid paying them the thirty-seven cents-an-hour minimum established by the Massachusetts Minimum Wage Commission. Harvard had been paying these employees only thirty-five cents an hour and thus directly violating the Commission's decree. This situation thoroughly aroused my indignation and I organized a group of distinguished Harvard alumni who publicly protested to the Harvard authorities and tried to persuade them to reverse their decision and pay the women the back wages due them. But President A. Lawrence Lowell and the Harvard Corporation stood pat. Acting as Secretary of the alumni group, I raised from them and a few other Harvard men a special fund of $3,000 with which we ourselves paid the fired scrubwomen the wages owing them. A few years later, when Dr. James B. Conant became President of Harvard, the University adopted a labor policy that was liberal and enlightened.

In 1932 I resigned my Columbia teaching post, which had been entirely satisfactory to me, because I needed more time for the writing I had planned and for certain public activities in which I was vitally interested. It was in the same year that I became a member of the Board of Directors of the American Civil Liberties Union, a position I held until 1945. The ACLU was dedicated to the defense of the Bill of Rights and the furtherance of civil liberties in the United States. The Board met every Monday for lunch to decide which cases to support and whether this or that issue really involved civil liberties.

In 1947 I returned to Columbia to teach a course, "The Philosophy of Naturalistic Humanism," in the School of General Studies. I gave this course for twelve years and from it drew materials for the writing of my book, *Humanism as a Philosophy,* later re-titled *The Philosophy of Human-ism.*[4] In 1971 I became a Columbia University Seminar Associate in Colum-bia's program of special seminars on important subjects that meet about once a month for free-wheeling discussion and analysis. There are some seventy-five of these seminars and the members include not only Columbia teachers and graduate students, but also competent outsiders, each inter-ested in a particular field. An effort is made to draw in both specialists and those with a general interest in the topic, so that a genuine cross-section of opinion is presented. My own Seminar has been on the many-sided subject of death.

I also maintained a close association with Columbia by serving on the Advisory Council of the Friends of the Columbia Libraries; and worked closely with Kenneth A. Lohf, the able Librarian for the Rare Book and Manuscript Library. In cooperation with him I helped establish special collections for artist Rockwell Kent, John Masefield and philosopher George Santayana. I presented my correspondence with both Santayana and John Dewey to the Columbia Libraries; and I have left to Columbia in my Will all of my letters, papers, manuscripts and some of my best paintings. In 1974 the University awarded me The Columbia Libraries Citation for Distinguished Service.

I always worked hard, in fact too hard because I let myself become involved in so many activities and organizations. But I played hard, too, and spent plenty of time in exercise and recreation. Weekends were set aside for sports of one kind or another, and I took off at least one summer month for an extended vacation. Although I sometimes worked evenings, more often I read or took in a movie or play or went dancing. My favorite dance partner was my second wife, Helen Boyden Lamb, a widow whom I married in 1962 after reluctantly divorcing Margaret. Helen was an econo-mist, teacher and graduate of Radcliffe College in the Class of 1928. She had taught at Bennington, Black Mountain and Sarah Lawrence Colleges. Helen had a deep, utterly contagious laugh and combined beauty, intellect and moral strength in her radiant personality. She had an enormous interest in Vietnam and we worked as a team in opposing the brutal U.S. invasion of that country.* Under her pen name, Helen B. Lamb, she wrote a penetrating study, *Vietnam's Will to Live: Resistance to Foreign Aggres-sion from Early Times Through the Nineteenth Century* (1972).[5] She was also an expert on India.

Much to my chagrin, considerable opposition developed among some of my relatives regarding my divorce and re-marriage. Two or three of them claimed that I was psychologically off balance and should consult with a psychiatrist. Two of them supported this recommendation by quoting me as saying, "Helen makes me feel like twenty-one again!" Now in my family circle I had always been something of a jokester and fond of making

---

*See Chapter XII.

far-fetched half-joking remarks just for the fun of it. My reference to age twenty-one was in that category and to cite it as a reason for psychoanalytic treatment was perfectly absurd. Not one of my critics warned that the divorce would seriously upset my children and would hurt Margaret irredeemably. Those were arguments that could have stopped me.

Helen, her immediate family and various relatives had found the small, unspoiled town of Tamworth in southern New Hampshire ideal as a summer retreat. Nestling at the base of the White Mountains, Tamworth offered magnificent scenery at every turn and tended to be deliciously cool during the summer months. Helen and I spent a month there every summer.

The intellectual life of the town centered around a summer theatre company, The Barnstormers, which produced a series of first-rate popular plays of the past during July and August, staging a different play each week. The able, sensitive Director and guiding spirit of the enterprise was Francis G. Cleveland, youngest son of President Grover Cleveland. We attended many of the Barnstormer plays and enjoyed them immensely. I thought some of them as good as anything on Broadway. The Fiftieth Anniversary of the Barnstormers was celebrated in August, 1980.

From Helen's many articles and reviews I edited a book by her entitled *Studies on India and Vietnam* (1976).[6] This volume of essays was published posthumously, for Helen had died in July, 1975. In February of that year the doctors discovered that she had incurable cancer of the liver. We did everything possible to prolong her life and to find some treatment that would show the doctors were wrong about the cancer being fatal. But to no avail. To see my beloved wife steadily and inexorably decline month after month for six months, knowing that the case was terminal, was the greatest ordeal of my life. During all those months Helen did not voice a single word of complaint. Despite my many interests, amusements and friends, I never fully recovered from Helen's death.

In the fall of 1975 we held a Memorial meeting for Helen in the Auditorium of the Ethical Culture Society of New York. The hall was full, as four or five of her close friends spoke in tribute. In opening the meeting I said: "We are gathered here this afternoon to pay tribute to the life and work of Helen Boyden Lamb Lamont. This is a *celebration*, in which we rejoice that such a beautiful, talented and compassionate woman as Helen Lamont could and did exist—and for full 69 years. Her life was a blessing for everyone who knew her." I was particularly pleased that my eldest grandson, Jonathan Lamont Heap, was one of the speakers at the meeting.

My feelings for Helen are expressed in my brief poem, "Victory":

> To you, my sweet, I am forever grateful
> For many new-found beauties in my life.
> You blithely turn the present into rapture
> And make the future promise sheerest joy.
> Even my bitter past you have redeemed,

Bestowing on it new significance.
It is the end that counts and gives to all
That went before its full and final meaning,
Transforming the defeats, humiliations,
Dead-end sorties, insane infatuations,
To merest incidents in my long search,
Or lessons fraught with wisdom for the heart,
Or stepping stones to our great victory
Of happy love and lasting comradeship.[7]

My final letter to Helen, as she lay dying, speaks for itself:

My dearest, darling Helen,

You have been a beautiful, wonderful, warm, loving wife to me for all these years, which now are almost thirteen. We have had so many happy times together and taken so many grand trips. And always you have been such a lively and joyous companion. Just think of the National Parks in the West, Mexico, the hill towns of Italy, Yugoslavia, England and Scotland and the Soviet Union. All so interesting and so much fun with you there beside me.

You are naturally a loving and outgoing person. Those qualities come from your inner being. And they have shone out especially in your relations with my four children. From the start you gave all of them love, and one by one they came to return that love,

I can hardly conceive of living without you at my side. What would Ossining and Tamworth and North Haven be without you? The whole world would be a desert with you gone. And many, many others would be stunned by your loss.

So you must keep on fighting hard to arrest and defeat this terrible disease and marshal every resource in the battle.

I doubt if any man in the history of the human race ever loved any woman as much as I love you.

So it is love, love, love,

Corliss

Chapter III   FIRST TRIP TO THE SOVIET UNION

I now go back to 1932 when I paid my first visit, with my wife Margaret, to the Soviet Union. Early in July we entered the country from Finland and so started our six weeks' tour in the north at Leningrad, formerly St. Petersburg, capital of the Tsarist regime. We traveled south by train to Moscow, the capital of the U.S.S.R., and one of the world's great cities. We spent three weeks studying life in Moscow and took interesting side trips to collective farms. From Moscow we drove to the Volga River and boarded a small steamboat that took us as far as Stalingrad. Shifting to travel by train and automobile, we finally reached Batum and Tiflis in the Armenian Soviet Socialist Republic. Turning north, we visited the historic cities of Yalta, Sevastopol, Kharkov and Kiev, and were able on the way to view the immense Dnieper River Dam.

Although our trip to the Soviet Union was superficial in some respects, we did see enough at first hand to convince us that the economy was functioning fairly well and that the First Five-Year Plan (1928-33) was a success. We believed that the Communist regime had done a remarkable job in view of the former backwardness of the country, the long disastrous years of World War I, the three even worse years of civil war and foreign intervention, and the terrible famine of 1921-22. The people in general seemed healthy and hard-working, friendly to us, eager to know about the United States and anxious for their country to live in peaceful co-existence with America and the other capitalist nations.

The Soviet Government was firmly in the saddle; there was no valid reason for the United States Government to withhold full diplomatic recognition of the U.S.S.R. When I returned to the United States, I publicly advocated recognition and shortly afterwards became Chairman of the Friends of the Soviet Union in order to further that end and to acquaint the American people with the basic facts about the U.S.S.R. In the Fall of 1933 President Franklin D. Roosevelt's Adminstration took the intelligent step of recognizing the Soviet Government.

For many years I continued to speak and to write on behalf of American-Soviet cooperation and taught two courses about the Soviet Union, one at Cornell University in 1943 and the other at the Harvard Graduate School of Education in 1944. I also published three books about Soviet Russia: the first, *Russia Day by Day* (1933),[1] which I co-authored with Margaret, told in detail of our 1932 trip; the second, *The Peoples of the Soviet Union* (1946),[2] was a study of the national and racial policy of the Soviet Union, which had outlawed all ethnic discrimination against the more than 170 national and racial minorities living in the U.S.S.R.; the third, *Soviet Civilization* (1952),[3] gave a general account of Soviet Socialism in its diverse aspects through the 1940's.

On April 12, 1953, my study of Soviet civilization aroused the ire of a mob in Chicago which had violently invaded a meeting of the Chicago Council of American-Soviet Friendship in the People's Auditorium, smashing the furniture, seizing the literature on display and making a bonfire of it on the street outside. Nineteen copies of my book were among those burned.

I called on Republican Senator Robert C. Hendrickson, Chairman of the U.S. Senate Judiciary Subcommittee on Civil Liberties, to investigate the outrage. In my letter to Senator Hendrickson I said: "I make this request as an ordinary citizen vitally interested in the protection of civil liberties and also as an author and scholar whose right to freedom of opinion has been in this case trampled upon and cancelled out." He replied that his Committee would look into the matter, but so far as I know it did nothing about it.

My attitude towards the Soviet Union has all along been that of critical sympathy. I was convinced that its planned Socialist economy was making enormous progress, that its standard of living was steadily improving and that the country was strong enough to withstand military assaults from either the West or the East. The majority of American economists, military experts, newspaper reporters and public opinion in general disagreed with me. After a second visit to the Soviet Union in 1938, I wrote: "It is my own feeling that the Soviet people are well-nigh invincible in an economic, moral and military sense. From without Soviet Socialism can undoubtedly be set back, but hardly destroyed." For this and similar statements I was widely misrepresented as an apologist for Soviet Russia.

In the summer of 1941, three weeks after the Nazi invasion of the Soviet Republic, I predicted—contradicting 95 percent of the American press and public opinion—that Hitler would never get to Moscow and that the Soviets would hold off the Germans and eventually defeat them. In a somewhat rhetorical yet truth-telling message I stated: "The Soviets will never yield. They will fight on their plains, they will fight in their mountains, they will fight along their rivers, their lakes and their seas, till the trampling march of Nazi power dies away into the silence of history." A few months later, George E. Sokolsky, an anti-Soviet die-hard and one of my most hostile critics, asserted in 1942 in his column in *The New York Sun:*

"So even those of us who are not given to seeing any good in Russia are faced by the very cold facts of the moment, and until we are proved right about our prognostications and doubts, we have to bow to such superior prophets as Corliss Lamont, who always said that the Bolshies would do it."

My chief criticism of the U.S.S.R. has been its continuation of a strict political dictatorship and the non-existence of free speech and civil liberties. While Joseph Stalin was in power, there was throughout the Soviet Union one of the most cruel and violent dictatorships in history, culminating in the judicial frame-up of Soviet leaders in the Moscow Trials (1935-38). Unfortunately, I myself had thought for a while that the trials were genuine, and even defended them. After Stalin died, the situation became considerably better and more in line with the promises in the 1936 Soviet Constitution regarding basic civil liberties. Article 125 of that document reads in full: "In conformity with the interests of the working people and in order to strengthen the Socialist system, the citizens of the U.S.S.R. are guaranteed by law: freedom of speech; freedom of the press; freedom of assembly, including the holding of mass meetings; freedom of street processions and demonstrations." Article 128 states: "The inviolability of the homes of citizens and privacy of correspondence are protected by law."

Unhappily, the Soviets have failed to live up to the promises in Articles 125 and 128, and in the Helsinki Agreement of 1975. It has tried to suppress criticism of official policies and doctrines by arresting dissenters, and sending them to labor camps. To anyone believing in a democratic political system, it has been extremely disappointing that the Soviet Union during its more than sixty years of existence still falls so far short of being a true democracy. Much of this backwardness stems from a centuries-old anti-democratic tradition, and I think it will take another century for the U.S.S.R. to establish civil liberties comparable to the guarantees in the American Bill of Rights.

As The New York Times Moscow correspondent David K. Shipler states: "For reasons of culture that go back before the Revolution, Western ideas of democracy remain alien, incomprehensible and unattractive to broad masses of Russians, much as the Russian ethic of collectivism is hard for an American to understand and admire. Deeply rooted values that have prevailed since Tsarist times foster a mystical respect for central authority, a yearning for order and unanimity, a distaste for disagreement and diversity, a dread of any turmoil of ideas. From this perspective American society looks chaotic and frightening." (The New York Times, June 14, 1979.)

The fundamental mistake that most Americans make in judging of democracy abroad is to neglect the principle of historical relativity, that is, the realizaton that every foreign country must be judged to a large extent in terms of its traditions and history. Nations such as Soviet Russia, China and Vietnam, which had little or no practice or tradition of political democracy prior to their Communist revolutions, cannot be expected to develop overnight democratic institutions comparable to those of the United States and Great Britain. The same considerations apply to the forty-six non-Communist countries of Africa which won their freedom from imperialist rule after World War II. Only two of the former colonies have been able up to 1980 to establish true democracy; the others are ruled by dictators, military or otherwise.

Columnist Max Lerner adopts the approach of historical relativity in commenting on the Middle East and Southest Asia: "The deeper truth is that most of the new Asian nations simply do not have the economic, political, administrative and social base on which a functioning democracy can yet be built. We are learning these days that a lasting democracy is the end-product of a long process of development, in which men learn in their daily lives to value and trust each other as equal persons, and leaders and administrators are trained to give them direction." (*New York Post*, October 23, 1959.)

Another weakness in America's criticisms of the low state of democracy in other countries is to overlook the defects in our own democracy. Here we are well over 200 years after our birth as an independent nation and we still have to fight tooth and nail, day in and day out, for the preservation of our democratic liberties as expressed in the United States Constitution and Bill of Rights. During the twentieth century there has been an unceasing battle to maintain our civil liberties and to guarantee ordinary civil and human rights to our racial minorities, especially the blacks.

Corruption in government—federal, state and municipal—has constantly violated democratic principles. Disregard for the law by elected officials has been a powerful factor in the subversion of American democracy. The worst instance in our history of government corruption combined with the flouting of law was in the Watergate case and the behavior of President Richard M. Nixon. Beyond his role in Watergate was his unbridled and unconstitutional extension of executive power, particularly in waging and continuing the American war of aggression in Vietnam and Cambodia.

Certainly the United States is far from having attained the democratic ideals that our forefathers wrote into the Declaration of Independence and the Bill of Rights. As long as that is the case, an element of hypocrisy taints our criticisms of the failings of democracy in foreign lands.

Chapter IV　　BASIC BELIEFS

By the mid-1930's, when I was thirty-three years old, I had worked through to my main positions in philosophy and public affairs. In philosophy I believed in naturalistic Humanism; in economics I supported democratic Socialism; in politics I usually voted Democratic and strongly upheld civil liberties and civil rights; in environmental control I supported far-reaching measures for the conservation of nature and the preservation of endangered species; in international relations I was militantly for world peace and disarmament, a backer of the League of Nations, opposed to imperialist exploitation and rule over so-called backward peoples. I described myself as a left liberal or moderate radical.

About this time I began to receive the customary brickbats for being a leftist. The first attacks stressed that I was primarily trying to build myself up by seeking personal publicity and that the easiest way to get such publicity was to take stands on fundamental issues that were in disagreement with my parents and the Establishment in general. I did not pay much heed to such shallow criticisms. What I regarded as a more serious charge was that my radicalism was owing to some sort of Oedipus complex.

As the weekly *New Leader*[1] expressed it: "As son and heir of the late grey eminence of the House of Morgan, Corliss early acquired a deep sense of guilt toward both his father and his money. He became the standard psychology textbook case: the son who wants to overthrow the father image, which, in his case, was so closely identified with capitalism." I reject as completely phony such pseudo-psychoanalytic explanations of my Socialist beliefs.

Before I graduated from college I had made the welfare of the human race my supreme commitment and was saying that I considered every individual my friend until he proved to be my enemy. On the emotional side I felt a deep compassion for my fellow human beings and a crusading spirit for the abolition of the many ills that beset them. I liked very much the maxim attributed to Stephen Grellet: "I shall pass through this world but once. Any good therefore that I can do or any kindness that I can show to my fellow creatures let me do it now. Let me not defer or neglect it, for I shall not pass this way again."

When I asked myself how the happiness of humanity could be achieved and evils such as war and poverty overcome, I used my intellect as best I could and came to certain conclusions, such as the necessity of democratic Socialism, for the actualization of those ends. I thought it absurd to attribute Oedipus hatred of my father and guilt feelings about his wealth as the main causes of my loving humanity and supporting Socialism.

I dearly loved and greatly admired my father. We argued about the important issues of the day, but I argued just as much with my mother; our family dinner table, as I have said, was a free-for-all in which everyone participated in a friendly and tolerant spirit. In any case, it is a social good that children should to some extent disagree with their parents. This is the key to progress in any community or country; and it stimulates constructive criticism by each new generation.

In the 1930's, in the middle of the Great Depression, Socialism as the way out was widely discussed and proposed by thousands of middle-class intellectuals and proletarian workers with nobody claiming that they had Oedipus motives and other psychoanalytic rigamarole, frequently used by the Establishment to try to show that radical proposals are irrational and merely emotional outpourings of suffering and discontented people.

Regrettably two eminent British radicals contributed to the psychoanalytic attack on radicals. Philosopher Bertrand Russell stated that while he himself believed that the rational arguments for radicalism are overwhelming, the fundamental incentives that lead persons, especially "educated men," toward the Left are non-rational and emotional. "Rubbish!" say I, to use a favorite British expression. Author John Strachey recounts that at his first meeting with Russell, the latter greeted him with the words: "What's the matter with you? I had a neglected childhood." And Strachey goes on to say, "Many and deep, I am sure, are the personal neuroses which have made me into a Communist."

I have never accepted the Freudian idea of an Oedipus complex that affects all children. I grant that some children develop antagonism or hatred toward one or both parents: others may suffer from different sorts of neuroses, resulting from social unpopularity or sexual maladjustment. Such troubles are important stimuli in thought and action, but do not in themselves determine the direction in which a person may turn in order to solve personal dilemmas. Individuals subject to such pressures do not necessarily land in the Socialist camp; they may enter the Catholic Church, become storm-troopers of Fascism, commit suicide, join encounter groups, develop into alcoholics, support the labor movement and Socialism, or become conservatives or radicals or apolitical.

The factors that bring people to or toward the Left are human sympathy and compassion plus reason or intelligence, whether they are of the working class, the middle class, or the most affluent capitalist class. I know that this has been true in my own case. I had a happy childhood and youth, was devoted to my parents and had the best possible education. It was when that education expanded while I was teaching at Columbia and the Great Depression stimulated me to thinking harder than ever before, that I began to consider Socialism as the way out for capitalist America. Many other young capitalists were coming to the same conclusion. Karl Marx, who was himself of bourgeois origin, called attention to this tendency in *The Communist Manifesto:* "Just as in former days part of the nobility went over to the bourgeoisie, so now part of the bourgeoisie goes over to the proletariat. Especially does this happen in the case of bourgeois ideologists, who have achieved a theoretical understanding of the historical movement as a whole."

My Oedipus-minded critics, unconsciously perhaps, assumed that a kind of deterministic law rules children by which they must necessarily revolt against the ideas and patterns of their parents. Even on a philosophical basis this is an obvious blunder, for every human being has freedom of choice, no matter what his upbringing or the nature of his parents. It is true, of course, that parents, teachers, friends, associates, the economic and political situation, all affect a person's life. But besides these common influences, every individual has free will at the moment of decision, to choose between genuine alternatives, whether important or unimportant. He can select the flavor of ice cream he wants at lunch or the woman he hopes to marry. As to political-economic issues, he can decide freely whether to follow a conservative, liberal or radical course. A thorough analysis of this entire matter is the basis of my book, *Freedom of Choice Affirmed*.[2]

The "psychoanalytic" attack on me fell apart by neglecting the important issues on which my parents and I agreed, as in our unrelenting efforts on behalf of birth control, civil liberties, the flourishing of poetry and international peace. We supported the League of Nations, and later the United Nations, as the best hope for doing away with war. A right-wing diehard by the name of Francis Ralston Welsh commented on the situation with an article about me and my parents called "Sowing the Wind and Reaping the Whirlwind." He pointed out that my mother was on the Board of Directors of such "Communist" organizations as the Foreign Policy Association and the New School for Social Research, that my father aided and abetted her subversive activities and was guilty of some rather liberal doings himself. "And so the wind was sown," concluded this dimwit writer, with the inevitable "whirlwind" following in the form of none other than my humble self.

In the 1940's the most vicious commentator about me and my family was the vituperative Westbrook Pegler, whose column appeared regularly in the Hearst newspapers. Pegler tied me in with the Communists, calling me "the voluptuous paradox of Wall Street and Union Square" and finally let loose on my parents. In his syndicated column of December 11, 1947, in the Dayton, Ohio, *Journal*, he made the absurd statement that my mother "was enthusiastic about the Bolsheviki and their revolution in Russia," and that she was at odds with my father.

Pegler wrote, "I am a fellow given to stern methods. I say a man should be head in his own home. When he lets a woman outman him he is done and everybody suffers. A punch in the snoot should be the last resort but Abraham Lincoln, F. D. Roosevelt and Thomas W. Lamont would have left the world in better shape when the squalling died down." I was not amused at Pegler's suggestion that my father beat up my mother.

In the same column Pegler hinted that I ought to be hanged. "In Galway," he wrote, "there was a Mayor named Lynch. He hanged his kid. Not that I am offering a serious proposal. I am only exploring the possibilities. I still think the idea wasn't too bad."

Another writer who took pleasure in attacking me was Benjamin De Casseres, author of a column entitled "The March of Events" for the New York *Daily News*. On October 14, 1944, referring to me as "Tovarisch," he made the remarkable statement: "The 'intellectuals,' from Plato to Karl Marx and Corliss Lamont, are the bane, the pests of the human race." I was delighted. My inclusion in the same category with Plato and Marx was surely the highest compliment I had ever received. I wrote De Casseres and thanked him, "It is comments like yours that in these days of blood, sweat and tears bring unalloyed pleasure to my soul."

Other columnists relished Red-baiting me. Austen Lake in the *Boston American* of April 9, 1935, wrote "Portrait of a Silk-Shirt Communist" and referred to me as a "young Park Avenue socialite whose palms have never known the corns and bunions of hard toil." Lake wound up with what he doubtless thought was a knockout punch: "The sight of a lounge lizard with his pants full of spending cash and a vault full of capitalistic bonds, knocking what the boys call 'his own racket' smacks of hypocrisy."

Francis Downing in *The Commonweal* and *Milwaukee Star* (September 8, 1952) took a different tack in an article about me titled "The Captive Mind," based on a debate about the Soviet Union with the author and teacher Peter Viereck. I had upheld my usual position of critical sympathy for the U.S.S.R., criticizing the Socialist Republic for its lack of civil liberties, its Iron Curtain, its labor camps and its support of Communist North Korea, but praising it for its drive for international peace, its care for women and children, its progress in science, its program of public ownership and its nationwide economic and social planning. Mr. Downing implied that, unless I made a total denunciation of the Soviets, I was a "captive" of their propaganda, "like a man in the toils of a vicious woman." He ignored the fact that for years I had shown independence of mind by rejecting, in a capitalist milieu, the capitalist economic system and traditional religion. Downing, I think, was a dunce.

Of course, during World War II, my entire family and I supported the Allies against the Fascist powers, with my elder brother Tommy a lieutenant colonel in the U.S. Air Force in England and my nephew Thomas W. Lamont II giving up his life on an American submarine fighting the Japanese in the Pacific. In November of 1942 my father and I were both speakers at a great rally in New York's Madison Square Garden, under the auspices of the Congress of American-Soviet Friendship, to express appreciation of and support for the Soviets' notable part in the conflict. Vice-President Henry Wallace and Soviet Ambassador Maxim Litvinov also addressed the meeting. This was the first and only time that my father and I spoke from the same platform. It was a thrill for me.

The columnists and the press in general were always playing up disagreements between me and my parents. But looking at our relationship as a whole, I think that there was genuine continuity between their beliefs and mine. Our main goals were much the same, though we frequently differed on the means to attain them. I can never forget my father saying when I was quite young, "The best way to find happiness is to make others happy"—clearly a Humanist ethical affirmation with which I am in complete accord.

Another charge that I was forced constantly to deny was that I was a Communist or a Communist fellow-traveler or even perhaps a member of the Communist Party (U.S.A.), an accusation made because I was in general sympathetic to the Soviet regime and willing to cooperate with Communists, as well as with everyone else, on specific reforms. I described my position as that of an independent, free-wheeling radical who did his own thinking and made his own decisions, often agreeing but more often disagreeing with Communist policies. Nevertheless, the newspapers, TV and radio took the lead in smearing me, ignoring the fact that philosophy was my main field of concentration and civil liberties after that, and doubtless unaware that my book *The Philosophy of Humanism* was regarded as the definitive volume on the Humanist movement in America.

For the mass media the Communist issue had the main news value, so they sought to discredit my economic and political views by making it seem that I was a secret mouthpiece for the Communist Party. Of course, the Humanist philosophy that I supported had fundamental disagreements with the Dialectical Materialism of the Marxists, which is faulty in many respects, including its awkward name.

Strangely enough, it was *The New Yorker* that first ran an article in the issue of June 4, 1932, calling me a Communist in a genial but foolish piece titled "Vagrant Lamonts," saying that my father was active in floating Japanese bonds while my wife and I were supporting a boycott against Japanese goods because of Japan's military aggression against China. While accurately stating that my wife, Margaret, was a member of the Socialist Party, the magazine alleged that "Corliss himself is a Communist and expects to see The Day" though I had never uttered a word in private or public favoring Communism, and had always advocated democratic Socialism democratically achieved. *The New Yorker* statement gave the Red-baiters the cue they needed, and I was constantly forced thereafter to deny that I was a Communist.

Several Federal government bodies joined the hue and cry: the Federal Bureau of Investigation, the Central Intelligence Agency, the House of Representatives Un-American Activities Committee and the Senate Judiciary Subcommittee on Internal Security. Louis Budenz, an ex-Communist perjurer, and Mrs. Hede Massing, an ex-spy, testified before the Senate Committee that they had known me "as a Communist," a deliberately vague and catch-all formula. In trying to prove that the American Institute of Pacific Relations was a subversive organization, the Committee counsel brought forth from the Institute's files a brief memorandum headed "C.L. from E.C.C." and suggested that I was the recipient of it. Everyone knew that "E.C.C." stood for Edward C. Carter, the head of the Institute. But nobody was permitted to testify at the hearing that the initials "C.L." were those of Clayton Lane, a former official of the Institute of Pacific Relations. So we had a new twist in the witch-hunt: frame-up by initials!

One of the most despicable tricks resorted to by the Red-hunters was to assert that this or that person had been "identified" as a Communist. An anti-Communist witness before a Congressional committee or a committee counsel himself might state that Mr. Brown was a Communist; and though no proof was given, the committee could then say with some plausibility that Mr. Brown had been "identified as a Communist," from which the average citizen would conclude that Mr. Brown was indeed some kind of Communist.

In my major philosophical works, such as *The Philosophy of Humanism* (first published in 1949) and *The Illusion of Immortality* (1935),[3] I have stressed the use of reason and modern scientific method as the best means of solving human problems. And I have challenged orthodox conclusions in various fields when analysis through intelligence led me to do so. The main thesis of my book, *The Independent Mind* (1951),[4] is that men's minds should be critical and free from control by any authority whatsoever—parental, religious, political or educational. It is inconceivable that as a scholar, writer and teacher I would ever lend my mind to the dictates of any political organization. The notion that I have at any time surrendered my autonomy to the Communist Party or "the Communist line" is preposterous. My only political ties have been with the American Labor Party, the Democratic Party and the Independent Socialist Party during its very brief existence.

Those who have claimed that I was a Communist have emphasized my activity with organizations they smear as Communist fronts, like the National Council of American-Soviet Friendship, of which I was Chairman for three years and a Director until late in 1950. They ignored my connection with other organizations—the American Civil Liberties Union, the National Emergency Civil Liberties Committee, the League of Nations Association, the American Association for the United Nations, the Foreign Policy Association, The Poetry Society of America, the American Philosophical Association and the American Humanist Association—because they could not pin a Communist issue on them.

My close connection with the Humanist Association since its founding in 1941 and with its official magazine, *The Humanist*, begun in 1943, illuminates my rejection of supernatural Christianity. Though my adoption of naturalistic Humanism was as much a break with my family tradition as going over to Socialism, my critics never cry "Oedipus" at me on that score: a person's philosophy has little news value and it has been impossible to inject the nonpolitical American Humanist movement with America's anti-Communist psychosis.

At first, I did not take the spurious charge seriously, laughing it off with the well-known lines:

> Breathes there a man with soul so dead
> That he was never called a Red!

But as the Red-baiting became more widespread, interfering with my work as a writer and speaker, in January of 1952 I finally published a brochure entitled *Why I Am Not a Communist*, giving fifty-three of my disagreements with Communism in thought and action in the United States and throughout the world. Meanwhile, I kept on teaching, writing and lecturing, my three main subjects being American-Soviet relations, the philosophy of Humanism and civil liberties.

As a lecturer I was usually received well, with no rude interruptions. I enjoyed the personal contacts with the audience during the question period, which might last about a half hour, and enabled me to bring in an occasional note of humor. The audience enjoyed it too and, though there were hostile questions, they were not asked harshly. The sour reactions came in the form of abusive letters, including the classic imbecility: "Why don't you go and live in Soviet Russia?" However, enthusiastic fan mail always vastly outnumbered my hate mail.

Since the Great Depression, starting in 1929, so many crises, national and international, have taken place that a mood of tension has swept the world, so deep-going that many people can no longer discuss calmly what should be done to overcome the chaotic problems of nuclear weapons, international war, mass unemployment, spiraling inflation, the hijacking of airplanes, corruption in the highest echelons of government. In American intellectual circles old friends will break off relations because of disagreement over some vital issue. I deplore the intolerance that leads to such actions and have never excommunicated anyone because of dispute about public affairs. My position here of course is bound up with my fundamental allegiance to free speech of every variety.

I inherited from my parents more money than I could put to intelligent personal use and was able to give most of it away for what I considered the good of my fellow human beings. My main gifts went to committees, journals and institutions of a left or liberal persuasion. I contributed to conventional institutions, especially those where I had been a student: St. Bernard's, Phillips Exeter, Harvard and Columbia, and I occasionally helped worthy liberal or left individuals in financial straits.

I also contributed to various publications: *The Churchman, The Guardian, The Harvard Advocate, The Humanist, In These Times, Journal of Philosophy, Monthly Review, The Nation, New China, New World Review, Science & Society;* and invested heavily in *The Daily Compass*, the only liberal daily in New York City. Edited by Ted O. Thackrey, *The Compass* attempted to present a progressive viewpoint, but was never able to become self-supporting. Mr. Thackrey did a fine job of editing and included a daily column by the independent liberal commentator, I. F. Stone. But after several years *The Compass* had to cease publication in 1952.

My wealth, however, became a burden in one respect. Like many other people, I was deluged by financial appeals in letters, phone calls and interviews. My name was on at least a score of lists used for charitable solicitations, and a large proportion of my mail consisted of financial appeals. On a typical day, Thursday, November 29, 1979, I received thirty-six pieces of mail, of which twenty were requests for money, three were advertisements, twelve were magazines and newsletters and only two were of a personal nature. In self-defense I have generally tossed into the scrap basket close to half of my mail unopened.

When it came to drawing up a Will, I left the bulk of my estate to the most important committees and causes that I have aided during my lifetime. I did not have to worry about my children and grandchildren, since my parents had set up generous trusts for them. I have established a foundation to carry on financially as long as possible on behalf of my basic interests: to concentrate on safeguarding the American Bill of Rights and civil liberties in general; to further education of the American people in the principles of democratic Socialism; to advance the philosophy of naturalistic Humanism as the best over-all way of life; to support far-reaching programs, both public and private, to conserve and develop America's beautiful natural environment; and to assist in every possible manner the abolition of nuclear weapons and the attainment of international peace.

Once in a while I received a nasty letter about my wealth. For a long time Mrs. Madalyn Murray O'Hair ("Mad Madalyn" as some of us called her) was very angry at me because I termed myself a Humanist instead of an atheist. I refused to identify myself as an atheist because I am in fact an agnostic and because the term "atheist" tied one in with the single issue of the existence or non-existence of God. "Humanism" has a broad connotation that not only denies the reality of the supernatural, but in an affirmative way implies devotion to the welfare of humanity. Mrs. O'Hair is an excessively voluble, intolerant woman who thinks all Humanists are hypocrites.

In the spring of 1976 I sent to her and others copies of my article in *The Nation*, exposing the FBI under the title of "What the FBI Had on Me." It summarized briefly some 300 papers I had obtained under the Freedom of Information Act from the absurd FBI file regarding me.* I thought Mrs. O'Hair might like to get away from atheism for a moment. But she answered with the following letter, the most vituperative I have ever received:

7th May, 1976

Corliss Lamont,

I have received the attached mailing from you, from the address above. I do not know why you are concerned about what I might think about you. You purchase your friends, your privileges, your honors, your associates—and while you support a pseudo-Atheist group (the American Humanist Association), you probably give to the Church too. You and the A.H.A. stink of the Communist technique, of the philosophy of the same, of the despiriting [sic] overreach of collectivism . . . and you totally turn off those of us who insist on individualism, freedom of the mind and freedom of association.

Convince someone else of how pure you are. I already have my opinion. The only thing that saved you from H.U.A.C. [House Committee on Un-American Activities] (which was an odious institution, I grant) was your money—not your philosophy or your purity.

Without your money, Corliss, baby, you are nothing. Your A.H.A. and other friends would desert you en masse.

SOCIETY OF SEPARATIONISTS, INC.
Madalyn Murray O'Hair
President

When Mrs. O'Hair said that I "probably give to the Church, too" she was correct, because for many years I made contributions to the Community Church of Boston, of which the Reverend Donald G. Lothrop was the pastor, and to the Third Unitarian Church of Los Angeles, of which the Reverend Stephen H. Fritchman was pastor. For half a century both of these liberal clergymen provided intelligent leadership on the main political and social issues of the day. Both combined regular Sunday services with addresses by prominent progressives, and their churches became centers of inspiration and liberal thought. I also donated annually to the

---

*See Chapter X.

Union Theological Seminary because of my use of its fine library and my friendship with two of its Presidents, John C. Bennett and Henry Pitney Van Dusen.

Although as a Humanist I disagreed with the theological doctrines of Christian churches on the existence of the supernatural, I was always ready to cooperate with religious individuals and organizations on behalf of honest government, civil liberties, progressive legislation and international peace. On the whole the Protestant churches of the United States opposed the Vietnam War, while the trade unions, for instance, with some honorable exceptions, were in favor of the American aggression. The churches in general oppose America's stupendous arms expenditures, while trade unions as a rule support them, mainly because they fallaciously believe that they make for maximum employment.

Chaper V   SPORTS AND RECREATION

From my childhood on, sports and the outdoor life were important to me. In my youth I played hockey, football, soccer, baseball, croquet, golf, tennis; I fished, hiked, sailed, canoed, skied, rode horseback, climbed mountains and went bathing along sandy beaches. For several summers my parents took us all to Easthampton, Long Island, where there was superb surf-bathing. At St. Bernard's School I played on both the baseball and soccer teams, and at Harvard I was on the Freshman hockey team. I was not a very good swimmer, but loved to ride in on the top of waves as they rolled toward the shore, though I never used a surf-board. While I played a bit of golf with my father, I dropped it after he died in 1948, primarily because it took so much time. As I grew older, I concentrated on skiing and tennis; after I was 70 I played a lot of croquet doubles, really a grand game with brainwork involved and a chance for grandchildren to learn easily and to participate naturally.

I did not take up skiing in a big way until after I was married in 1928, and then it gradually became my favorite sport. Usually I would go off skiing for a whole weekend with my wife and children, or friends. We concentrated on the New England area, often driving to ski centers such as Bousquet's and Jiminy Peak near Pittsfield, or to Big Bromley, Mt. Snow or Stratton in Southern Vermont; the air was always fresh and pure. I never became more than an intermediate skier and especially liked to traverse broad slopes leisurely while looking at snow-mantled mountains and lakes stretching away in the distance, or feeling the pervasive pleasure of gliding and weaving across the white expanse of open fields glistening in the sun. Once I saw a fox running into the woods; and often there were the multitudinous branches of massed evergreens all etched in the night's new fallen snow.

This continual variety in natural beauty is matched by the variety possible in the very act of skiing. On a hill that was high and wide I could take a different route every time I came down, and use different techniques in my descent. The sheer exultation of a fast *schuss* down a steep slope had its special appeal; but what I liked best was to wander and explore more slowly, pioneering my own trail in fresh powder snow, and sometimes branching out from a main hill to twist and turn among the trees. As my skis pressed ahead through the virgin snow, I felt almost like an artist creating a new and unique pattern. One advantage of skiing is that it can be done alone.

At the end of the afternoon with twilight coming on, I would stand for a minute or two at the top of the hill and breathe in the beauty of the winter landscape before making a last run. The tows had shut down; I would go into the lodge for a cup of hot chocolate; then with legs stretched out before an open fireplace, I would talk to other skiers about the adventures of the day and enjoy the cordial good fellowship of the skiing fraternity. I admit that I am romantic about skiing, for in all my experience there has been nothing more joyous, in its own way, than skiing days and skiing weekends with good snow and good company.

During four or five winters I flew out for a week to Aspen, once a booming silver camp, in Colorado, where there were four large mountains, each with scores of ski hills and chairlifts. Since the town was at an altitude of almost 8,000 feet, the air was wonderfully invigorating, and there was always plenty of snow. The wide, long hills were ideal for my type of skiing. I always came back to New York feeling on top of the world, though once I returned home with a broken rib and once with a broken collarbone, both slight injuries that healed automatically.

A favorite ski companion was the novelist and poet, Norman Rosten, whose abilities on the hills just about matched mine. After a perfect weekend with other friends and me at Mt. Snow in Vermont, he wrote these verses:

> *The Ballad of Mt. Snow*[1]
>
> (for Corliss Lamont)
>
> The day was clear and sunny
> Upon the mountain peak.
> What thinkest thou, friend Corliss?
> I pray thee, master, speak!
>
> He answered me serenely
> In syllables precise:
> Methinks the weather glorious
> But the trails are full of ice.
>
> Must we ski today,
> Or strike it from our list?
> Ski we shall, said Corliss,
> No existentialist!

The wind was strong and blew
As we mounted through the air.
Corliss smiled at the trees,
I shivered in the chair.

We rose into the summit,
The skiers crossed beneath.
Some were doing parallels,
Others not so neat.

Who needs this sport? I wondered.
What am I doing here?
I should be out with girls.
I should be drinking beer.

As we reached the last unloading,
My knees were cold and tight.
I thought that curfew certainly
Would not ring that night.

Ready, boy! called Corliss,
His cap a gaudy red.
Ready, I mumbled, wishing
I were safely back in bed.

Corliss took the turns
With Norman close behind.
Corliss would not rest.
Corliss was not kind.

He was a steady skier,
He let the speeders pass.
But he was passing later
While they were on their ass.

Near the bottom run,
My buddy let it whiz,
He cut across the hill
Like a bottle with a fizz,

Then rode a draft of air
That lifted to the trees,
Pursued by howling winds
Like the Eumenides,

Then cleared the trees and ridge,
And back upon the trail.
I watched in admiration
As I do the U.S. Mail.

I have been thinking lately
Of exploits I still want—
But I have reached Nirvana,
Skiing with Lamont!

I kept skiing in my seventy-ninth year, though with increasing care and reduced speed. I was pleased when on arriving at the age of seventy-five I was presented with a special card at Stratton Mountain, one of the best ski areas in Vermont, denoting me as a "Super Senior" and granting me free skiing for the rest of my life. In the winter season of 1980, this privilege was extended for me to Big Bromley, which had merged its Association of Senior Skiers with that of the Stratton Association.

In all my athletic activities I had great fun and the vigorous exercise was doubtless a factor in my good health. I never got sea sick, car sick or train sick and in crossing the Atlantic on a steamer I welcomed stormy weather, with the big foaming waves breaking over the prow. My only serious illness until I reached seventy-seven was a burst appendix. I did, however, have continual trouble with my teeth, I don't know why, but I do know that the dentists had a field day putting in inlays and pulling out teeth, until only three uppers and one lower were left. The dentist's chair became a place of supreme torment for me, where even the injections of novocaine could not offset the excruciating pain.

In 1929 Father and Mother moved from Englewood to their new country house atop the Palisades at Sneden's Landing in New York. Their land extended out to the cliffs and into some fifty acres of woodland interspersed with trails. It was all a paradise for me. One path led straight into the Palisades Interstate Park and on to the top of the great cliffs, some fifteen miles long, that are known as the Palisades of the Hudson. A well-worn trail runs along the top of the cliffs, and another along the bottom at the edge of the river. I came to know both pathways very well.

Following a narrow path carpeted with pine needles at the summit of the precipice, you come every hundred yards or so to lovely natural lookouts, often half-hidden in the foliage, which yield long, leisurely views along and across the river, at times of the great span of the George Washington Bridge and the upper skyline of Manhattan and reaching on clear days to the far side of Long Island Sound. And there are breathtaking moments as you peer over the edge—down four or five hundred feet to the water—or admire the sheer drop of the precipice and the lofty stone columns that rise in many a strange and picturesque shape from the base of the wall. Great oaks and pines grow from every possible crevice at every conceivable angle. Even the dead trees, losers in a fight to survive, contribute to the living beauty of the place. Grey, weatherbeaten, frequently grotesque, they protrude from the rocky ramparts like gargoyles from a cathedral.

No more appropriate spot could be found for a modern Omar Khayyam than these quiet watchtowers on the crest of the Palisades. Lying on your back, there is the expanse of blue sky and white masses of clouds moving in every kind of shape. Behind you, the breeze stirs in the trees, making a music of rustling leaves and swaying branches. Birds call and the chirp of crickets adds a pleasant, lazy note. The scent of wild flowers hangs upon the air; and the air upon these heights is good to breathe.

The bottom of the Palisades is almost as fascinating as the top. So are the slopes, with their huge rockpiles that extend far up from the water front. These masses of giant boulders, heaped one upon the other in profuse and wayward splendor, are simply broken-off sections of cliff, pried loose by erosion and sliding down with a mighty roar, overwhelming trees, underbrush, everything in their path. Some of these immense landslides clearly occurred in the distant past; others more recently, in 1938 opposite North Yonkers after a big storm just prior to the Munich Conference. For at least a year it left a configuration of rock distinctly resembling the face of Adolf Hitler!

In his poem, "The Western Hudson Shore,"[2] John Masefield gives a graphic description of the Palisades:

> In a long life's first independent day,
> As a Septembral mistiness grew bright,
> I saw the Hudson River where it lay
> Westward, all silver in the windless light.
> There, like a giant guard,
> Ranked as a rampart, proud yet battle-scarred,
> Were precipices silent in array.
> Endurance in eternity grown gray,
> Sentinel in implacable regard,
> Watching the ending of another night.
>
> "What is the cliff?" I asked. "The Palisades."
> Thereafter, daily, I would look across
> And watch the silences of their brigades,
> Enduring their eternity of loss,
> The sun, the wind, the cold.
> Often I watched the setting sun glow gold
> Down to their summit at a day's decline.
> I saw no dwelling in the rocky line,
> No lighted window starred the dusking shades,
> Sombre the fort, from rampart-top to fosse.

It is an enrapturing experience to stay atop the Palisades, perhaps with a picnic supper, as the sun goes down and twilight gently takes over. The sky turns blue velvet and, all along the New York shore and slopes on the east side of the Hudson, lights come on, twinkling one by one, and then, as darkness falls, shining in spreading clusters. The entire stretch of the Palisades at any time of day or night is ideal for romance. Appropriate here may be some sentimental lines from my poem, "Palisades Memoir":[3]

> Treading leafed, pine-needled paths
> And coming on those towering
> Ramparts of long-crumbling cliff
> Older than all our ancestors

Ten thousand generations back,
We looked, enchanted, far beneath,
Across the lush and swaying green,
To the river, wind-rippled white;

To the foaming wake of motorboats,
To slow barges of grey gravel,
To hawks and seagulls flying low
And floating on the fitful breeze.

Then for a single exquisite moment
The whole pulsating world was ours;
Ours to hold close, together,
As Time stopped at our bidding.

When my mother died in 1952, she left most of the Lamont Palisades property to Columbia University as a Geological Observatory, which, because of an additional bequest, later became known as the Lamont-Doherty Geological Observatory. However, I had persuaded Mother to set aside in her Will some 25 acres of her land as a permanent Nature Preserve. She willed this area, adjacent to the Observatory, to me and my younger brother Austin, with the statement: "It would be my wish that this tract of land be preserved in its natural beauty, either through maintaining it as an unspoiled private area or through turning it over to some public authority or through any other means that my sons in their discretion may deem wise and necessary."

This park was given the name of Lamont Nature Sanctuary. Although it was owned technically for several years by the Nature Conservancy, I was in charge of the Sanctuary for approximately twenty-five years. This meant primarily keeping the trails open and cleaning out the beer cans and Coca Cola bottles left by vulgar visitors heedless of natural beauty. With my clippers I loved to snip the growing branches ever encroaching on the trails from trees and shrubs alongside. Every storm would leave scattered branches and fallen trees blocking the rather narrow paths. It was enjoyable exercise to clear the paths and saw through the trees.

I was able to interest Columbia in the Sanctuary, students and faculty put it to good use, and the University finally set up a special Lamont Sanctuary Committee which negotiated the Nature Conservancy's official transfer of the area to Columbia. Should Columbia ever violate its agreement to keep the Sanctuary free of buildings or other man-made contrivances that interfere with its wildness and beauty, the land will revert to the Nature Conservancy.

The Lamont Sanctuary has been a valuable asset for me; it is but twelve miles north of the George Washington Bridge and only a half hour's drive from the Columbia University area where I have lived since 1928—and ideal for an afternoon walk. The Palisades are so near Columbia that all during my adult life I have hiked along these magnificent cliffs.

My health and happiness were enhanced by vacation family trips arranged by my parents. During the summer of 1913 they introduced us to the Alps, and after we had spent some days at Geneva and taken boat trips on Lake Geneva that included a visit to the antique Castle of Chillon, we drove across the border to Chamonix in France. There we climbed some lesser mountains, always with snow-capped Mont Blanc towering in the background, and fought our way up the glacier known as the Mer de Glace. Particularly exciting was climbing the glacier and peering down into the perilous crevasses. We were intrigued by the story of the man falling to his death on the Mer de Glace whose frozen body emerged at the outlet of the glacier seventy-five years later. Glaciers move very, very slowly.

That summer we took a cottage in southern England for two or three weeks. After the first week the caretaker of the place began to refer to me and my two brothers as "them three imps." We crossed the English Channel and stayed for a while at a house in Le Touquet-Paris Plage where there was fine bathing on the wide sand beach. My parents had engaged a Mr. Strickland to help look after their three sons. The only thing I can remember about him was that one day when we were all bathing, I came up suddenly from under a wave head first, collided with Strickland and knocked out two of his front teeth. Strickland badly stricken!

Following our European excursion, my parents took us on exciting expeditions to the Rocky Mountain West. The first was in 1914 when I was twelve and the family traveled to Flying D Ranch, at an altitude of over 5,000 feet, near Salesville, Montana. Our cabins were only a stone's throw away from the swiftly flowing Gallatin River. In the distance were glorious views of the jagged Spanish Peaks. All summer long we rode horseback, fished, climbed and went on pack trips. I did a lot of trout fishing with my father in nearby streams, both of us wearing high hip boots, and casting our many-colored flies into the eddying pools. That was grand fun and I became a pretty good fisherman.

In the following summer of 1915 we all went out to Oregon and stayed at White Pelican Lodge on the edge of Klamath Lake, named after the nearby Indian tribe and at the base of the Cascade Mountains. There we did most of our trout fishing by trolling from boats on the lake. The flat meadows alongside Lake Klamath were excellent for riding; we galloped our horses over them in high glee. But the fishing seemed a little tame compared with wading and casting down the fast-flowing waters of Montana.

Those two thrilling summers in the heart of the West gave me a lifelong appreciation of America's rugged mountain scenery and National Parks. At the end of the 1914 trip Father and Mother took us through Yellowstone National Park, with its remarkable geysers, hot springs, brightly pigmented canyon and waterfalls. We proceeded to Glacier National Park in Northern Montana and its massive snow-capped mountains and glaciers, and numberless opportunities for hiking or riding or fishing. At the end of the 1915 adventure, we visited the unique Crater Lake National Park, not far from our Lake Klamath Lodge, a huge body of water that had filled in a large crater when ages ago a volcano blew off the top of the mountain.

Those vacations in the West were a grand introduction to America's great system of National Parks, most of which I have visited. Besides Glacier National, I recall with particular nostalgia the magnificent Grand Canyon of the Colorado; its miniature duplicate, Zion in Utah; Yosemite in California; and Grand Teton in Wyoming where I spent part of two summers riding and hiking. In this sphere of National Parks the United States excels every other nation in the world.

After experimenting with various places for a permanent summer retreat, Father and Mother finally settled down on the island of North Haven, Maine, in the middle of Penobscot Bay. There in 1920 they constructed a large, sprawling, informal dwelling that merged several houses into one. Their house, named Sky Farm, stood on a bluff more than a hundred feet high, near the entrance to incomparable Pulpit Harbor. From the porch on the western side of the house we looked across West Penobscot Bay, with its islands, and reveled in most beautiful sunsets as the sun went down behind the Camden Hills on the mainland.

North Haven was a Mecca for summer sports with its informal life of golf, tennis, boating and especially sailing. While I participated to some extent in the sailboat racing, I preferred to sail a seventeen-foot knockabout in and out of the innumerable small islands that dot Penobscot Bay, often landing for a picnic lunch and exploring the islet, at times with a pretty girl as companion. The outermost White Island, south of North Haven, became my favorite anchorage, with its huge and high pink-white granite cliffs and dramatic views of bay and mountains. The Lamonts fell in love with this fascinating island and my father eventually bought it. Later we gave the Nature Conservancy a share in the ownership. Every summer we would stage a grand picnic at the White Island with all the Lamont families and relatives. For the young folk the water was warm enough for a swim, but in general I found Maine waters too cool for swimming.

After my father died in 1948, I acquired a fine house with some thirty acres at Ossining, New York, about a fifty-minute drive from my New York City apartment. The place had a lovely pond with an outdoor swimming pool at one end presided over by a large stone frog; an excellent tennis court a step away; an ample croquet field; and a complex of inviting trails through the woods. I called the main walks the Inner Circle, the Outer Circle and the Great Circle. From the house we had an enchanting view of the Hudson and the highlands on the west bank of the river. Several small paths bordered with flowers completed the picture. Again, we had grand headquarters for sports, the outdoor life and full appreciation of Nature. My wife and our four wonderful children—Margaret, Florence, Hayes and Anne—enjoyed it all as much as I.

My grandchildren, seven of them, and six step-grandchildren, felt the

same way. They came to love our Ossining haven. The grandchildren
families would come from time to time for a whole weekend; that was the
greatest fun of all for two or three very active days. Most of the time we had
a cat and kittens in the house. One spring our tri-colored Rainbow gave
birth to six kittens; as we fondled and played with those warm, lovable
creatures ecstasy reigned.

Every so often I gave over my Ossining place for the day to some
organization for a big outdoor money-raising affair. Two or three hundred
people would turn up for the picnics of the leftist weekly, the *National
Guardian*, or the Westchester Peoples Action Coalition (WESPAC). There
would be brief speeches, music and sometimes singing by folk artists such
as Pete Seeger.

In my Will I left all of my property at Ossining to the Brooklyn Botanic
Garden to be used as one of the special units of that prestigious institution
established in 1910 for the scientific study and display of plants.

Among many visitors to our Ossining house were two close friends,
Albert Rhys Williams and his wife, Lucita. Early in the 1950's they came to
Ossining for a weekend and liked the place so much that they stayed about
ten years. We saw them usually on weekends and became very fond of
both. Rhys Williams was a skilled writer who concentrated on the Soviet
Union. He was one of the few Americans in Petrograd (Leningrad) at the
time of the Communist Revolution, and wrote two books describing the
upheaval, *Through the Russian Revolution* (1921),[4] reprinted in 1967, and
Journey into Revolution (1969).[5]

Williams was a large jovial man and quite handsome with his shock of
grey hair, a mobile mouth, an expressive face with blue eyes; and his build
suggested his coal mining ancestors in Wales more than his preacher
ancestors. A gifted conversationalist, he talked endlessly of his experiences
in the U.S.S.R. and of his opinions on world politics. We went for many
hikes on nearby woodland trails, continuing our discussions as we walked. I
can see him now standing in front of our blazing wood fire and telling
amusing stories about strange happenings. No doubt about it, Rhys Williams had charisma.

In this chapter I have been praising man's ability to appreciate the
beauty and magnificence of Nature, one of the most significant of all arts in
developing human sensitivity and the enjoyment of existence. In my
Humanist philosophy, a keen responsiveness to the natural loveliness of
this earth and the universe beyond is particularly important. Since Humanism rejects belief in any form of the supernatural, it encourages all the
more man's sense of oneness with the eternal Nature that is his home, his
feeling of kinship with other living creatures, and his understanding of the
intimate interrelations between him and the cosmic matrix.

Constant awareness of Nature's pervasive patterns of beauty refreshes
and enriches the soul; it is an aesthetic pleasure, a spiritual delight and a
simple, healthy mode of recreation. In the world around us there is an

infinity of things for the alert person to enjoy—ocean waves breaking white and foaming along a sandy beach; a flowing river shimmering in the light of sun and moon; the incomparable Milky Way on a clear night; a rainbow's arc spanning a wide vista of hills; a panorama of lakes and evergreens from a high mountain; a white-streaked waterfall hurtling over a precipice; the big swirling flakes of a snowstorm; a hawk or seagull floating gracefully along the breeze; the gentle swish of a canoe gliding through still water; rural churchbells ringing in the distance; sweet-scented violets growing in a rock garden; the caress of a hot sun or warm breeze; the autumnal burst of glorious colors from trees and shrubs.

Americans are indeed blessed with innumerable rivers, lakes and bays; our enthralling mountains, valleys and plateaus, our extensive forests and plains and rolling hills. No country on earth surpasses the United States in variety and magnificence of scenery. I know at first-hand many of the wonder spots of Europe—regions like the towering Alps, the Soviet Caucasus, the French Riviera, the fjords of Norway, the Breton coast, the Rhine valley, the Scottish highlands, the English countryside and the lagoons of Venice. They are all superb and thrilling places. Yet all the natural splendors of Europe combined cannot outmatch those of America.

Indoors my favorite games were chess and bridge, both of which my parents taught me at an early age. As I grew older and took up permanent residence in New York City, I chose for evening entertainment the theatre, the movies and the ballet. Opera did not appeal to me very much.

In the movies I came to prefer Katharine Hepburn and Jane Fonda, Gary Cooper and Sir Laurence Olivier. Marilyn Monroe and Elizabeth Taylor never appealed to me. Early on, I felt that Miss Hepburn was a truly great actress and in fact America's best. I loved her slightly metallic voice and her lithe athletic figure. A character of profound sensitivity and artistic integrity shone through her acting. Like her mother, Mrs. Thomas Hepburn, Katharine was a liberal.

I first met Katharine Hepburn in the winter of 1950 when she was acting in Shakespeare's *As You Like It* in New York City. After I first saw the play, I sent her this telegram on February 8:

> No actress in this century or probably in any century has ever put on a more magnificent performance of Shakespeare than did you last night in "As You Like It." You have made the role of Rosalind as noteworthy as that of Lady Macbeth, bringing out with such understanding humor all the tender colors of life and love, and giving your audience those moments of sudden glory and poetic rapture that lift them out of and beyond the formidable crises of existence today. This was the great play that was waiting for your great talents and now indubitably you go down in history, for those with judgment, as the most memorable actress America has yet produced.
>
> Corliss Lamont

She responded with an appreciative note:

> Theatre Guild
> 23 West 53 Street
> New York, New York
>
> 3/10/50

Dear Corliss Lamont:

What a wonderful wire. I have been secretly waiting for you to come and see it as I remember that years ago you suggested that I should step out a bit so I was very pleased to hear from you and at the same time disappointed that you did not come backstage. However, I can frame your wire and read it whenever I get depressed.

It is, I must say, a really exciting experience. I get an enormous thrill out of doing it and a feeling that every minute I am learning something. Oddly enough, I think the audience has the same experience, so we lift each other up and that is always good.

Thank you for your great enthusiasm.

> Yours faithfully
> Katharine Hepburn

[P.S.] Next time for heaven's sake—come back.

I went to *As You Like It* again on my birthday, March 28, and was able to see Hepburn after the show. My memo of the time tells the story:

Went backstage at Cort Theatre after performance of *As You Like It*. I gave my card to an attendant and stood in a little hallway for about five minutes. To the left was the dressing room of William Prince, who played Orlando, and on his way into it he passed me just as I handed over my card.

Hepburn's dressing room was at the other end about fifty feet away. When the attendant thought she was ready, he went down and gave a maid my card. When I walked in, we shook hands and said hello. She was dressed in white slacks and a white sweater, and was wearing slippers. She offered me a cigarette and we both lit up.

I told her the play was just as splendid tonight as when I saw it before. She replied she was afraid it wasn't so good because it was so hot on the stage. It had been the warmest night since spring officially began. I said I had sat in the back row, the seventeenth, and could hear every word very well. I asked whether it would be done in the movies and she said she hoped so and that it certainly ought to be. It had been done once as a film and was a terrible flop. I suggested that some movie house ought to put on a general Hepburn revival at this point and she countered by remarking that her movies had been revived to the limit already. I told her about the remark I had heard coming in, that *As You Like It* would have closed in two weeks, except that it turned out not to be Shakespeare at all. I attacked *The*

New Yorker for its statement that it was such a baffling play, when really it was so simple, the quintessence of romantic love. She claimed Brooks Atkinson, who disliked the play, also disliked her, and considered her a rich Connecticut girl who had bought her way into the theatre. I remarked on how people always insisted that the tragic characters in drama were the greatest and she answered that it was true; they wouldn't allow comedy as great. However, she corrected me by stating that Rosalind *was* considered one of Shakespeare's great characters. She remarked that though she had received the Academy Award for *Morning Glory*, her role in *Little Women* was much harder.

She asked me what I was doing now, and I replied that I was treasurer of the Progressive Party, for which she had done such a fine job at Hollywood in 1948. She told me what a great thrill it was to talk through the mike to so many people and also what trouble she had gotten into with her movie employers. She remarked she was always afraid that I was going to land in jail. By this time we had smoked our cigarettes and I felt it was about time to go. She kicked off her slippers and put on some socks, talking all the time, and started to hunt for her shoes. She agreed Washington had become a perfect madhouse and that you never get anywhere by this sort of thing. She felt it must soon get better, but I cautioned against optimism and said it might get worse. They were so afraid of everything, I said. She said passionately, "But fear never accomplishes anything." She wondered if the situation didn't get me down. And I said, "Not usually, because I wake up in the morning feeling pretty good and rather enjoy the battle anyway."

Going back a bit she asked me whether I didn't have a sister in Hartford. I told her yes, that her husband Charlie Cunningham was director of Hartford Athenaeum. Did I go to Hartford sometimes? Yes, occasionally. You know my mother, don't you? Yes, she's a great liberal and I had lunch with her when I went through Hartford a few years ago.

Later that spring of 1950 Hepburn accepted my suggestion to go for a walk along the trail at the top of the Palisades. Thereafter, since she liked to hike, we took many walks along both the top and bottom of the Palisades, and in Central Park as well.

I wrote her again on May 5, 1950:

Dear Katharine,

After seeing you act or talking to you personally I, as a writer, am simply *compelled* to write something. This I have done for years after going to any movie in which you appear. Now more than ever I must write; and since I have more or less gotten over my stagefright I dare to send you this letter.

Do you really know the effect you have on people? For me at least you raise life to the pitch of ecstasy; make me want to dance before breakfast and sing all day; fill me with visions of the great things I might achieve; give me a continuing series of quite fruitful brain-storms. It is a hundred times more potent and effective than benze-drine.

There is for me something remarkable and unprecedented in this situation; and if I could unravel the mystery, I would possess the secret of the universe and would tell other people and make them happy. I have enough confidence in my own instincts and intelligence to be convinced that you are an absolutely phenomenal person and that an actress equal to you walks this earth only about once in a hundred years.

This is why I, as one generally interested in the advancement of art, want to see your influence spread; your name and splendor become immortal. You, too, with all your loveliness and vitality, will go some day

> "To pillow your bright head
> By the incurious dead." . . . .

Devotedly yours,
Corliss

I was so enthusiastic about my actress friend that I established in 1952 a special Katharine Hepburn scholarship at Bryn Mawr College from which she had graduated, to be awarded annually to an undergraduate with promising acting ability. I kept this matter confidential because I was afraid that my reputation as a radical and possibly a Communist might somehow harm Miss Hepburn's career.

Our correspondence continued. We settled down to the nickname "Kate" for her. She airmailed a letter from Venice in September, 1954:

Grand Hotel
Venice

September 4, 1954

Dear Corliss,

It was nice to hear from you. I get all the printed matter from Dad. I should think that you would be so disgusted that you would snarl all day long. It is a good thing that you have such a warm sense of humor—I must say I do think that you have a very superior brain and lovely character. I think of you very often. The days come and go as they always do when one is working very hard. It is a thrilling place to be. The people are angelic—generous and truly artistic. They make one feel entirely fascinating and mutter the most flattering things as one passes. We (Constance Collier—her secretary and I) have had the good fortune to live in a very sweet palazzo of only 140 rooms. Wow! What luxury—and slaves to work for you. They get nothing and they never take a day off. There is a very frightening contrast between rich and poor here.

Send me a photograph of the Rivera portrait. Love your letters about him. Sounds fascinating.

With many affectionate thoughts.

K—

On June 5, 1968, I wrote Kate how terribly upset I was over the assassination of Robert Kennedy in Los Angeles. She replied:

> Victorine Studio
> Nice, France
>
> [June, 1968]
>
> Dear Corliss,
> Your letter about the enormous danger you felt for Robert Kennedy barely preceded the disastrous happening. Shattering to feel that all this wonderful potential for the vigorous doing has just been ended. I always had an enormously warm reaction to him—what in the world can one do to stem the tide—this tide of sudden disaster.
> Our movie "Lion" is about the same thing in 1183. I'll be back sort of July 7th, 8th.
>
> Affectionately,
> Kate

For more than two months in the Fall of 1976 I rejoiced in the Hepburn Festival at the Regency Theatre in New York City, and wrote Kate:

> November 19, 1976
>
> Dear Greatest Actress of Twentieth Century America:
>
> "Holiday" last night was a magnificent ending for me of the Hepburn Festival. It was a superb piece of acting on your part; and the other characters, including especially Cary Grant, were all excellent.
> I left the theatre so exhilarated that I felt ready to commit some wild, extreme act like jumping through a store window or making sudden love to my female partner. I once wrote a poem to you entitled "The Gift of Exaltation." So it is Exaltation and Exhilaration combined!
> Well, these nine weeks of the Festival have been a great thing for me, a deep-felt, moving experience that has brought me to almost full recovery (it can never be complete) from my wife's death. There is no friend to whom I owe more gratitude than you.
> The movie future now is not too dim. For the Regency Theatre next week is starting a five-week Fred Astaire Festival. And I am very fond of his films.
> Good luck and happy Thanksgiving, Kate, and all the best as you continue to conquer the West.
>
> Corliss

I will conclude with one more letter from Kate Hepburn that came in 1976:

November 23rd [1976]

Corliss,

Your letters are a delight. You make me feel very fascinating at a time when I really feel like a great Lug. Can you imagine being so stupid. Anyway, the Wheel Chair Version is on. Some things are improved—others are difficult. But it seems to work.

Now for five more weeks I will be in the cast. Broke fibula-tibia and tore the ligament.

Your pamphlet on your trip to China is excellent. Most interesting. Your enthusiasm over my dramatic efforts makes me very happy.

Affection,
Kate

[P.S.] It is indeed wicked to lose someone you love. Must recover. Must get accustomed. But it ain't easy.

Jane Fonda I hardly knew personally, but admired her acting in such films as *Coming Home* and *China Syndrome*. I first met her as one of the public figures opposed to the military aggression of the United States in the Vietnam War. At the risk of ruining her career in motion pictures, she took a principled position against the American invasion. Then in 1979 *China Syndrome*, the dramatic film about an incident at a nuclear reactor plant, was released only a week before the actual and very dangerous accident did take place at the Three Mile Island reactor station in Pennsylvania.

Some months later Miss Fonda went on a nationwide tour with her husband, Tom Hayden, lecturing on the menace to human life of nuclear plants and calling for their abolition. Their position was supported by the October 30, 1979 Report of President Carter's Commission on the Accident at Three Mile Island, which stated that even if all of its suggested controls were adopted for nuclear reactors, there was "no guarantee that there will be no serious future nuclear accidents." (*New York Times*, October 31, 1979.) There was plainly a possibility that the entire billion-dollar plant might never reopen.

Chapter VI THE MYTH OF IMMORTALITY

It was in 1932 that I took a significant step in my philosophical development. In that year I finished my thesis "Issues of Immortality" and received
my Ph.D. degree in philosophy from Columbia University. In accordance
with Columbia's regulations, the thesis was published as a small book. In
that study I did not state any opinion as to whether or not personal
immortality existed, but made clear, following the monistic psychology of
Aristotle, that body and personality were intimately and inseparably con-
nected; and I demonstrated that traditional religions gave much convincing
evidence of this very point.

The question of immortality seemed to me central to a rounded philosophy. As I continued to study it for several years, I became less impressed by
the dualist or Platonic psychology with its assumption that man was a
twoness of body and soul, and that the soul was separable from the body
and could go on into a future life after the death of the individual. Common
sense, scientific fact and philosophical analysis all pointed, I thought, to the
oneness of man, to the indivisible unity of body and personality. Religious
acceptance of this doctrine can clearly be seen in the Bible.

The Old Testament Hebrews could not conceive of a robust, happy
afterlife without the body. They either looked upon death as the end or
thought the enfeebled spirits of the departed went to a sad and somber
place called Sheol. The ancient Greeks had a similar view of survival after
death in what they called Hades. According to Homer,[1] the shade of
Achilles told Ulysses: "Better to be the hireling of a slave and serve a man of
mean estate than to be ruler over all these dead and gone." Plato wanted
such passages to be deleted from the poets, because he thought that they
would make warriors less willing to give up their lives in battle.

The New Testament Christians had a different attitude toward post-mor-
tem existence. Their brilliant solution was the resurrection of the natural
body become glorified and incorruptible. The orthodox Christian conception of the resurrection and immortality brings out clearly that body and

soul must be inseparable in the afterlife just as in this life. The foundation stone of Christianity is faith in the bodily resurrection of Jesus into the realm of immortality as recounted in the New Testament. The resurrection extends to everyone; it is to be the identical body of this world, without a hair or fingernail missing, that rises from the tomb. The Roman Catholic Church still frowns on cremation for its members because it psychologically weakens belief in the resurrection of the corpse. Primitive religions also associated immortality with the body. The ancient Egyptians, for example, believed that a desirable future life was bound up with the mummification and preservation of the dead, natural body.

But in modern times more and more people in the Western world have become unable to believe in the literal resurrection of the body. Yet, in the ideas of immortality held by certain modern religious sects it is clear that some sort of body is necessary in the hereafter. The Spiritualists give the soul an *etheric* body. The Swedenborgians have invented the *crystalline* body. The Theosophists talk of *astral* bodies. And the Modernists in Protestant churches, like that masterly preacher, Harry Emerson Fosdick, assume the existence of *spiritual* bodies in the future life as essential vehicles for the personality or soul. Reincarnation supplies the departed soul with a body, even if it be that of a monkey or cobra, as we know from a study of the Buddhists and Hindus in India. There is a strong Buddhist following in Japan. When I was travelling in that country in 1959, I read in the newspapers that, since Crown Prince Akihito and his wife were expecting a baby very shortly, it was estimated that at least 1,000 suicides would probably soon take place so that the dead person's soul could enter the body of the baby at the precise moment of its birth. The individual thus reincarnated then might one day become Emperor.

What my studies showed was that Christianity in its main divisions, primitive religions, modern cults in the West, and reincarnation in the East, all stressed the necessity for some sort of body in the afterlife and thus lent support to the monistic psychology of the unity of body and personality. Looking at the alternatives, I concluded that the best way to achieve immortality is through the resurrection of the natural body, or through its continuing to stay alive on this earth.

As to the prolongation of individual human lives, the science of medicine has made such advances during the twentieth century that the average length of life has been greatly extended in many countries. Life expectancy in the United States in 1980 was almost seventy-four. The science of medicine is still grappling with the problems and diseases of old age such as heart attacks and hardening of the arteries. Even if they are finally overcome, it is doubtful that medicine can prolong human life indefinitely, with the billions of cells in the human body probably continuing to wear out and ceasing to function properly. It is barely conceivable that far in the future a human being might live to the age of 969, which the Bible tells us Methuselah reached.

We must consider now the Life Extension Society and Trans Time, both of which have their headquarters in California. These societies claim that if you freeze a man at the moment of death and then resurrect him and thaw him out fifty or a hundred years later, advances in medicine will enable doctors to cure him of the disease from which he had died, so that he might keep on living indefinitely. The advertising slogan of the Life Extension Society is "Freeze, Wait, Reanimate!", while the motto of Trans Time is "Never say die." It is true that some unicellular animals and bacteria frozen for centuries into Arctic tundra or Antarctic ice have come alive when thawed out. But we must doubt whether the same result would take place in the case of so complex an organism as that of the human, with the circulation of the blood always a vital factor.

Arthur Quaife, president of Trans Time, states that the company had, as of 1980, nine bodies in storage and explained that these " 'patients' were suspended in capsules refrigerated with liquid nitrogen at 106 degrees below zero centigrade." The cost for each deceased person was $60,000 for this extraordinary process of resurrection that does not wait for the Christian Day of Judgment. The California Cemetery Board believed that the whole business "is a gross consumer fraud and ought to be stopped."[2]

We have to admit that these experiments are in principle on the right track, because they do proceed on the basis that body and personality are inseparable. Such experiments remind us of the solid truth that the only way to be immortal is to stay alive forever in this natural world, and thus actualize the original meaning of immortality as "not-death."

When we turn from religion and philosophy to science, we find conclusive evidence of the intimate and inseparable association of body or physical organism, on the one hand, and personality, including the mind, on the other hand. Modern biology, psychology and medicine all support the monistic viewpoint. Biology shows that the species Man is the culmination of a long evolutionary process that began at least three billion years ago when the first living forms appeared on this earth. Personality and mind appear only when the physical organism has reached a very complex stage, as in the human animal; and mind has developed during the most recent stage of evolution. It is the complexity of the brain in Man, and especially of the cerebral cortex, that gives him the power of thought.

Just as in the evolution of species, mind and personality appear when bodily organization has reached a certain stage, so it is in the history of every normal human being. Neither the embryo nor the newborn infant possesses the distinguishing features of mind. The laws of heredity and of sex, based on genes, are fundamental in determining what sort of personality develops.

More than two thousand years ago Lucretius[3] summed up the situation in his great poem, *On the Nature of Things:*

> Again, feeling doth prove that mind is born
> Along with body, and with it step by step

Doth grow, and equally must waste and age.
For e'en as children totter with a weak
And tender frame, so doth a slender wit
Attend thereon; but as with riper years
Their strength doth wax, wisdom will grow apace
And force of mind gain increase. And at last,
When time's stern strength hath sapped the frame, and loosed
Are all the limbs, their powers benumbed, anon
The wits are lamed, tongue raveth, mind is shaken,
All things give way and in one breath are fled.
'Tis meet, then, that the nature of the mind
Should all be scattered likewise, e'en as smoke
Into the high-flung breezes of the air:
Since side by side with body do we see
It brought to birth, and side by side they grow,
And worn with age together droop and fade.

Psychology, especially, demonstrates the unity of body and personality. The mind and thinking processes are vital to the sense of personality, to its development and to most of its activities. Those thinking processes are centered in the cerebral cortex which has more than ten billion neurons (nerve cells). In the brain's cortex the interneuronic connections, actual and possible, approach infinity. In this extraordinary cortex our memory patterns are laid down; and memory is of crucial importance for personal immortality because it is necessary for connecting the mortal and the immortal self, just as it is essential for connecting the self that goes to sleep at night with the self that awakens in the morning. In the body as a whole there are 265 trillion cells. And one must ask, "Really, can all those numberless intricacies of body and brain be resurrected as functioning entities on the great Day of Judgment after the corpse has decayed in the grave for untold eons or been reduced to ashes in the crematory?"

We must remember that mind in Man comes into being only through social intercourse, through the give-and-take of language and speech in the family and the larger community. We are born with brains; we *acquire* minds by association with other minds. Thus, there is an inseparable connection between the body-mind-personality and the human community. This fact further undermines the dualist psychology.

In this discussion the scientific Law of Parsimony is of particular significance. This law holds that any scientific explanation be based on the fewest possible assumptions that succeed in accounting for all the facts. Sir Arthur Conan Doyle, the creator of Sherlock Holmes, came to think that the spirits of the dead could be contacted, and even believed that invisible fairies tended the flowers at night. We discard this charming idea about fairies because the science of botany adequately explains in naturalistic terms why flowers grow in the spring. They don't need the help of fairies. The Law of Parsimony rules them out as an unnecessary assumption.

The dualist assumption that man has a separable, supernatural soul violates the same law because it is superfluous for explaining the emotional profundities and intellectual powers of human beings. The infinite intricacy of the brain and its cerebral cortex is fully competent to sustain the manifold activities and achievements of human personalities. To add a special soul to a man's native equipment is like conjuring up devils or demons as the cause of insanity or hysteria. Well into the nineteenth century physicians still believed in the devil theory; and I gather from the newspapers that many of our fellow citizens are coming back to it today. The Catholic Church has never given up belief in *The* Devil and a multitude of little devils.

To summarize, the sciences of biology, medicine and psychology have accumulated an enormous amount of evidence pointing to the oneness and inseparability of personality and physical organism. The Law of Parsimony leads to the same conclusion. It is inconceivable that the characteristic mental activities of thought, memory and imagination could go on without the cooperating potencies of the brain and cerebral cortex. Moreover, the monistic view of the nature of Man is supported or implied by Christianity and other religions which insist that both soul and some kind of body are necessary for personal survival.

The resurrection of the dead body is in some ways the most sensible way to save the day for immortality. But that is a miracle in which, in this modern age, I and probably a vast majority of the human race cannot possibly believe. This supposed solution in any case has a fatal flaw. The world refuses to come to an end and no resurrection has taken place, despite the repeated predictions of the Seventh Day Adventists. Meanwhle, the souls of the dead are supposedly biding their time in places like purgatory; but they do not have their original bodies with them. And their survival as naked souls, as it were, runs into all the difficulties I have pointed out in relation to personal survival in general.

Since I was unable to believe in the resurrection or in any of the supernatural bodies offered, my research and reflection after the publication of my first book led me to conclude that it is very probable that death marks the end of the conscious personality. This is the theme of my later volume, *The Illusion of Immortality* (1935). When one of my teaching colleagues learned that I planned to publish the very unorthodox *Illusion*, he warned me that such a publication would probably put an end to any academic advancement for me. But I was not seeking that anyhow, and it did not come my way. In America *The Illusion of Immortality* became accepted as a prime reference book on the non-existence of a hereafter. And I made the problem of immortality my specialty in the field of philosophy. Probably a majority of American philosophers in colleges and universities agree that immortality is impossible, but to this day very few wish to take the academic risk of saying so publicly.

I deeply regret that personal immortality seems impossible. Approaching the age of 80, I do not relish the prospect of complete extinction within the next ten years or so. As the sole survivor of my original family, I should like nothing better than to awake after death in the Utopia that is heaven, to be once more with my beloved parents, brothers and sister and to mingle with my many dear friends, men and women, who have passed on. So it is that I feel sympathy and compassion for everyone who ever longed for immortality.

The main motive for desiring an afterlife is the simple wish to keep on living. We are enjoying life on this earth (or a lot of us are), and we want to prolong it. And so, since we have to die, we should like to go on existing somewhere else. It is an extension of the instinct for self-preservation. The idea of personal immortality, if we exclude the concepts of hell and purgatory, is a pleasant myth or dream, but we should not treat it as reality.

In 1933 I initiated a lively correspondence with H. L. Mencken when he was Editor of *The American Mercury* and had recently published *Treatise on the Gods*.[4] I wrote him (July 24, 1933) to take issue with his position in that book that *fear* was the chief motivation for belief in supernatural religion and immortality. I claimed that *hope* was more important in this regard. He answered on July 27:

Dear Mr. Lamont:

Unquestionably, a good case may be made out for hope as a religious motive, but I am inclined to think that analysis will show that hope in many cases is scarcely more than a sort of escape from fear. In other words, fear is the primary emotion.

Not many people would hope for pie in the sky if they did not fear annihilation, or worse. I am speaking here, of course, of the more elemental sort of human beings. On higher levels religious ideas become immensely complicated, and motives appear which would be quite incomprehensible to the average country Baptist. Many years of observation of backwoods Christians have convinced me that fear is almost the sole motive behind their faith.

Unfortunately, I haven't read your "Issues of Immortality", but I hope to do so very soon. Incidentally, have you anything under way that suggests publication in The American Mercury? If so, I surely hope you let me hear of it. It would be a pleasure indeed to print you.

Sincerely yours,
H. L. Mencken

Far more relevent for Humanists than speculations about immortality is to work for the permanence, which might extend to immortality, of institutions that they consider important—schools, colleges, libraries, scientific institutions, museums, nature sanctuaries, committees for civil liberties and human rights, outstanding cities, one's country and the United Nations. And beyond all that is the possible immortality of the human race.

The most potent obstacle at present to the immortality of Man is the danger of a worldwide nuclear war, in which death-dealing fallout could bring about the extinction of humankind upon this planet. The continued production of nuclear weapons by the Great Powers is mad; nevertheless, the armaments race in both conventional and nuclear weapons continues. The United States maintains a huge number of military bases abroad—more than 400—at the cost of tens of billions of dollars. These enormous military expenditures, requiring $500 billion annually worldwide, are a deadly menace to America and all mankind.

Humanity's ultimate fate is of course bound up with the sun, which some day will not give off enough heat to maintain life on this planet. Harlow Shapley, Professor of Astronomy at Harvard, estimated that it will be ten billion years before the sun cools off that much. Other astronomers say it will be five billion or less. These figures are of course all speculative. Such vast stretches of time seem to me practically immortality in itself. In any case, we must not accept inevitable doom. Modern science is only some 400 years old. Imagine what advances science will have made in 400 million or four billion years.

The development of nuclear energy opens up vast possibilities. Some scientists are talking of sending up artificial suns to encircle the globe; and others talk of utilizing nuclear power to speed up the revolution of the earth around the sun, so that our planet would get nearer to the sun as its heat diminished. And it has long been dreamt that humans will eventually be able to emigrate to other planets in space ships when and if this earth becomes uninhabitable. The American astronauts who landed on the moon in 1969 foreshadowed this possibility.

Whether or not these speculations have validity, it is exciting and consoling to think that in other parts of the infinite universe, including our own galaxy, forms of life different from or similar to humankind may have been evolving. To cite Professor Shapley again: "We can no longer doubt but that wherever the physics, chemistry and climates are right on a planet's surface, life will emerge and persist."[5] And if extraterrestrial life *has* emerged here and there, it is possible that beings more highly developed than Man have evolved.

It is a fact that in the observable universe billions upon billions of stars exist—10 to the 21st power. There are 150 billion stars just in our own Milky Way galaxy. It is reliably estimated that if only one out of a million stars in the universe has at least one planet, there are in the cosmos planets numbering 10 to the 15th power, which means 100 trillion. And if only one planet in a million is of a sort that can support life, there are at least a billion such planets in the cosmos. The distinct probability that life exists scattered throughout the universe may mean that life, if not Man, is immortal in this stupendous array of stars, planets, suns and galaxies.

Chapter VII   THE PHILOSOPHY OF
                HUMANISM

As I was working through to definite conclusions about the meaning of
death and the impossibility of personal immortality, a very important
intellectual event occurred in the United States. That was the publication
in 1933 of *Humanist Manifesto I*, signed by twenty-four leading professors
of philosophy, clergymen and authors who rejected all forms of theism and
supernaturalism. The *Manifesto* stated that "Humanism considers the
complete realization of human personality to be the end of man's life and
seeks its development and fulfillment in the here and now . . . in the light
of the scientific spirit and method. . . . Holding an organic view of life,
Humanists find that the traditional dualism of mind and body must be
rejected."

I found the *Humanist Manifesto* too vague and incomplete to express the
Humanist philosophy adequately. I was also critical of its reference to that
philosophy as "religious Humanism." Nonetheless, I realized that it constituted the best expression of my own beliefs yet formulated. My book *The
Illusion of Immortality* was a natural stepping stone to Humanism in
general. The American philosopher, William James, had stated: "The
popular touchstone for all philosophies is the question, 'What is their
bearing on a future life?' "[1] He went on to say that for most men and women
God has been primarily the guarantor of survival beyond the grave. James
was right.

Some of the *Manifesto*'s signers, under the leadership of Edwin H.
Wilson, a Unitarian minister, pressed on to establish in 1941 The American
Humanist Association to educate the American people on the Humanist
viewpoint. Mr. Wilson became the able and energetic Director of the
Association for twenty-five years and also Editor of the organization's
monthly magazine, *The Humanist*, likewise founded in 1941. I promptly
joined the AHA and have worked closely with it ever since. In 1974 I
became Honorary President of the Association and was honored in 1977
when it bestowed on me the Award of Humanist of the Year.

The Humanist Association has cooperated with the American Ethical Culture Societies and the American Ethical Union which in general support the Humanist philosophy. This cooperation is seen best in the International Humanist and Ethical Union (IHEU), founded in 1952, which has its headquarters at Utrecht, Holland, and publishes its own quarterly, *International Humanism*. Actually, the Humanist Association and individual Humanists are glad to cooperate on social, economic and international issues with *anyone*, no matter what his over-all philosophy or religion may be.

In 1973 more than 200 intellectuals, including myself, issued *Humanist Manifesto II*, edited by Paul Kurtz, Professor of Philosophy at the State University of New York at Buffalo, and Edwin H. Wilson. This statement gave a more extensive and up-to-date summary of the Humanist outlook than *Manifesto I*. In 1980 another basic Humanist Declaration was published, signed by sixty-one scholars and writers, and decrying the "reappearance of dogmatic authoritarian religions" as a danger to "intellectual freedom, human rights and scientific progress." This same group announced the founding of a new Humanist magazine, *Free Inquiry*, edited by Professor Kurtz.

The word *Humanism* itself is so warm and attractive that in the twentieth century it has been adopted by various groups, often diametrically opposed in ideology. Thus we have *Catholic* Humanism, *Socialist* Humanism, *secular* Humanism, *scientific* Humanism, *democratic* Humanism, *religious* Humanism and *naturalistic* Humanism. For my own part I prefer the phrase *naturalistic Humanism* and to describe it as a philosophy or a way of life. To define naturalistic Humanism briefly: It rejects every form of supernaturalism, theism, pantheism and metaphysical idealism, and considers man's supreme aim to be the welfare, happiness and progress of all humanity in this one and only life, according to the methods of reason and science, democracy and love.

The ultimate goal is not Christian service to an improbable God, but service here and now to our fellow human beings. Reserving the word "love" for his family and friends, the Humanist takes an attitude of *compassionate concern* toward his fellow humans in general. To sum up specifically my understanding of naturalistic Humanism in a dozen or so brief propositions:

First of all, the Humanist finds that Nature or the universe makes up the totality of existence and is completely self-operating according to natural law, with no need for a God or gods to keep it functioning in a fairly harmonious way. This tremendous cosmos, unbounded in space and infinite in time, consists fundamentally of a constantly changing and evolving system of matter and energy. It is entirely neutral in regard to Man's well-being or values. The origin of the universe, if there was an origin, and its final destination, if any, are as much a mystery to Humanism as to any other philosophy.

The very immensity of the universe tends to make the Humanist an agnostic regarding the existence of God. We find no convincing evidence of God functioning upon this planet and in the sun-guided solar system. But what about the billions of stars out there in our own Milky Way galaxy and in other star-studded galaxies whirling through space billions of light-years from one another, a light-year being the distance—approximately six trillion miles—that light travels in a year? We are not justified in absolutely denying the existence of God until we have checked the nature of things in at least half of the universe. And we know that this is impossible. Accordingly the Humanist prefers to call himself a *non-theist*. In fact everyone ought to be an agnostic about the reality of God, since religious "proofs" of his existence pertain only to this planet Earth.

The astronomical findings of the twentieth century about this gigantic, expanding, runaway universe have made the earth increasingly insignificant in terms of space and time. Spatially speaking, our planet is a mere speck on the edge of our great galaxy. Reflecting on these things, human beings may experience a sense of cosmic loneliness and unimportance, and thus long for a cosmic companion in the form of a benevolent God. I sympathize with all who may feel this way.

Next in the Humanist world-view is that the race of Man is the present culmination of a time-defying evolutionary process on this planet that has lasted at least three billion years; that Man exists as an inseparable unity of mind and body; and that therefore it is extremely improbable, if not impossible, that after death there can be any personal immortality or survival of consciousness.

During the past decade fundamentalist religious groups such as the Moral Majority have been carrying on a concerted campaign to discredit the concept of Darwinian Evolution. They have demanded that American educational institutions, especially public schools, teach, on an equal basis with evolution, God-guided Creationism as the origin of Man. Actually, theists would make more sense if they argued that the progressive evolution of life upwards to the appearance of Man shows a divine power at work.

Fundamental to Humanism is that in working out its basic views on Man and the universe, and in attaining the truth in general, it relies on reason, and especially on the established facts, laws and methods of modern experimental science. In general, Man's best hope for solving problems is through the use of intelligence and scientific method applied with vision and determination. Courage, love and perseverance provide emotional drive for successfully coping with difficulties, but it is reason that finds the actual solution. Intuition may offer brilliant ideas, but they must always be double-checked by reason or scientific procedures.

On an issue of constant controversy, I oppose all theories of universal determinism, fatalism or predestination and believe that human beings possess genuine freedom of choice (free will) in making decisions both important and unimportant. Free choice is conditioned by heredity, education, health, the external environment (particularly economic conditions) and other factors. Nonetheless, it remains real and substantial. Humanism rejects alike Christian and Islamic theistic determinism, Marxist economic determinism and the determinism of behaviorist psychologists such as Professor B. F. Skinner. My recent book, *Freedom of Choice Affirmed,*[2] attempted to refute these various kinds of determinism.

I was happy to receive a letter from Sir Julian Huxley with significant comments on the question of free choice:

31 Pond Street
London, N.W.3

3rd September, 1965

Dear Corliss,

. . . . As regards Freedom of Choice, I arrived at similar conclusions to you, but by a rather different route. I take the purely objective view that the number of "choices", i.e., of different courses of action, open to different organisms increases as you go up the evolutionary scale, culminating in man. The *range* of choice is increased, and I would say this is one important aspect of freedom.

In any case, the particular actual choice is determined or conditioned (a) by external environment, (b) by the individual's genetic outfit and personal history, (c) by his particular mental state at the moment. As it is quite impossible to evaluate the result accurately, the philosophic basis of so-called determinism, and also of freedom, falls to the ground. The question, in these terms, is impossible to answer, and therefore should not be asked. In the same way, especially as the actual choice may be influenced by unpredictable changes in single neurones (just as unpredictable changes in atoms underlie the uncertainty principle, which has made hay of the idea that if we knew enough—which we never could!—we should be able to prophesy the future of anything in the universe). This, if you like, is pragmatic, but none the less valid for that!

I am so glad you are having a nice time in Maine. Juliette joins me in all very best wishes. I am exceedingly busy with a lot of writing!

Yours ever,
Julian H.
Sir Julian Huxley

In ethics or morality I advocate a position that grounds all human values in this-earthly experience and relationships. Since we live only once, we should make the most of it in terms of an abundant and reasoned happiness, unmarred and unrestrained by the conscience-stricken suppressions of the past. Such a philosophy heartily welcomes all life-enhancing and healthy pleasures, from the rollicking joys of vigorous youth to the contemplative delights of mellowed age. This way of life draws no hard-fast line, sets up no confusing or corrupting dualism between the personality or mind on the one hand, and the body or physical organism on the other. For in whatever he does Man is a living unity of personality and body, an interfunctioning oneness of mental and emotional and physical qualities. Thus it should be clear that the so-called goods of the spirit—of culture and art and responsible citizenship—are, like all other natural goods, an integral and indispensable part of the ideal life, the higher hedonism, for which Humanism stands. This is a philosophy of continuing and expanding joy: for the individual, for the community, for all humankind.

It cannot be said too often that although Humanism regards as myth the supernatural aspects of Christianity, it embodies in its philosophy much of the Judeo-Christian ethic as set forth in the Old and New Testaments. In America and the world at large we need nothing so much as a firm allegiance to precepts of the Ten Commandments such as "Thou shalt not steal," "Thou shalt not bear false witness," and "Thou shalt not kill." We cannot stress too much the cardinal importance of plain, old-fashioned honesty in every walk of life.

Turning to the New Testament, we find that the gospels have much to offer a generous and humane ethical philosophy such as Humanism's. Jesus spoke out repeatedly on behalf of broad Humanist ideals: social equality, the brotherhood of man and peace on earth. Certain of his teachings presented in the Sermon on the Mount possess an ethical import that will always be an inspiration to Humanists and everyone else. And what could be more Humanistic than Christ's statements: "Ye shall know the truth, and the truth shall make you free"; and "I am come that they might have life, and that they might have it more abundantly."?

I believe that the good life is best attained by an individual in combining personal satisfactions with significant work and other activities that contribute to the welfare of one's family, university, trade union, city or nation. Worthwhile work is likely to make a person happier. Everyone must also exercise some self-interest to keep alive and healthy. Normal and legitimate self-interest can be harmoniously united with ethical idealism and altruistic endeavors on behalf of the community. I do not favor the "selfless" life, because it denies to the altruistic individual his own right to happiness.

In the controversial realm of sex relations, Humanism rejects entirely dualistic theories that separate soul from body by claiming that the highest morality is to keep the soul pure and undefiled from physical desire and pleasure. The Humanist regards sexual emotions and their fulfillment as healthy and beautiful, Nature's wonderful way of making possible the continued reproduction of life on earth. While Humanism advocates high standards of conduct between the sexes, it rejects the puritanism of the past and looks upon sexual love and pleasure as among the greatest of human experiences and values.

In aesthetics Humanism encourages the widest possible development of the arts and awareness of beauty, so that aesthetic experience may become a pervasive reality. The Humanist eschews the artificial distinction between the fine arts and the useful arts and asserts that the common objects of daily use should embody a fusion of utility and grace. The mass production of industrial goods by machinery need not defeat this aim. Humanism calls for the planned architectural reconstruction of towns and cities so that beauty may prevail in urban life.

Humanists give special emphasis to man's appreciation of the beauty and splendor of Nature. There is no heavenly Father in or behind Nature; but Nature is truly our Fatherland. Humanists back efforts for conservation, for extension of park areas and protection of wildlife. Long before a sound ecology and anti-pollution measures became accepted as national goals, they were campaigning for these very things. The Humanist's responsiveness to every sort of natural beauty evokes in him a feeling of profound kinship with Nature and its myriad forms of life.

As to political philosophy, Humanism believes that the best type of government is some form of democracy, which includes civil liberties and full freedom of expression throughout all areas of economic, political and cultural life. Reason and science are crippled unless they remain unfettered in the pursuit of truth. In the United States, the Humanist supports the democratic guarantees in the Bill of Rights and the Constitution.

In international affairs and for the actualization of happiness everywhere on earth, the Humanist advocates world peace, democracy and a high standard of living throughout the globe. In their concern for the welfare of all nations, peoples and races, Humanists adopt William Lloyd Garrison's aphorism: "Our country is the world; our countrymen are all mankind." It follows that Humanists are opposed to all forms of racial and nationalist prejudice. Humanism is international in spirit and scope, as is evidenced by the activities of the International Humanist and Ethical Union. This organization meets every five years and everywhere decries the danger of nuclear war and nuclear weapons which menace the entire human race. The date set for the eighth IHEU Congress was 1982.

The invention of nuclear bombs has made the matter of international war versus world peace the most important ethical issue of all. Robert Johansen, President of the Institute for World Order, gives the Humanist viewpoint when he states: "The human race—not simply one segment of it—is the important constituency to consider even in national policymaking . . . . To one who identifies with the human species as well as with the nation, all wars become civil wars—conflicts of brother and sister against brother and sister."[3]

Finally, Humanism, in accordance with scientific method, encourages the ceaseless questioning of assumptions and convictions in every field of thought. This includes, of course, philosophy, naturalistic Humanism and the summary I have here presented. Humanism is not a new dogma; it is a developing philosophy ever open to experimental testing, newly discovered facts and more rigorous reasoning.

I am convinced that there are millions of Americans who have adopted naturalistic Humanism as their philosophy without knowing its name— without ever having heard of the American Humanist Association. That Association has never had more than 6,000 members and must be considered a *pilot* organization that points the way rather than aiming to become a mass membership group. It points the way not only through its journal, *The Humanist*, but through TV and radio programs that it has managed to have broadcast in recent years, programs that have constituted an important breakthrough for Humanism.

Professor Emeritus of Philosophy at the University of Florida, Morris B. Storer, says: "A large majority of the educators of America and the western world are Humanist in their outlook. The faculties of American colleges and universities are predominantly Humanist, and a majority of the teachers who go out from their studies in the colleges to responsibilities in primary and secondary schools are basically Humanist, no matter that many maintain a normal attachment to church or synagogue for good personal or social or practical reasons."[4]

Three men whom I consider the greatest philosophers of the twentieth century were all essentially Humanist, although they did not choose that word to describe their position. John Dewey preferred to call himself a humanistic Naturalist; Bertrand Russell termed himself a Rationalist; and George Santayana wished to be known as a Materialist. While these thinkers differed on technicalities, their comprehensive philosophy was definitely that of naturalistic Humanism.

Although I was acquainted with all three, I knew Dewey best because he lived during the latter part of his life in New York City and taught at Columbia University when I was a student and teacher there. In his extensive writings he covered all the main fields of philosophy with such books as *Experience and Nature*,[5] *How We Think*,[6] *Ethics*,[7] and *Reconstruction in Philosophy*.[8] He also signed *Humanist Manifesto I* of 1933. The Center for Dewey Studies at Southern Illinois University issued *The Poems of John Dewey* posthumously.[9] Dewey wrote the universally known book *Democracy and Education*[10] and was considered the founder of progressive education in the United States. In 1934 Yale University Press published his controversial book on religion, *A Common Faith*,[11] in which he offered a new definition of God. Pointing out that intelligent human action, utilizing available social forces and the experimental methods of modern science, is ever attempting to transform the ideal into the actual, Dewey stated:

"It is this active relation between ideal and actual to which I would give the name 'God.' I would not insist that the name *must* be given. There are those who hold that the associations of the term with the supernatural are so numerous and close that any use of the word 'God' is sure to give rise to misconceptions and be taken as a concession to traditional ideas."

Dewey's arresting redefinition did indeed cause numberless misconceptions, confounding equally philosophers, theologians educators, students and even myself. Most of the commentators rejoiced that naturalist and Humanist John Dewey had returned to the bosom of God in his old age. I was not convinced and so wrote him a letter on July 28, 1935, asking him to clear up the confusion. He replied a month or so later from his summer place at Hubbards, Nova Scotia:

Dear Mr. Lamont,

Thanks for your note which explained something I hadn't been able to understand. I suppose one of the first things I learned in grammar was the difference between *will* and *shall*, and the consequent difference between *would* and *should*. But nevertheless I made a bad slip which accounts for the fact that you thought I was making a recommendation. The meaning in my mind was essentially: If the word "God" is used, this is what it *should* stand for; I didn't have a recommendation in mind beyond the proper use of a word . . . . I got my auxiliary verbs mixed.

Sincerely yours,
John Dewey

His letter to me constituted decisive evidence for settling the long argument as to his use of the term "God." He did not incorporate that word into his "common faith" or into his philosophy, as outstanding naturalist philosophers have often done—Aristotle and Spinoza, for example—to the lasting befuddlement of their readers for centuries, indeed right down to the present day.

It is no mere quibbling over words when we try to assign correct and unequivocal definitions for such a significant term as "God." I like that old Chinese proverb, "The beginning of wisdom is calling things by their right names." The whole philosophic enterprise starts with what various thinkers have called the ethics of words or, as Dewey himself phrases it, "the integrity of language."

I had another exchange of letters with him, again about a semantic problem. Since he was one of the signers of the *Humanist Manifesto I* and was on the Advisory Board of the First Humanist Society of New York, I suggested in a letter of August 30, 1940, that he should call his philosophy "Humanism" rather than "Naturalism." I thought, too, that the term "Humanism" was less formidable and more meaningful for the average person than "Naturalism." Dewey answered on September 6:

I have come to think of my own position as cultural or humanistic Naturalism. Naturalism, properly interpreted, seems to me a more adequate term than Humanism. Of course I have always limited my use of "instrumentalism" to my theory of thinking and knowledge; the word "pragmatism" I have used very little, and then with reserves.

Dewey was born in 1859, the same year in which Charles Darwin's *Origin of Species* was published. Of immense vigor and robust health, he was active to some degree in public affairs, supporting the League of Industrial Democracy and various committees working for international peace. He believed in democratic Socialism and backed for President of the United States the perennial Socialist candidate, Norman Thomas. Dewey lived to the grand old age of ninety-two.

To celebrate his Centennial year of 1959, I brought out a small book, *Dialogue on John Dewey,*[12] based on the taped transcript of an evening's discussion on him at my Riverside Drive apartment. The eleven participants had all known Dewey fairly well; they included several Columbia professors, as well as Professor Horace M. Kallen of the New School for Social Research, Alvin Johnson, Director Emeritus of the New School, and author James T. Farrell. Aware of Dewey's epigram, "Democracy begins in conversation," we talked and reminisced for three hours about the man who had meant so much to us, to his country and to the whole world.

Although I disagreed with John Dewey occasionally on political issues, especially on affairs in the Soviet Union, our personal relations were cordial. He invited me to parties now and then, where I enjoyed the "Dewey cocktail," which was simply a species of rather strong Old-Fashioned. More important, he permitted me to use his favorable review of *The Illusion of Immortality* as an introduction to the second edition and subsequent editions of that book. I never knew his first wife, Alice Chipman, who was an able teacher in her own right and shared his intellectual interests to such a degree that she was able to give him valuable advice. Her death in 1927, after forty years of happy married life, was a shattering blow to him. In 1965 Dewey's likeness was printed on the 30-cent stamp, part of a commemorative series issued by the Post Office.

In 1946 when he was eighty-seven, Dewey took the bold step of marrying for the second time. His bride was an old friend, Roberta Grant, who was forty-seven. I was on good terms with her until the publication of my *Dialogue on John Dewey*, which caused her to take umbrage at the discussion about Dewey's relation to Dr. Matthias Alexander, who believed that many human ills were caused by bad posture and movement. Having been troubled by a very stiff neck, Dewey claimed that Dr. Alexander cured him, and wrote an introduction to the doctor's book, *Man's Supreme Inheritance*.[13] Alvin Johnson, an elderly man of phenomenal memory, remarked, "Well, Dewey was enamored of Alexander." At this innocent observation, Roberta Dewey hit the ceiling; she had the absurd notion that homosexuality was implied.

For several years the Deweys lived on a farm at Huntington, Long Island, actually selling eggs to neighbors. If their farm supervisor failed to show up, Dewey would deliver the eggs himself. One day he went to a cocktail party and as he walked in, the hostess said, "Oh my God! The egg man!" Mrs. Dewey had another fit when she read this item and came up to Columbia, where I was giving a course on philosophy, and cornered

Professor James Gutmann of the Philosophy Department. She ranted to him for an hour, claiming that Columbia should fire me because I was the editor of that terrible book *Dialogue on John Dewey* that so grossly insulted her husband. Professor Kallen suggested that the egg incident might have been the origin of the word, "egghead."

Some months later a Japanese edition of the book was published. Mrs. Dewey got in touch with the publisher and insisted that the introduction to the Japanese edition should include a statement that Dewey and Alexander had no homosexual attraction for each other. We must conclude that this lady's reactions were idiotic.

Like Dewey, Bertrand Russell took a Humanist stand on the main issues in philosophy and was active in public affairs, especially in the struggle for peace and the eventual abolition of nuclear weapons. His literary style was eminently readable and often caustic in criticism of some philosopher or other. He was one of the few philosophers who ventured into the precarious realm of sex relations. His notable book on the subject, *Marriage and Morals* (1929),[14] advocated a liberal and rational approach.

During his last decade I had the privilege of visiting Russell twice at his home in Wales. In his eighties, though somewhat spare physically, his mind seemed as acute as ever as he discoursed on the burning issues of the day. I was much gratified when he wrote a foreword to my book on civil liberties, *Freedom Is As Freedom Does* (1956).[15]

In December, 1962, the Emergency Civil Liberties Committee presented its annual Tom Paine Award to Earl Russell in absentia at its yearly dinner to celebrate the ratification of the Bill of Rights by Congress. I made a brief presentation speech of appreciation on behalf of the Committee, and Russell sent me a gracious acknowledgment:

Dear Dr. Lamont,

It was a great pleasure to receive your kind letter of December 13 and to read your presentation speech for the Tom Paine Award.

My disappointment at not being present at your dinner was more than matched by my delight in noting both the generosity and the wisdom of your remarks.

I once wrote of Paine that ". . . he set an example of courage, humanity and single-mindedness." I am indebted to the Emergency Civil Liberties Committee for the honour it has conferred by associating me with the memory of Tom Paine.

With warm good wishes for the New Year,

Yours sincerely,
Bertrand Russell

Active in public affairs to the end, Bertrand Russell died in February, 1970, at the extraordinary age of ninety-seven. Some years earlier he had

written: "Three passions, simple but overwhelmingly strong, have governed my life: the longing for love, the search for knowledge and unbearable pity for the suffering of mankind." In June, 1970, I flew to London to
represent the American Humanist Association, of which Russell had been
an honorary member, and the National Emergency Civil Liberties Committee at a Memorial Meeting for Russell. I spoke briefly, saying that
"American Humanists long have regarded Bertrand Russell as the world's
outstanding representative of the Humanist philosophy. He was a modern
Socrates continually challenging the Establishment and outworn traditional beliefs. . . . He was one of the few philosophers of the twentieth
century who stepped out of the study to put ethical ideals into action."

During the last decade of his life I had a voluminous correspondence
with Lord Russell covering his support of civil liberties, his unceasing
campaign for international peace and the abolition of nuclear weapons, and
his opposition to the American aggression in Vietnam. Here is a short note
from him in answer to my letter of November 14, 1967, in which I
mentioned my contribution of $2,000 toward his activities in exposing U.S.
atrocities and other war crimes in the Vietnam war:

Dear Dr. Lamont,

I was very pleased to receive your good letter of November 14th and
to learn of your further generous gift to our work. This is not only a
great encouragement to me personally, but is also, of course, of great
practical importance.

The final public session of the International War Crimes Tribunal is
now being held in Copenhagen and I am hopeful that it will help in a
small way to make more widely known the full horror of the war in
Vietnam.

With all good wishes,

Yours sincerely,
Bertrand Russell

Turning to the realm of philosophy, I had a very important exchange of
letters with him on the issue of freedom of choice or free will. I had set him
down as a determinist until I read in Erich Fromm's essay, "Prophets and
Priests" (1968),[16] that Russell "is not a determinist who claims that the
historical future is already determined; he is an 'alternativist' who sees that
what is determined are certain limited and ascertainable alternatives."
Now this fits in precisely with my own viewpoint on freedom of choice.
Opposing the extremes to which Sartre goes on this question, I claim that
free choice is *always* limited by one's heredity, environment, economic
circumstances—all deterministic elements in the picture. But beyond
them, though established by them, are real alternatives between which a
man can choose. That is where free choice comes in.

Russell answered me on August 16 with a noteworthy letter:

Dear Dr. Lamont,

Many thanks for your letter of August 3, I am in broad agreement
with what you say about the free will question. Anything that one says
on this is sure to be wrong! It is difficult to find a form of words, and the
difficulty is due to linguistic problems. There are no laws of nature
which make the future certain. Any scientific investigator would
always have to assume determinism as a working hypothesis, without
complete belief or complete denial. I cannot be described as a determinist, and my views are closer to yours than to Sartre's.

With kind regards,

Yours sincerely,
Bertrand Russell

I have called Russell's letter "noteworthy" because for the first time in
his long career he subscribed to the idea of limited freedom of choice. This
question is of such great significance in philosophy, religion and our
day-to-day life that an outstanding philosopher's opinion on it is most
persuasive.

Another of my philosophical heroes is George Santayana, a writer of
enormous creativity, not only covering the entire field of philosophy, but
also producing poetry, plays, essays such as those in *Soliloquies in England*
(1923),[17] a first-rate novel, *The Last Puritan* (1936),[18] and a volume of
fascinating letters, among which, I am happy to say, were several to me.
His superb literary style, the most felicitous of any philosopher since Plato,
makes him a joy to read. In his classic book, *The Life of Reason* (1905-06),[19]
he presents an integrated summary of the Naturalist (or Humanist) philosophy that can be understood by the average educated person. The broad
sweep of this great work becomes clear from its principal divisions, each
incorporated in a separate book: *Reason in Common Sense*, *Reason in
Society*, *Reason in Religion*, *Reason in Art* and *Reason in Science*.

For me Santayana is the most quotable of philosophers, as can be
discerned in these typical observations:

"That rare advance in wisdom which consists in abandoning our illusions
the better to attain our ideals."[20]

"In Aristotle the conception of human nature is perfectly sound; everything ideal has a natural basis and everything natural an ideal development."[21]

"Those who cannot remember the past are condemned to repeat it."[22]

"Trifles, as Michelangelo said, make perfection, and perfection is no
trifle."[23]

In 1935 I began an occasional exchange of letters with Santayana and on
February 20 of that year wrote him:

Dear Mr. Santayana:

I have taken the liberty of sending you under separate cover a book of mine just published entitled *The Illusion of Immortality*. Because you have yourself spent a good deal of time in the field of religion it occurs to me that there may be certain things in this book which will interest you. And you will see, too, how very much I am indebted to you and your own work.

In fact, it has been not only in the writing of this book that I have felt your influence, but throughout the whole of my work in philosophy. And I have long meant to express my thanks for the immense stimulation and clarification that I have received from all of your books. No philosopher, living or dead, has given me more than you, and few as much. . . .

Sincerely yours,
Corliss Lamont

Santayana replied with surprising promptness:

Rome, March 5, 1935

Dear Mr. Lamont:

Thank you very much for your book and your letter. As far as your argument is concerned, you know that you are preaching to the converted. The subject of immortality has long ceased to be a living issue with me: and though I know that some people agonize about it, I am confirmed in my old impression that this is a verbal or mythical obsession of the human mind, rather than a literal belief. Everything, in myth and religion must be understood with a difference, in a Pickwickian sense, if we are to understand it truly, and not to import an unnatural fanaticism into the play of poetic fancy.

I have been particularly struck by your quotation from Keyser, on p. 129. I suppose he has got this from Heidegger, whom you don't mention, but who, as you doubtless know, has made a great deal of this notion of death as the totality of life, or as I should say, as the *truth* of life, which is something eternal. With this insight on the one hand, and the insight that life is movement, on the other hand, I think a rather new and profound analysis might be made of the notion of immortality. Orthodox heavens are peaceful: souls are not supposed to change and pass through new risks and adventures: they merely possess, as in Dante, the truth of their earthly careers and of their religious attainment. In other words, souls in heaven are mythical impersonations of the *truth* or totality of those persons' earthly life. At the same time, this life, and anything truly living, is something dramatic, groping, planning, excited, and exciting. It is dangerous: and Nietzsche needn't have told us to live perilously: it would have been enough to tell us *to live*. Put these two points together and you have a demonstration of the necessary transitiveness and finitude of any real life.

On hearing that you belonged to the Delphic Club,* I took the Catalogue of 1932, which I happen to have here, to see what class you were in, and incidentally I glanced over the early lists of names more familiar to me. Those are very pleasant memories: and they illustrate our philosophy of life: because it is what those young men were then, in the flush of youth, that is worth returning to and congratulating oneself upon, and seldom, perhaps never in the end, the later transformations which they may have undergone.

Yours sincerely,
G. Santayana

My last letter from him came in reply to my cable to him of December 16, 1951:

To George Santayana

By chance today read your thoughtful letter about *Three Philosophical Poets* to a group of enlightened spirits, old and young. Then we discovered it was your 88th birthday and send this message of sincere greetings and warm congratulations, feeling it a high privilege to be in contact with one of the greatest minds in the philosophic Pantheon.

Corliss Lamont

Via Santo Stefano Rotondo 6
Rome. Dec. 19, 1951

Dear Mr. Lamont

Your long cablegram with its picture of your philosophic circle listening while you read my afterthoughts about Goethe's Faust and sending me their congratulations on being 88 years old, was very pleasant and unexpected. In general I should agree with Ecclesiastes and other old fogeys that living after eighty is not a blessing; but in my case I cannot complain of misery or decrepitude of a moral kind. My little ailments are physical and quite endurable, and I was less fortunate in my early youth than in my late old age. The world has grown steadily kindlier and more interesting to me (though less satisfied with itself) and my mind less *dépaysé* than it felt itself at first. I never expected to have much support from my contemporaries; but now that I have survived most of them I find ample sympathy, if not agreement from many quarters, and also much more to attract and absorb me in the history of the past. It is history rather than philosophy that I read now with satisfaction. It is often, if not always, tragic, but it is a rich and varied dramatic spectacle; and how should natural existence be anything else?

Yours sincerely,
G. Santayana

---

*Santayana, Harvard Class of 1886, and I, Harvard 1924, both belonged to the Delphic Club, one of the College's social clubs familiarly called the Gas House.

In August of 1950, two years before Santayana's death at eighty-nine, I visited him in Rome near the Colosseum at the Catholic Convent of the Blue Sisters of the Little Company of Mary where he had retired. A Sister ushered me to a sitting room into which Santayana shuffled in his dressing gown, and took me to the end of the hall to show me the view of the old city wall. Then we went into his simply furnished room for tea and talked for two hours without interruption as I asked him question after question about his philosophy. He seemed to me exceptionally keen intellectually and I was impressed by his alert and sparkling eyes.

"I was brought up on English philosophy," he stated, "but it never suited me. Then when I read the Greeks, I knew that was *It*. The way I think is the way Aristotle and the pre-Socratic philosophers thought, though in a different idiom and a different civilization. Socrates too much moralized philosophy and prepared it only too well for the topsy-turvy system of Christianity. As for modern philosophy, I think that perhaps my greatest inspiration was Schopenhauer. I like his pessimism."

When I got up to go, I did not expect to see Santayana again; but he suggested that I come back when convenient; so I returned two days later for another rewarding talk. This time he was dressed in a brown cassock and looked a bit like a monk. As we chatted, he made caustic comments about some of his opponents in philosophy and amusing observations about people he had known. He even censured the Pope by remarking that perhaps he had been foolish to declare the dogma of the bodily Assumption of the Virgin Mary to heaven. When I said my final goodbye, Santayana remarked he had been glad to see me and that it seemed to wake him up. His parting words were: "I shall be right here next year if I am still alive."

Several of the persons who participated in the John Dewey dialogue met for a similar evening at my residence to talk about their memories of George Santayana. And again I reproduced from the tape-recording a slender volume, *Dialogue on George Santayana* (1959).[24] Horace Kallen, Emeritus Professor at the New School for Social Research, led the discussion. He had been assistant to Santayana when our philosopher was teaching at Harvard and came to know him well. Kallen recalled: "Santayana simply had allure. It wasn't merely the voice; it was the way he addressed you. He talked pretty much as he wrote, and he wrote pretty much as he talked. . . . It was rare for a class to applaud at the end of a lecture, but usually once a week there would be a spontaneous outburst of applause."

Our evening, in the genial give-and-take of reminiscence, turned out to be truly delightful. We gained fresh insights into Santayana's philosophy and learned a great deal about his character and personality. One interesting point that emerged was that his handwriting was so perfect. All of his books and letters were meticulously handwritten; from the few letters that Santayana sent me, I felt that his handwriting was a miniature work of art.

Chapter VIII   THE MASEFIELD SAGA

In 1916 John Masefield came to the United States on a lecture tour to arouse sympathy for England in World War I, and it was in February after an address in New York City on "The Tragic Drama" that the Lamont family's long association with him began. My mother was introduced to him after the meeting and volunteered to drive him to his hotel in her car. He accepted the invitation, and my parents soon were entertaining the poet at their house in New York, establishing a warm and fruitful friendship that lasted the rest of their lives. In 1918 Masefield visited America again with the same purpose of evoking support for the cause of Britain and the Allies. In the same year he dedicated his book *The War and the Future*[1] to my father, Thomas W. Lamont.

Nineteen-sixteen was, however, not the first time that Masefield came to America. He had originally arrived in 1895 when he was seventeen years old. He had jumped ship at New York and after unhappily drifting for a while found his first steady job as a general clean-up boy in Luke O'Connor's saloon in Greenwich Village. A little later he moved on to Yonkers, where he worked for almost two years in the Alexander Smith carpet factory and found time to fulfill his insatiable appetite for reading, especially the classic English poets. Already he was experimenting with poetry himself.

It was after reading Keats that the youthful Masefield felt all at once that "life is very brief, and that the use of life is to discover the law of one's being, and to follow that law, at whatever cost, to the utmost. I knew then . . . that my law was to follow poetry, even if I died of it. Who could mind dying for a thing so fair?"[2]

At Yonkers in 1895 Masefield boarded for a time with the Mac Lachlan family, who took a liking to the young man. Mr. Mac Lachlan, who was superintendent of the Worsted Mill in the carpet factory, gave him a much-needed overcoat and taught him how to shave. Many years later, when Masefield had become well known, he designated the lovely daughter of the family, Helen, as his goddaughter. Subsequently they carried on a brisk correspondence, which Miss Mac Lachlan finally presented to the Rare Book and Manuscript Library of Columbia University. I regret that I did not meet this charming lady until 1977.

From Yonkers Masefield could see the magnificent Palisades on the other side of the Hudson River, and he occasionally rowed across to explore them. He eventually composed one of his finest poems about the mighty cliffs, "The Western Hudson Shore,"[3] and made a beautiful voice recording of this poem, which was released commercially in 1977 by Folkways Records. The daily sight of the majestic Palisades undoubtedly stimulated Masefield's appreciation of the beauty of Nature, which became a constant theme in his writings.

Masefield returned to England in 1897, worked at odd jobs and kept writing poetry. In 1902 he had a sufficient sheaf to publish (in an edition of 500 copies) his first book, *Salt-Water Ballads*.[4] It included his most famous poem, "Sea-Fever," with its memorable opening line, "I must go down to the seas again, to the lonely sea and the sky." The first poem in the volume was "A Consecration," with its Humanistic tone. I quote a few lines:

> Others may sing of the wine and the
>   wealth and the mirth. . . .
> Mine be the dirt and the dross, the dust
>   and the scum of the earth!
> Theirs be the music, the colour, the glory,
>   the gold;
> Mine be a handful of ashes, a mouthful
>   of mold. . . .
> Of the maimed, of the halt and the blind
>   in the rain and the cold—
> Of these shall my songs be fashioned, my
>   tales be told.

It was primarily *Salt-Water Ballads* that led to his being heralded as "the poet of the sea." But the title is misleading. Masefield, who was prone to seasickness, deserted the seafaring life when he was seventeen. After *Salt-Water Ballads*, he published scores of other books on many subjects: the great rhyme-flowing narrative poems, such as "The Widow in the Bye Street,"[5] "Reynard the Fox,"[6] "Right Royal,"[7] "Dauber,"[8] and "The Everlasting Mercy"[9]; philosophical sonnets; exceptional novels and plays; penetrating essays; and brief prose works about the two world wars such as *Gallipoli* (1916)[10] and *The Nine Days Wonder*(1941)[11]. More appropriate than "poet of the sea" for John Masefield is "poet of the people," because of his sympathetic portrayals of the poor and unfortunate.

While entranced by his sea ballads and by some of his philosophical sonnets, I preferred most his long narrative poems, especially "Reynard the Fox" and "Right Royal," describing a horse race. The English critic, G. Wilson Knight, wrote: "Our twentieth-century literature shows a dearth of narrative poetry; it is as though our poetic consciousness were losing contact with the springs of action. But the achievement of Mr. John Masefield stands in splendid contrast to the prevailing tendency. He is a poet of vivid life in men and animals; of the earth and of the sea; and of spirit-powers. Man has risen through action, contesting with the elements, with beasts and with other men, impelled by mind; and of this striving it is right that a strong poetry should be from time to time, the voice."[12]

My friendship with Masefield and his family began in the Fall of 1924 when I became a student at New College, Oxford, for the academic year 1924-25, after graduating from Harvard in June of 1924. My mother had earlier introduced me to them. Since 1917 they had lived on Old Boar's Hill about four miles outside Oxford. I would often bicycle to the Masefield house, Hill Crest, for tea or supper and then enjoy coasting easily down the long incline back to Oxford. Sometimes on the same day I would stop and call on Professor Gilbert Murray, the author and classicist, and his wife Lady Mary, at their house, Yatscombe, near Hill Crest. Murray was a keen supporter of the League of Nations; from him I learned a great deal about the functioning of the League and international affairs in general.

During my student year at Oxford, the Masefields on several occasions took me in their car for all-day drives through the countryside or to the theatre. I remember going with them to Stratford-on-Avon for performances of *Macbeth* and *The Winter's Tale*. We drove also to Bradfield for the *Agamemnon* of Aeschylus, with its stirring choruses. Masefield remarked that he thought this was the greatest play ever written.

After supper at Hill Crest, he occasionally read aloud some of his poems, commenting on them as he went along. His voice was mellow and haunting. When I got back to my lodgings at Oxford I would jot down Masefield's comments, insofar as I could remember them, in the margins of my volume of his *Collected Poems*.[13]

I recall a memorable evening at Hill Crest on Friday, February 1, 1925, when for almost two hours Masefield read a number of his poems and talked about them. He chose several selections from *Lollingdon Downs*,[14] including some of the finest sonnets in that work. When he came to "No Man Takes the Farm,"[15] he explained that one day he had stopped by the roadside to look at a deserted house. A man nearby told him the story of the place—a narrative of drunkenness, savagery and killing all in the same family—and Masefield put the harrowing tale into verse. I quote the first five stanzas:

> No man takes the farm,
> Nothing grows there;
> The ivy's arm
> Strangles the rose there.

Old Farmer Kyrle
Farmed there the last;
He beat his girl
(It's seven years past).

After market it was
He beat his girl;
He liked his glass,
Old Farmer Kyrle.

Old Kyrle's son
Said to his father;
"Now, dad, you ha' done,
I'll kill you rather!

"Stop beating sister,
Or by God I'll kill you!"
Kyrle was full of liquor—
Old Kyrle said: "Will you?"

Masefield then read his "Sonnet V"[16] and his wife commented that she was particularly fond of it:

I could not sleep for thinking of the sky,
The unending sky, with all its million suns
Which turn their planets everlastingly
In nothing, where the fire-haired comet runs.
If I could sail that nothing, I should cross
Silence and emptiness with dark stars passing;
Then, in the darkness, see a point of gloss
Burn to a glow, and glare, and keep amassing,
And rage into a sun with wandering planets,
And drop behind; and then as I proceed,
See his last light upon his last moon's granites
Die to a dark that would be night indeed:
Night where my soul might sail a million years
In nothing, not even Death, not even tears.

Another passage he read that evening was the Madman's soliloquy at the conclusion of his play, *Good Friday* (1916).[17] My penciled note is explicit: "M. doesn't like *Good Friday* much; in fact he dislikes most of it. Was to have been sort of a Christlike Bible story. But was writing it in 1915 when war cut loose and he felt he couldn't go on. Simply cut it short. Then took it up in form of new play, 1924-25."

Toward the end of the evening he reached "Right Royal" and the rousing verses about the finish of the horse race at Compton Course. Here I wrote: "M. read these last few pages. Marvelous tone and expression. This his favorite of the longer poems." Later, Mrs. Masefield told me her husband thought more highly of his noted war poem, "August, 1914,"[18] than of any other poem he had written.

As my friendship with the Masefields grew over the years, we developed a lively correspondence. Almost all their letters to me were handwritten. In 1932 they moved to Cirencester in Gloucestershire, calling their place Pinbury Park. I went to see them there only once, but well remember the splendid row of walnut trees on either side of the long driveway leading to the house, trees said to have been planted from nuts that came from Napoleon's table at Elba. Just before World War II, the Masefields moved to their Burcote Brook house at Abingdon near Oxford where from their living room they could look out upon the narrow upper reaches of the River Thames.

On trips to England every few years, I made a point of dropping in on them for lunch or tea. Masefield was a conversationalist of the old school and entertained his guests with droll stories, anecdotes of literary figures, and reminiscences of the sea. What was to be my final visit was at Burcote Brook in August of 1965, when he was eighty-seven. He seemed to be in good health, his complexion as ruddy as ever, and his voice undiminished. When it was time for me to leave, he came down the steps from the front door to bid me goodbye. We both felt, I think, that this might well be the last time we would see each other.

As I look back on my association of more than forty years with John Masefield, who was British Poet Laureate from 1930 until his death in 1967, I realize more clearly than ever that his friendship was among the most inspiring and meaningful experiences of my life. One of the truly great men I have known, both as a poet and a personality, he was ever warm and gracious, highly sensitive, sometimes sad, often smiling. Not the least of his gifts were a keen sense of humor and a contagious chuckle. Masefield lived these words of his: "No profession is enough . . . nor any art, all through life, unless it be linked to some spiritual enthusiasm which does not die as the body begins to die."

Mrs. Masefield, the daughter of Nicholas de la Cherois-Crommelin, came from County Antrim in Northern Ireland. Eleven years older than her husband, and a schoolteacher by profession, she was serene and attractive when they were married in 1903. When I first met her in 1924 the good looks had disappeared and she dressed rather shabbily, but she was one of the most amiable and interesting women I have ever known. Generally liberal in her opinions, her breadth of knowledge and depth of mind were apparent in her conversation and her letters. For thirty-five years, until her death in 1960 at the age of ninety-two, Mrs. Masefield was a warm, understanding friend to me. It was always a treat to receive a letter from her discussing some new book or telling about life in England.

The Masefields had a daughter, Judith, and a son, Lewis Crommelin. Two or three years younger than I, Judith was a talented woman, illustrated some of her father's books with pen-and-ink drawings and wrote several first-rate children's books. She was somewhat of a recluse. Lewis, who went to Rugby and Balliol College, Oxford, was away from home when I was at Oxford, so that I rarely saw him. He became a journalist and

published two novels. In 1942, at the age of thirty-two, he was killed during
World War II while serving with a Red Cross unit attached to the British
Army in Africa.

Masefield and his wife built a little theatre close to their house on Boar's
Hill and called it the Music Room. There they staged some of his plays and
a number of the lesser known English classics; and also presented concerts.
I sometimes acted as ticket-taker at the door. I remember the Saturday
evening, May 9, 1925, when Masefield's play, *The Trial of Jesus* (1925),[19]
was given, and both Julian and Juliette Huxley were in the cast. When
George Bernard Shaw and his wife entered the hall for this play, I took
their invitation, which was their entrance card, and have preserved it ever
since.

Every summer from 1923 to 1929 the Masefields arranged and presided
over the Poetry Recitations, in an Oxford University hall—a competition
for amateurs in which men and women, young and old, came from every
part of the country to recite verse. One of the more frequent prize-winners
was the fiery Betty Bartholomew from Scotland who later came to live in
New York City as the wife of Henry Pitney Van Dusen, President of Union
Theological Seminary. She became a good friend of the Lamonts.

What Masefield said at a festival in honor of William Butler Yeats was
precisely relevant to the Poetry Recitations: "The best poetry comes like
life itself from a high state of the soul. It comes as a living image, upon a
rhythm out of eternity, into the minds of men and women, who are thereby
toucht into generosities. It is the work of most unusual men working in
their moods of power by a concentration of mental strength. It is for the
speaker, therefore, to strive into those moods of power, so that he or she
may be lighted or exalted; and the words luminous to them may be
luminous to others; so that something of the mental glory from which the
words came may be in speaker and hearer, and all that is living and lovely
may be brought near, and all sorts of givings and forgivings quickened."

Reflecting upon the rich program of plays presented at the Music Room
on Boar's Hill and the hard work of carrying on the Poetry Recitations, I am
struck by how Masefield not only continued his writing at full blast, but at
the same time furthered the poetic awareness and cultural life of the
community in two important enterprises. This man was a veritable demon
of energy; I know of no other great poet whose extra-curricular work was so
extensive and significant.

He had a deep understanding and love of modern painting, and occasionally remarked that perhaps he should have taken up painting as his profession instead of poetry. His pen-and-ink sketches on letters and in gift-books
showed genuine talent. Masefield's reputation as an art critic led to his
appointment in 1902 as the director of a large exhibition of paintings at
Wolverhampton, the industrial capital of the northern midlands, and the
show was a great success.

Still another aspect of Masefield's life was his prodigious writing of letters. As in conversation, he displayed encyclopedic knowledge of history and culture. After I left Oxford, he and I developed a considerable correspondence, which I later embodied in a brief book, *Remembering John Masefield*,[20] in 1971. More important, over a period of thirty-six years he wrote to my parents, particularly to my mother, more than 2,100 letters now permanently preserved in the Houghton Library of Harvard University. My nephew, the writer Lansing Lamont, and I selected about 300 to my mother and published them in the book, *Letters of John Masefield to Florence Lamont* (1979).[21] My mother's letters to Masefield were sent to me by Judith Masefield, but were lost in the transatlantic mail.

His letters are enthralling, covering a vast field of literature and history, from the horrors of the Western Front in World War I to the sounds of water he liked best and a running critique of writers and poets, many of whom were his friends. The letters are studded with Chaucerian parodies; Masefield's own delightful, satirical rhymes; his pen-and-ink drawings of sailing ships; and aphoristic wisdom, such as: "The novel exists because life is not exciting enough; the poem exists because life has excited the poet." Anne Morrow Lindbergh commented on the Masefield volume: "The book is a moving tribute to a friendship that spanned the ocean, two world wars, and age, sharing the profound and the trivial, and remaining to the end vigorous, humane and witty."

In his letters Masefield mentioned so many persons and places that it was difficult to provide adequate footnotes. In working on them, I almost committed the prize boner in literary footnotes. In two letters Masefield mentioned that he had been off with Black Nag. Since he liked to ride horseback, I footnoted "Black Nag" as the Masefields' favorite horse, but discovered at the last minute that it was the name they had given to their erratic Overland automobile.

Mr. and Mrs. Masefield were very sympathetic to me in my battle with Senator Joseph McCarthy. When Judge Weinfeld dismissed my indictment for contempt of Congress in July, 1955 I wrote the Masefields about my court victory. On August 9 Masefield replied:

> How very kind of you to send us the glad news of your release from anxiety, and the triumph of your stand for Liberty. Thank you so much for writing to tell us. What a grand success for you, and for your very able attorney, and what a relief to you all.
>
> I hope that there will be no trouble about the passport, and that we may have the pleasure of seeing you before the days shorten.

In March, 1964 I sent the Masefields a copy of my pamphlet "The Enduring Impact of George Santayana," and later an explanation. I mentioned Santayana's remarkable letters and added "They were always handwritten, and the handwriting itself was, I thought, a work of art. In this Santayana's hand resembles yours." Masefield replied on April 24:

You are the first discoverer of beauty in my handwriting; and this gives you "another" uniqueness among mortals.

Alas, I often say, that now I will try to better my handwriting, and then, the next day, I have to write, in a hurry, many letters or other matter, and the results are what you see, and the world laments.

Your Father and Mother wrote admirable hands. Thomas Hardy and Robert Bridges wrote beautiful hands; so did Gilbert Murray and Neville Lytton, and (in the past) Ben Jonson.

So did a Mr. Nathaniel Clutterbuck, who lived in the 17th century and owned a book that I have, and wrote his name in it.

Do come to see it, and admire.

Shakespeare wrote his Christian name fairly well, but did rather wallow about in his surname.

I thank you for your kind Spring wishes, and wish you the like. But this here is not yet a Spring, but a late winter, alas.

In the Fall of 1964 I wrote Masefield enclosing a feature story about him by journalist Milton Marmor who said: "Many times, too, he sat at desks next to that smiling man, Vladimir Lenin." Masefield replied on November 15, 1964:

Many grateful thanks for the cutting about me, and for your kind letter.

No. I *never* sat next to Lenin; no such luck.

I often saw him in the Brit Mus Reading Room (I suppose about 57 or so years ago) and always said to myself "I wonder who that extra-or-dinary man is", for anyone must have seen that he was an extra-ordi-nary man, certain to make a mark in the world.

Once, as I was leaving the room, I saw that he was just behind me, so that I held the door open for him till he had passed. He smiled at me and muttered some words of thanks, and that was the nearest I ever got to him.

Later, when things had happened, a lot of young English writers came to know who that marvellous being had been. He was at the Room often for some considerable time, and people noticed him; no-one could have failed to notice him.

In April of 1967 my elder brother, Thomas, who had been suffering from heart trouble, underwent a serious open-heart operation that proved too severe a strain for him. He never recovered consciousness and died on April 10. I immediately wrote to Masefield and he replied a few days later on April 14:

I grieve to have your sad letter with the heart breaking news of the death of Tommy for so long the honoured head of your great house. Your Father and Mother did me the great honour of making me almost one of the family and I cannot but grieve to the heart that that family is so stricken and cruelly hurt. I send my sad thoughts to you across the sea, with my very warmest wishes.

Masefield dictated this letter from his sickbed, where he lay extremely ill from gangrene. He refused to allow the doctors to amputate his foot, or later his leg below the hip. The fatal infection spread and he died at Abington on May 12, 1967, about three weeks short of his eighty-ninth birthday. Judith Masefield wrote me later "he was so merry and we laughed right to the end."

There had developed between the Lamonts and the Masefields a bond of affection and devotion that endured without interruption for more than half a century. Two lines from Masefield's poem "The Western Hudson Shore" express the feelings our families had for each other:

Friendship is sunlight scattering man's cloud,
Making a life a sunbeam's spangled dust.

The Centenary of John Masefield's birth came in 1978. In the United States Columbia University took the initiative in celebrating the occasion by staging in February a splendid Masefield Exhibit. It included first editions, photographs, the exquisite oil portrait by the English painter, Sir John Lavery, original letters handwritten by Masefield, often illustrated by lively pen-and-ink drawings, and a small barque constructed by Masefield himself. The prize book was a copy of *Reynard the Fox*, inscribed by the poet to his wife and embellished with more than one hundred of his watercolor and pen-and-ink sketches. Many of the items I had myself presented to the Columbia Library's special Masefield Collection. Other educational institutions that mounted exhibits were Harvard, the Phillips Exeter Academy, the University of Texas and the University of Vermont.

In England the high point of Masefield commemorations was the Memorial Service in Poets' Corner at Westminster Abbey on June 1, 1978, the poet's 100th birthday, for which a small delegation of Americans, including myself, flew to London. There were readings from Masefield's poetry by Sir Bernard Miles, the noted actor and founder of the Mermaid Theatre in London; an address by the English poet, Patricia Beer; and the laying of a wreath on the Masefield stone by Jack Masefield, nephew of the poet. As the service was about to start, a silvery grey pigeon suddenly settled on Masefield's stone, and a verger pushed it away with his staff. Sir Bernard read from Masefield's earliest poetry beginning with the well-known "Cargoes" from his first book, *Salt-Water Ballads*.

A few days later our American contingent drove to the beautiful town of Ledbury in Herefordshire where Masefield was born. We visited his original red-brick home, known as Knapp House, now occupied by the poet's nephew, William Masefield, and his wife. They reminisced entertainingly about the family, observing that one sister of the poet was still much alive at ninety-three and that another sister lived to be a hundred. From the living room of the house there was a view of the rolling English downs stretching away in the distance, a scene that Masefield recalled vividly in his autobiographical poem, "Wonderings (Between One and Six Years)," (1943).[22]

We visited also the fine Ledbury Library where an excellent Masefield Exhibit had been mounted by the attractive librarian, Mrs. Alice Paice. The Library is situated on Bye Street, a name the poet used in his noted narrative poem, "The Widow in The Bye Street." (In September, 1978, Ledbury's separate Grammar and High Schools were consolidated as the John Masefield School.)

Our expedition continued to Cambridge University to call on Constance Babington Smith, author of a biography of Masefield. Miss Babington Smith, a lineal descendant of Thomas Babington Macaulay, was busy with the page proofs of her book when we rang the bell at her little eighteenth-century house on Little St. Mary's Lane. She graciously stopped her work to serve us sherry and then gave us a personally conducted tour of Peterhouse College with its stained glass windows by Edward Burne-Jones. Only a few days previously *The Times* of London had devoted a full page to an excerpt from the Babington Smith manuscript, recounting the poet's meeting with W. B. Yeats.

The final excursion in our pilgrimage was to Oxford and the former Masefield home, Hill Crest, a short way outside the city. At the gate now is a sizeable sign, "Masefield House," while the nearby small theatre or Music Room has its own sign, "Masefield Cottage." I easily recognized the house as the one I used to visit on my bicycle when I was a student at Oxford. In 1978 the house was occupied by Professor of English Literature Godfrey Bond of Pembroke College, Oxford, and his family. They greeted us cordially and showed us the study on the fourth floor where Masefield did much of his work.

In recent years it has been the fashion among some literary circles in the United States and England to look upon John Masefield as passé and of little interest to generations subsequent to his death. I think this is a most doubtful proposition. And I cite as evidence a remarkable article published in 1980 by journalist Russell Landstrom that three or four centuries from now Masefield will be regarded as the greatest man of the twentieth century. Landstrom writes that when other eminent figures are more or less forgotten, "Masefield's poetry will still be alive. . . . He was a heartening man, simple and noble, like everything he wrote and every quality he exemplified."

Chapter IX   THREAT OF ASSASSINATION

It was shortly after the end of World War II that I encountered a new sort of problem when a middle-aged gentleman with whom I was slightly acquainted began to make strange phone calls to me and to send even stranger letters, always in a blue envelope. The trouble began in March, 1946, when Jack phoned me out of the blue and said, "Corliss, do you remember the supper you attended at my apartment back in 1935?" I answered, "Why Jack, that was an awfully long time ago, but, yes, I vaguely do recall coming to dinner one night."

Jack said, "I understand you came to my house that night with an ulterior purpose." I said, "What the devil do you mean, 'an ulterior purpose'?" and he replied, "People have been calling me on the phone and telling me that you came to dinner that night for reasons more than the ordinary social ones." I said, "Why Jack, this is absolutely crazy! I like to discuss things with you once in a while; but please tell me what the dickens the alleged purpose was and who the hell these people are who are calling you on the phone." Jack responded, "Well, I can't go into the details, but I didn't think you were that sort of a guy and I just wanted to check with you." I said, "Well, it's all a complete mystery to me" and we rang off.

About a month later he phoned again à propos of nothing at all and revealed that he and his wife were separating. I remarked, "I'm sorry to hear about this. Why are you getting separated?" Jack replied solemnly, "I'm separating from her for the usual reasons for which a man separates from his wife. And I understand you are involved in this business." "But Jack," I said, "this is absolutely fantastic! I would hardly recognize your wife if I saw her on the street. I have met her only a couple of times in my life, and those were when she was with you." (Jack's wife, as I recall her, was a plump, rather unattractive woman).

He kept insisting "These people keep calling me on the phone about you." I said, "Jack, will you please tell me the names of these people so that

I can punch somebody in the jaw or bring a libel suit?" He answered, "That's just the trouble, I don't know their real names." Then I said, "What the dickens is all this about, anyway? I have enough trouble on my hands with the Un-American Activities Committee charging me with contempt of Congress. Please take it easy and let me alone." Jack now brought in his ex-butler as one of those who kept phoning him and added that there were two other men besides myself who were involved in the affair with his wife. Jack had a country place at Purdy, New York, that had a small lake, and he said that during the last three months he had walked frequently along the lake, wondering whether life was worth living any more and why he shouldn't throw himself in.

This was followed by a phone call from his daughter who said that his family knew what was going on and she apologized to me for her father's paranoid behavior. She added that he was claiming that the baby recently born to her was really her mother's by one of the men he was threatening. She also said that she and her mother were trying to get her father into a mental health clinic.

Jack's phone calls ceased for a while, but then in the middle of August, 1946, there came, in the familiar blue envelope, a clipping from the *New York Daily Mirror* of August 13 telling how a man had found his wife and her lover in a hotel room in Chicago. His wife was nude and the lover, who it turned out, was his best friend, in a bathrobe. After some wild talk and a scuffle, the husband shot the lover dead—and was acquitted of the charge of murder. A small slip of paper in the envelope read: "YOU CONTEMPTIBLE SCOUNDREL AND FRAUD."

After this episode, I decided to consult both my lawyer, Basil N. Bass, and the well-known psychiatrist, Dr. Carl A. L. Binger.

Jack kept sending me short notes in the blue envelopes. That of September 30, addressed to Corliss S. B. Lamont, read: "I have just started to make you *pay in full* for your foul deed. You are a cheap, filthy double-crossing son of a bitch."

November 13 brought: "The party concerned is now in a state of prostration with threats of self-destruction. If this should occur then blood will be upon your hands and murder upon your head. And you thought you had gotten away with it. Just wait. You'll pay."

The blue envelope arriving on November 22 had in it only Walter Winchell's column in *The Daily Mirror* of November 21, with a large black arrow pointing to "Corliss Lamont is having trouble other than political."

The November 26 message warned: "Watch out when you cross the streets; you may be hit by an automobile."

On December 10 Jack brought my father into the mess with a note to him with Shakespearean overtones:

> Tis true, tis pity, tis pity, tis true that a legitimate father can have a bastard for a son.

A second note for my father arrived on December 10. Because he was extremely ill, my mother would not allow it to be delivered to him. It read: "He is now bellyaching that he has a wife and four children. Why didn't he think about my family before he committed this foul deed?"

On December 19 the blue envelope was addressed to Corliss S. C. B. Lamont, 450 Riverside Drive, and the note was in poetic form:

> The ball has been set in motion,
> It cannot be stopped.
> It must strike!

S. C. B. means Sneak, Coward, Bastard.

Now we enter the year 1947. New York City newspapers listed in their radio columns that on Sunday evening, January 26, I was going to debate with Dr. Ruth Alexander on station WMCA on the subject "What is Capitalism?" in a series called "Wake up, America." Sure enough, a day or two later my blue envelope turned up in the mail, containing the warning: "Something unexpected may happen at the Studio Sunday night." I immediately phoned my lawyer and asked for his advice. Mr. Bass insisted that a special guard should escort me to the Studio. A city detective was assigned and accompanied me to the WMCA headquarters in Rockefeller Center. Dr. Alexander and I had our debate and nothing unusual occurred.

Meanwhile, Jack's family, their lawyer, the two other men involved and their lawyers had been conferring to decide how to get him committed to an institution. They finally succeeded the first week of February, 1947. Jack remained incarcerated for six months or more, was able to resume his normal business, and never bothered me again.

After the commitment had taken place I went to see Dr. Binger to rejoice that the threat to my safety had been eliminated. As we were sitting there in his office, he suddenly said, "Corliss, I don't like the look of your eyebrows. I think you may have a thyroid deficiency." I couldn't have been more surprised. We arranged for a medical test the following week and, sure enough, it showed I had a bad thyroid deficiency. Dr. Binger prescribed one two-grain pill for me daily and within two or three weeks I was feeling much better than I had for the past two years. It was the greatest medical triumph of my life. Would it ever have happened were it not for my old friend Jack? I have taken the thyroid pills ever since.

My second encounter with the threat of dangerous violence occurred in 1974. One morning about the middle of June, in preparing for a summer vacation, I cashed a check for $300 at my bank. I was living in an apartment house nearby. After receiving the money from the bank teller, I walked leisurely to a delicatessen store, where I bought some bananas, walked home and entered the lobby of my apartment house. There were a couple of people milling around there, one of them a tall, slender man with a moustache. He was wearing a straw hat. I took it that he was waiting to see some friend and paid no notice to him. As I entered the elevator he followed and as it started to ascend to my floor, this man suddenly blurted out, "Give me the money you just got from the bank."

Remembering police advice not to resist a mugger, I quickly handed over my $300 to the robber. I never knew whether he was armed or not. But since he was somewhat bigger than I, he probably would have prevailed had I tried to resist him, or even killed me. He got off the elevator at the fourth floor and disappeared down the back staircase. I had forgotten about the alarm button in the elevator. If I had pushed it when the robber got out, the superintendent might well have been able to intercept him on the ground floor.

The robbery remains a mystery. Since he was waiting for me in the vestibule of my apartment house, it is clear that the man had not followed me from the bank. He must have been observing my movements for some time, or there may even have been collusion with somebody observing me at the bank. The police detectives could not throw any light on the incident. They showed me pictures of about a hundred criminals from their files, but I could not identify my robber. The police comforted me by saying that in such situations the thief seldom comes back a second time.

Chapter X   ADVENTURES IN CIVIL
             LIBERTIES

From the time of my undergraduate days at Harvard and my attempt to establish academic freedom by having the Harvard Union occasionally invite radical speakers for its lecture program, I developed a considerable interest in civil liberties in the United States. I was deeply aroused by the infamous prosecution of the instructor John T. Scopes in 1925 for violating a Tennessee state law against teaching the theory of biological evolution. The trial was doubly dramatic because the celebrated attorney Clarence Darrow was one of Scopes's attorneys and the former Secretary of State William Jennings Bryan, an ardent believer in old-time religion, aided the State prosecutor. Scopes was convicted, but later released by the State Supreme Court on a technicality. Tennessee did not repeal its absurd law until 1967.

During that same decade, 1920–30, another civil liberties issue much in the public eye was the right to write and lecture about safe methods of birth control, and to establish birth control clinics where the necessary information would be available. The courageous Mrs. Margaret Sanger led the birth control movement at this time as President of the American Birth Control League and I contributed funds to this organization.

In the summer of 1932 I became personally involved in my first civil liberties case when I made a trip to the Soviet Union with my wife and brought back to the United States in September a number of lively posters, which illustrated public health work, reproduced works of art and ridiculed them as seditious. The National Council on Freedom from Censorship, them as seditious. The National Council on Freedom of Censorship, affiliated with the American Civil Liberties Union, immediately protested and two months later secured the release of all except three of my posters. The U.S. Customs confiscated them because they showed mini-reproductions of American paper currency, an inch long by half an inch high. According to the Treasury Department, this violated U.S. counterfeiting laws. The Council on Censorship argued that the reproductions were too small to be useful to counterfeiters.

The *St. Louis Star Journal*[1] ran a derisive editorial entitled "When Bottom the Weaver Rules" on the seizure of my posters:

> Corliss Lamont, son of Thomas Lamont, last September imported a set of reproductions of art classics from the Hermitage Museum in Russia and a collection of Soviet posters. The posters were seized by the United States Treasury department on suspicion that they were seditious. Finally, after spending two months translating the Russian inscriptions on the posters, Treasury agents have released all but three of them, which are now held on the charge that they *violate the laws against counterfeiting United States currency*.
>
> The "counterfeiting" consists of poster representations of American currency, an inch and a half long, and an inch wide. The denomination of the bills is not stated, hence it is not revealed whether Mr. Lamont is supposed to have imported the posters with the intention of cutting out and passing $1 or $1,000 bills, an inch and a half long, on the unsuspecting public.
>
> Of course, the Treasury Department may have figured that by the time it recovered from its asininity sufficiently to release the posters, the American dollar would have shrunk to an inch and a half in length. Quite possibly. Indeed, in such a length of time it might totally disappear, in which case there could be no counterfeiting and the posters might as well be turned over to Mr. Lamont at once.

That same year, 1932, I was elected to the Board of Directors of the American Civil Liberties Union. During those times, starting with the Roosevelt regime, came the great battles for trade union organization and the founding of the Congress of Industrial Organizations (CIO). In the early thirties we also had the antics of Jersey City's autocratic mayor, Frank Hague, who stated: "I am the law." His law was that there should be no workers organized into trade unions in Jersey City, so that the employers could do pretty much as they pleased in terms of labor policy. One fine day in the spring of 1934 the American Civil Liberties Union sent me over to Jersey City on a test case to picket peacefully on behalf of the Furniture Workers Industrial Union. One of the organization's able counsel, A. L. Wirin, accompanied me as an official observer.

For about twenty minutes I walked up and down carrying a sign in front of the factory where the workers were on strike. At the end of that time a couple of policemen came by, arrested me for disorderly conduct, herded me into a police van and hauled me off to jail, where I was finger-printed. What I remember best about that Jersey City jail is that I was compelled to remove my necktie, shoelaces and belt, so that I wouldn't commit suicide.

I was in jail for only a few hours, because the ACLU got me bailed out quite promptly, and I was able to go home to New York for a pleasant supper. We appealed my arrest right away, but my case never came to trial because there were similar cases already in the courts; and one of the higher courts reversed previous anti-picketing decisions in New Jersey, establishing the right to peaceful picketing in Jersey City on the ground that it was a legitimate exercise of freedom of expression. My case was automatically dropped. Though my picketing episode was a distinctly minor occurrence, the experience of being in jail for even a short time was psychologically disturbing.

During the next ten years I was involved in little struggles here and there, and with my work in the American Civil Liberties Union. My next important case was in 1946 when I was subpoenaed by the Un-American Activities Committee of the House of Representatives. This Committee had been established in 1939 and after World War II became a constant menace to civil liberties in the United States. They subpoenaed me as Chairman of the National Council of American-Soviet Friendship, demanding that I bring to their hearing in Washington all our correspondence and financial records from the time the organization was founded. We considered this a violation of the First Amendment.

We didn't think that the "Un-American Committee" had a right to investigate us at all and that its mandate for "the investigation of Un-American propaganda" was unconstitutional on its face. I refused to bring those papers. I had a heated session with Representative J. Parnell Thomas, the Chairman, who later went to jail for graft, and with John E. Rankin from Mississippi, who shouted at me at the top of his voice, and wanted to know why I hadn't told the American people about the crimes of Soviet soldiers everywhere throughout Eastern Europe.

The House cited me for contempt of Congress because I didn't bring the papers. But actually I did not have custody of those papers. The Executive Director of the organization, Richard Morford, had the responsibility for them. The U.S. Attorney General soon dropped my case because he knew it couldn't stand up in the Courts, but he obtained the indictment of Mr. Morford, a stalwart ex-minister, for contempt of Congress and brought him to trial on the contempt charge. Morford took the position that to surrender the papers would be a violation of the First Amendment, and so pleaded. He lost his case in the lower Federal courts and then appealed to the U.S. Supreme Court, which refused even to hear his case. He was sentenced to three months in jail and a fine of $500.

After my clash with the Un-American Committee in 1946, it continued year after year to roam the country in its delirious anti-Communist witch-hunt. In addition to the House Committee in this conspiracy against the democratic rights of all Americans there were the Senate Subcommittee on Internal Security and the Senate Permanent Subcommittee on Investigations of the Committee on Government Operations. Republican Senator Joseph McCarthy was Chairman of this Subcommittee. One result of the frenzied campaigns of these committees was to foment an atmosphere of suspicion and tension that helped to build public support for the Cold War of the United States Government against the Soviet Union.

All three of these inquisitorial committees rampaged rough-shod over the Bill of Rights by asking unconstitutional questions about political beliefs, associational activities and personal or private matters. They attempted to destroy careers and reputations through public smears and innuendos, and through the abhorrent doctrines of guilt by association, guilt by accusation and guilt by gossip or rumor; and so threw overboard the time-honored legal concepts that guilt is always personal and that a man is deemed to be innocent until proved guilty.

These Congressional committees of inquisition usurped the powers of the judiciary by holding trials of individuals, finding them guilty and bringing about their punishment, while denying witnesses most of the legal safeguards long established in the administration of justice in English-speaking countries. The committees did not ordinarily inflict punishment directly; but the witnesses who were questioned suffered severe penalties through the wide publicity given to charges against them and frequently through losing their jobs and being put on blacklists that made future employment almost impossible. Many teachers and government employees were summarily dismissed, either because of unproved accusations which placed them under a cloud of suspicion or because, standing on the Fifth Amendment to the Constitution, they refused to answer questions calculated to make them witnesses against themselves.

This well-recognized guarantee against compulsory self-incrimination is only one of five provisions in the Fifth Amendment; and actually is not as important as the provision which states that no individual shall "be deprived of life, liberty or property without due process of law." This principle was repeated in the Fourteenth Amendment as applying to the States. What the Congressional committees constantly did was precisely to neglect or negate "due process of law," which is fundamental to the whole American system of justice.

These Congressional committees purported to be exposing and counteracting far-reaching Communist plots for wrecking the American Republic; but in fact they were engaged in a paranoid witch-hunt against all ideas and associations that did not conform to right-wing orthodoxy. The investigations in general, as Professor Henry Steele Commager of Amherst College has pointed out, "do not deal with acts for the very good reason that there are already laws on the statute books that take care of all conceivable subversive acts. They deal, instead, with imponderable things like intentions, thoughts, principles and associations, with that shadowy realm which has ever been the happy hunting ground of tyrants."[2]

Actually the Federal Bureau of Investigation possessed long dossiers on almost all those called before Congressional committees. But since these witnesses—most of them radicals, liberals or dissenters of some sort—had not violated any law, the committees attempted to cause their ruin through extra-legal, and often illegal, methods of inquisition. Furthermore, the questions that Joseph McCarthy* and other Senators asked were infrequently of the sort that might reveal useful information, but designed to hold the victim up to abuse or, worse, to trap him into a perjury indictment.

We must all agree that the investigative function of Congress can be helpful and important in its authorized purpose of preparing the way for new legislation. But it is obvious that in the present era some Congressional committees have constantly gone far beyond their proper authority and arrogated to themselves powers never delegated to them by the United States Constitution or by any federal law.

Public sentiment against the Un-American Activities Committee grew increasingly vocal and widespread, influencing even the House of Representatives. In 1970 the Committee was transformed into the House Internal Security Committee, which was abolished in 1975. So after thirty-six years we were finally rid of one of the worst political engines of evil in the history of the United States.

My free speech troubles extended even to Canada. In May, 1956, I was on a continental speaking tour, scheduled to give two lectures at the First Unitarian Church of Toronto under the auspices of the Toronto Humanist Association, a philosophical organization that was completely non-sectarian and non-political. My topics were "Humanism and Civil Liberties" and "Humanism versus the Traditional Religions." When my train from Detroit to Toronto stopped at Windsor, Ontario, Canadian immigration officials came on board, arrested me and had me deported back to Detroit as an "undesirable visitor." Within hours the news of this incident spread widely, and angry protests exploded in the Canadian press and Parliament. "Cut out this nonsense," said the *Toronto Globe and Mail*[3] in an editorial castigating my deportation.

The protests became so serious and widespread that the next day the Canadian Minister of Immigration, John W. Pickersgill, reversed my deportation. He excused the earlier action on the grounds that the National Council of American-Soviet Friendship, which he called a "Communist Front," had arranged my lectures—an absolute lie, since that organization had nothing to do with my tour. The consequence of my deportation was that I missed my first meeting and a TV broadcast. However, by racing 240 miles through the rain in a drive-your-own car, I managed to arrive at the Toronto church just in time for my second address. I am reasonably certain that the FBI or CIA, or both together, incited the Canadian authorities to the folly of my deportation.

In that mad and maddening era of McCarthyism we had trouble with passports. I had engaged passage on the S.S. *Queen Mary* with my wife and family to go abroad in the summer of 1951 and thought I would easily get my passport renewed, but unexpectedly I received a letter from Mrs. H. B. Shipley, long the tyrannical Chief of the State Department's Passport

---

*I tell of my own battle with Senator McCarthy in the next chapter.

Division, denying me a renewal of my passport. She stated: "Your travel abroad at this time would be contrary to the best interests of the United States." What was I going to do traveling abroad? I would go to museums, see the sights, visit old friends, admire the cathedrals and do a little research. However, Mrs. Shipley and her associates always pretended that I was planning to conspire with foreign Communists against the U.S.A. They knew this was poppycock. In reality they wanted to punish me for my radical views and to pressure me to change them. This was concretely demonstrated when Senator Jacob Javits of New York informed me that everything would be all right if I publicly renounced my dissenting opinions on public affairs. This "liberal" Senator knew that the Government's position was outrageous, but did not offer to protest it in any way.

The passport nonsense went on for a long time and instead of going to Europe that summer of 1951, we went to Mexico, which does not require a passport, and had the time of our lives. We might never have gone to that marvelous country except for the State Department's refusal to grant me a passport.

In 1957 I again made formal application for a passport. However, the applications forms since 1956 had added three entirely new questions about whether one was or had been a member of the Communist Party.

I had sworn under oath before the McCarthy Committee in 1953 that I was not and never had been a member of the Communist Party. But I declined to answer the new passport questions because they were unconstitutional political inquiries by the State Department, and because every American has a natural right to travel regardless of his political, economic or religious views. The Passport Office refused to grant me a passport or even to give me a hearing on the grounds that my application was incomplete and therefore not duly executed. Hence I filed suit against Secretary of State John Foster Dulles in order to re-establish my right to travel.

In a letter to Mr. Dulles I said: "As an American citizen deeply concerned with the freedoms guaranteed in the Bill of Rights, I must oppose on principle and in practice State Department procedures that encroach upon my civil liberties and those of the American people. I bring this suit against you, Mr. Secretary, not for myself alone, but also to help safeguard the fundamental rights of my fellow Americans against a capricious and tyrannical bureaucracy."

Commenting on the general situation prevailing in America during those mid-century years, I wrote a little poem printed in *The Daily Compass* of New York City that was entitled "Chant for Progressives":

> MacArthur, McCarran, McCarthy and McGrath
> All richly deserve the people's wrath;
> Happy are we that one Mac was fired;
> Now let's make sure the others are retired.

General Douglas MacArthur, in command of U.S. troops in the Korean war, was dismissed by President Truman in 1951 for publicly releasing statements disagreeing with U.S. Government policy. Pat McCarran was a reactionary Democratic Senator from Nevada who sponsored the McCarran-Walter Act tightening beyond all reason immigration into the United States. Joseph R. McCarthy was the notorious Republican Senator from Wisconsin. J. Howard McGrath, appointed United States Attorney General by President Truman in 1959, was especially active in attempting to enforce the U.S. Attorney General's list of subversive organizations.

My good friend Rockwell Kent had started suit for his passport for reasons similar to mine and somewhat earlier than I. Hence his case, together with that of psychiatrist Dr. Walter Briehl, were ahead of mine in the courts and reached the U.S. Supreme Court in the spring of 1958. Soon afterwards that Court handed down a favorable decision for Kent and Briehl, declaring that it was unconstitutional for the State Department to make political qualifications for an American citizen to obtain a passport. I then automatically won my suit and was able to get my precious passport in June, 1958.

I had another encounter with government illegality in 1963 when Congress passed a law requiring the U.S. Postmaster General to screen all incoming mail from foreign countries—except first-class sealed letters—for Communist political propaganda. If the Postmaster found something containing one sentence of alleged Communist political propaganda, he was to send a postcard to the addressee saying in effect, "Do you really want to receive this subversive literature?" And if the addressee wrote back "Yes," the Post Office mailed the literature to him. My lawyer, Leonard Boudin, discovered later than when the Post Office forwarded such literature to the addressee it also sent his name to the Un-American Activities Committee, which would then subpoena the poor man who was getting some piece of mail from China or the Soviet Union or Poland, and there would be another victim for the Committee to harass.

I received a postcard in 1963 informing me that a copy of the *Peking Review* was addressed to me and was being held by the Post Office in San Francisco. I hadn't subscribed to the *Peking Review;* but somebody was sending it to me. I was annoyed at getting the postcard, and instead of returning it and saying "Yes, I want it," I sued the Postmaster General on the grounds that he was violating my First Amendment rights and acting as a censor in the delivery of something I wanted to read. We lost my case in a special three-judge Federal District Court in New York and then were able to appeal directly to the U.S. Supreme Court, which took the case.

It was one of the most memorable days of my life when I went to Washington in April, 1965, to hear Mr. Boudin argue my appeal before the Supreme Court. I had never attended a Supreme Court session before, so that the whole experience was new and fascinating to me. Boudin, of course, was brilliant and the U.S. Solicitor General, Archibald Cox, weak and wobbly. A delegation of about ten students from the Harvard Law School came down from Cambridge to listen to the proceedings. Less than a month later when the decision was announced in the case of *Lamont* v.

Postmaster General, we were as surprised as could be that the Court decided unanimously, 8 to 0, that the statute was unconstitutional on First Amendment grounds.

Mr. Justice Douglas wrote the main opinion, stating that this law was unconstitutional because it interfered with the "unfettered exercise" of First Amendment rights. Douglas said that the requirement that addressees must request in writing that mail be delivered "is almost certain to have a deterrent effect, especially as regards those who have sensitive positions. Their livelihood may be dependent on a security clearance. Public officials, like schoolteachers who have no tenure, might think they would invite disaster if they read what the Federal Government says contains the seeds of treason. Apart from them, any addressee is likely to feel some inhibition in sending for literature which federal officials have condemned as 'Communist political propaganda.' The regime of this Act is at war with the 'uninhibited, robust and wide-open' debate and discussion that are contemplated by the First Amendment."[4]

This was the first time in the history of the Supreme Court that it had declared a Congressional law unconstitutional because it violated the First Amendment. The Court's verdict in *Lamont* v. *Postmaster General* was well received throughout the country. The press in general approved of it and many newspapers ran special editorials praising it. It was considered a landmark decision and was cited repeatedly in other civil liberties cases. Naturally, I felt very happy about it all.

In the 1970's the Freedom of Information Act gave American citizens who think that the FBI or the CIA has a file on them the right to see its contents. In 1975 Mr. Boudin and I made a reasoned guess that there was a file on me at both the CIA and the FBI. That guess turned out to be justified in both cases. After corresponding for about eight months in a delaying action, the FBI confessed that it had a file on me of 2,788 pages. I was somewhat surprised at the size of the file, but then friends started to congratulate me. After another long delay we obtained 2,055 of those pages, with the FBI initially holding back approximately 733 and considerable portions of the released letters, "in the interest of national security and foreign policy." Through steady legal pressure, we finally got a good many of those 733 papers.

I forced myself to read most of my FBI file, and it was really very boring because they had monitored my radio speeches, and copied my articles and pamphlets. They could have obtained all this from me free. But they had to assign an agent to do all that work and I had to read it many years later. Nonetheless, I found some very important and amusing material. For instance, when in 1961 John Kenneth Galbraith was appointed Ambassador to India by President Kennedy and had to have a security check by the FBI, one of the questions they asked was: "Professor Galbraith, why were you living fourteen years ago in the same apartment house in New York City as Corliss Lamont?" He and I were teaching at Columbia at the time.

Galbraith took an attitude of affronted dignity and brushed the matter off humorously by calling it a case of "dangerous cohabitation." A new crime—not only guilt by association but guilt by cohabitation!

Another incident occurred there which was quite ludicrous. One day the elevator man, Johnny, stopped me and said, "You know, the FBI was here asking me about you." I said, "Why, Johnny, what did they say?" This occurred some twenty years ago, but I'll try to reconstruct the conversation. The FBI agent asked, "What does Mr. Lamont say on the way up in the elevator?" Johnny answered, "He don't say much." FBI agent: "Does he ever mention Soviet Russia?" Johnny: "No, I can't remember that." Then the FBI man became very firm and said, "Well, I suppose he *did* talk to you about Communism?" Johnny: "No, he never mentioned that." Johnny was getting nervous at this point because he felt he was failing a test and that somehow he must supply some valid information to a Government agent. So he said to the FBI man, "Well, I tell you, Mr. Lamont sometimes carries a tennis racquet." We will stop there, except that I must add that somewhat later a U.S. Government employee was quizzed by the FBI as to why he had played tennis doubles with me.

About this time the FBI came around to a friend of mine and asked him a number of questions about me. One was, "Does Lamont have a grand piano?" Another was, "Is he influenced by women?" I enthusiastically plead guilty here in the affirmative. Has there been a single man in the history of the human race who was not influenced by the female sex?

The FBI perpetrated its worst outrage against me and my family when it engaged Mr. Jetson Dyer, the head of my parents' staff at the Lamont summer place in Maine, to spy on me. He was supposed to report on those with whom I played tennis and went sailing during my summer vacation, and to tail me in general. The FBI also arranged for the ticket office of the State of Maine Ferry Service to report whenever I took the regular boat from the island of North Haven to Rockland on the mainland. Such absurdities justify my saying that FBI stood for Federal Bureau of Idiots. The FBI also constantly harassed the superintendent of my weekend place at Ossining, New York, demanding the names of all visitors, if possible, and at least the numbers of their auto license plates.

From the papers obtained from the FBI it is evident that J. Edgar Hoover and his cohorts considered me a terrible menace and were trying hard to get something on me that would land me in jail or show I was a secret member of the Communist Party. An FBI agent or informer was always listed with a "T"; thus "T-1, T-2, T-3" and so on. No fewer than twenty-seven different "T's" or agents reported on me to Hoover from time to time for some thirty years.

On January 11, 1944, Director Hoover sent out the following memo concerning me:

> While the Bureau's files contain a great volume of information concerning this individual which indicates he has played an important

role in numerous Communist front or Communist controlled groups, it does not appear that a comprehensive investigative report has ever been submitted concerning him.

It is, therefore, desired that your office prepare a summary report setting forth fully his birth, citizenship, background and Communist connections and activities.

My main impression from reading the more than 2,000 pages about me in the FBI file was that this agency of repression's chief interest in me was to prove that I was or had been a card-carrying member of the Communist Party. The FBI knew that I was not guilty of any major crime such as murder, robbery, arson, criminal assault or treason. So it concentrated on criminal perjury, as with many other radicals, and thrashed around desperately for "proof" that could be convincing to a grand jury. Of course, the FBI was constantly tapping my phone.

Their efforts to obtain this proof were redoubled after I stated under oath before the McCarthy Committee in 1953 that "I am not and never have been a member of the Communist Party." FBI reports on me were usually headed, "Corliss Lamont SM-C. Perjury." "SM-C" means "Security Matter-Communist." The FBI persuaded the U.S. Internal Revenue Service to make a special check on my 1951 and 1952 tax returns—wherein I had reported certain business losses—in hopes that some grounds for perjury could be discovered.

For many years the FBI had me on its Security Index, which listed those persons to be immediately arrested and thrown into concentration camps in case national security were threatened. However, in the NECLC suit *Lamont* v. *Department of Justice*, Federal Judge Edward Weinfeld in 1979 held that the Government failed to show that the FBI's surveillance of me under the Security Index program was "related to the FBI's duties to enforce federal law." In other words, the FBI had no legal right to investigate me at all. The court's decision was of far-reaching significance because the FBI frequently invoked the Security Index for its wide-ranging political surveillance.

Among other despicable things, FBI men came into my bank at the end of every month, looked at all my cancelled checks and then demanded that they receive copies of them in Washington. This was against the law and has made me more nervous than anything else because I am always afraid of filing a tax return on gifts that may not be quite accurate. With the FBI maybe reporting on all these checks to the IRS, I might get into real trouble, but nothing like that ever happened. For all I know, the FBI is still looking at my cancelled checks.

A bizarre action by the Nixon Administration was its compilaton of an "Enemies" list—of almost 500 Americans whom President Nixon considered inimical to him and to the United States. My wife Helen and I were on the list and thought that was an honor. Helen appeared on the list twice, first as Mrs. Corliss Lamont and second as plain Helen Lamont. It was obviously too much of a brain strain for U.S. Intelligence to figure out that these two names represented the same person.

Turning now to the Central Intelligence Agency, we shall see that its conduct towards me was just as discreditable and obnoxious as that of the FBI. Senator Frank Church's investigating committee established that from 1953 to 1975 the CIA had secretly examined international mail entering or leaving the United States, had opened and copied some 21,000 letters mailed first-class to or from Americans in foreign countries and had fed about 1.5 million names acquired in this way into computers. During a period of twenty years the CIA snoopers had photostated every piece of mail I had sent from the Soviet Union or received there, about 155 in all. Under the Freedom of Information Act, I obtained some 300 photostats of the CIA photostats. From a notation in the upper right-hand corner of each letter it was evident that a copy had been sent to the FBI at the time it was originally procured.

Of course, the CIA's opening of my mail was illegal, for it directly violated the Fourth Amendment of the Bill of Rights: "The right of the people to be secure in their persons, houses, papers, and effects, against unreasonable searches and seizures, shall not be violated, and no Warrants shall issue, but upon probable cause, supported by Oath or affirmation, and particularly describing the place to be searched and the persons or things to be seized."

The bulk of my U.S.-U.S.S.R. correspondence was with an old friend, Vladimir D. Kazakevich, a Russian economist working in Moscow. He left Russia with his parents after the 1917 revolution and came to the United States in the early 1920's. Kazakevich took various jobs in the field of economics, including teaching at Columbia and Cornell Universities, and returned to the Soviet Union permanently in 1950. Our correspondence was of a scholarly sort dealing with economics, philosophy, international affairs, American-Soviet relations and civil liberties. Both the CIA and the FBI must have been terribly disappointed in the harmless character of the Lamont-Kazakevich correspondence.

Early in 1976 my lawyer, again Mr. Boudin, and I decided that I should sue the Central Intelligence Agency for $150,000 damages for its unconstitutional action in opening 155 letters to or from me. The case came to trial early in 1978 before Judge Jack B. Weinstein of the Federal District Court in Brooklyn, N.Y. On February 8, 1978, I testified in the witness box for an hour and a half responding to the questions put by the U.S. Government lawyer and my own trial lawyer, Michael Krinsky.

Only 10 days later Judge Weinstein handed down a decision in my favor awarding me $2,000 in damages and directing the United States Government to send me a "suitable letter of regret." The CIA case was extremely weak, since it admitted that the letter-opening was illegal, but justified in the interests of "national security," the standard governmental excuse for violating the Constitution.

In his opinion the Judge stated: "Mr. Lamont's reaction to his discovery of these illegal mail openings was one of 'surprise,' 'indignation,' 'depression' and a 'sense of failure'. His sense of despair upon realizing that his lifelong work on behalf of civil liberties had not prevented this major breach of his own rights is understandable." The Judge was particularly incensed over two "love letters" that I had written to my wife, Helen. He declared: "In describing the opening of these letters on the witness stand Mr. Lamont was obviously deeply upset. . . . Illegal prying into the shared intimacies of husband and wife is despicable."

The Judge went on to say: "The sums being awarded are in large measure symbolic. They probably substantially underestimate the deep sense of personal affront and the psychic loss suffered by a distinguished man of the world writing to friends, associates, and his wife. Certainly the wound to his sense of freedom and pride in our Constitution is enormous. . . . These damages will not be paid by the bunglers responsible for the wrongs, but by the taxpayers who were unaware of the program."[5]

Naturally I was very happy to win this suit against the Central Intelligence Agency. But more important than my personal satisfaction was that the victory upheld the Fourth Amendment and the right of privacy against a dictatorial government disregarding the principles and procedures of democracy. I did not receive my check for the $2,000 damages from the United States Treasury until more than a year later. I immediately turned over this check to the National Emergency Civil Liberties Committee for a special project on human rights.

It was almost sixty years ago that I first became involved in the struggle for civil liberties. Since that time it has been a mixed picture, with a sharp decline during the McCarthy era and the Presidency of Richard Nixon, and with no more than 50 percent of U.S. Supreme Court decisions uncompromisingly upholding the Bill of Rights and the Constitution. The United States was certainly heading in the direction of a police state. But after the Watergate scandal of 1973 and the exposures of innumerable illegal actions on the part of the Federal Bureau of Investigation and the Central Intelligence Agency, the tide turned in favor of civil liberties. The Freedom of Information Act has been an important factor in alerting the American people to the danger of unscrupulous government bureaucracies running wild and heedlessly violating both the Constitution and criminal law.

Another important factor in the improvement of the civil liberties situation was the détente with the Soviet Union and the Communist world. That was matched by a domestic détente in which the old anti-Communist witch-hunt of the McCarthy days largely subsided. As James Madison wrote Thomas Jefferson (May 13, 1798), "Perhaps it is a universal truth that the loss of liberty at home is to be charged to provisions against danger, real or pretended, from abroad."[6] President Madison was right. The state of civil liberties within the U.S.A. is always closely related to the success or failure of American foreign policy and the real or fabricated menace of international war. There will never come a time, no matter what kind of economic system we have, when we can afford to lean back and say: "We don't have to worry about civil liberties any more." The repressive tendencies latent in Man will forever spring back if given half a chance.

The flourishing of civil liberties is a precondition for the free pursuit of every other good cause. I have enjoyed working for civil liberties because of its immense social importance; because it has brought me into touch with a wide variety of interesting Americans, including both scoundrels such as Joe McCarthy and Congressman Martin Dies and outstanding leaders such as Arthur Garfield Hays and Harry F. Ward; and because in fighting for human rights I have won several significant cases in the courts of my country, including one in the United States Supreme Court.

As this chapter has illustrated, I ran into a good deal of trouble in speaking and in other activities on behalf of the Bill of Rights. I was eventually barred by most radio and TV stations. Then came the founding of the Pacifica Foundation in 1950 and its Eastern division. Radio Station WBAI-FM in 1960, with their promise to give liberals and radicals a chance to present their views. I thought this offered a great opportunity for voicing dissenting opinions, a true civil liberties radio station, which was to operate by listener-sponsorship, without any commercial advertising and financially supported by its subscribers. The man behind it was Louis Schweitzer (1890-1971), a generous philanthropist who owned the building where WBAI was located and who agreed to forego the station's annual rent.

I decided I would do everything possible on behalf of this station and joined others in raising funds for its operations. Harold Winkler, President of the Pacifica Foundation, called me into conference to discuss the general situation, saying that he knew of my abilities as a speaker and expressing the hope that I would take on some sort of series at WBAI. I replied that I would be glad to work something out and that I was enthusiastic about the educational and cultural program he had outlined for WBAI. I felt that an independent radio station that could not be controlled or influenced by advertisers would be a major asset for the people of greater New York and all who could tune in. It was clearly in the public interest that such an enterprise should flourish.

Winkler wrote me from Berkeley, California, on December 17, 1959, saying "we would like your series now in KPFA in Berkeley, and I think in KPFK, Los Angeles," and suggesting that I make tapes at WBAI, which would mail them to California. Winkler noted that Pacifica's commentators were heard either bi-weekly or monthly, and concluded by asking me "how frequently you plan to do your commentary" for WBAI and Pacifica.

I drew up for Winkler a suggested outline of nine broadcasts, January through March, 1960, with the emphasis on civil liberties, and with two talks on the philosophy of Humanism. Early in January, 1960, I gave this outline to Winkler when he was in New York again. He thought it excellent and said he would hand it on to WBAI. He also noted that the station needed to raise $100,000 for the year 1960 and asked me to help garner some funds. I said I would try.

During the next few months I obtained from an interested friend a pledge of $10,000 and a gift of $20,000 from the Palisades Foundation, a Lamont family enterprise that had been set up many years previously by my father. These donations were to be given to Pacifica earmarked for WBAI. Winkler agreed that he would announce the $20,000 gift simply as coming from the Palisades Foundation. However, he promptly revealed to the Pacifica Board the relationship of my father and me to the Foundation. This touched off a heated debate on the Board, a minority arguing that Pacifica should refuse to accept a contribution originating even indirectly with a militant radical like myself.

Meanwhile, I heard no word from WBAI about my projected radio series that Winkler had approved. However, I made separate broadcasts over WBAI May 12 and October 18, 1960, and when I saw Winkler again in New York in January, 1961, I asked him what had happened to my program. He answered in considerable embarrassment that Louis Schweitzer had taken the position that though the large donation to WBAI was in fact from the Lamont family, my initiative in the matter would make any broadcasting by me over the station look like "payola." Accordingly, Winkler added, my appearance on WBAI had become most doubtful, although he hoped they could squeeze me in very occasionally. And that's the way it turned out.

Never had I felt more outraged than by this surprising message from the President of Pacifica and Mr. Schweitzer, the chief financial angel of WBAI. I felt I had been trapped in a thoroughly dishonest maneuver. It seemed to me that WBAI was at the outset violating my rights of free speech and betraying its own principles by subverting the public interest in open and honest broadcasting. Schweitzer was perfectly aware that I, as a well-known figure among American liberals and radicals, was in frequent demand as a speaker and that nobody in his senses would ever make a "payola" accusation against me. Furthermore, unless Pacifica itself called attention to my connection with the Palisades Foundation, in all probability the public would never have learned about it. In fact, the "payola" business was so inherently absurd that I knew in my bones it was a phony alibi for something else, namely, Schweitzer's hostility to me as an uncompromising leftist.

During the next three years—1962, 1963, 1964—various officials at WBAI made efforts to straighten out the situation and to obtain large contributions from me. Before Winkler had informed me of the "payola" angle, I had intended to make substantial gifts to WBAI each year. However, I felt the Schweitzer dictum was so scandalous that I dropped my original plan. I had three meetings with WBAI officials at which they insisted that Schweitzer did not control the station's policies and that no "payola" rule had ever been in effect.

My most important meeting with WBAI personnel took place on January 29, 1964 at the home of Dr. Harold Taylor in New York City. Besides Dr. Taylor, a member of the WBAI Board of Advisors, there were present Louise Berman, another member of the Board, and Joseph Binns, Manager of the station. When I told the group the story of my relations with WBAI, they all agreed that I had been treated shamefully and that steps should be taken to rectify the situation. Mr. Binns said he would promptly arrange a number of broadcasts for me over WBAI. But nothing ever resulted from that commitment.

A few months later, on the evening of May 13, 1964, I was introduced to Louis Schweitzer after a dinner meeting of the *Monthly Review* at the Hotel Sheraton in New York. I had never met him before. He said he was glad to meet me, because he had wanted for a long time to tell me frankly that he was the person who had kept me off WBAI. He spoke in an aggressive manner, and I was surprised that anyone would want to boast about interfering with my radio rights. I protested that WBAI should have informed me in advance that anyone who made or arranged a large contribution to it would be barred from its broadcasting facilities. When I asked Schweitzer how large a donation would bring the ban into effect, he answered, "Anything over $100." This policy against "payola" he claimed, was "a rule of thumb" that had been instituted when the station was established. Schweitzer concluded our short talk by a bitter attack on my political views. I got the impression that he had a sort of personal obsession about me.

I wrote letters of protest about my encounter with Schweitzer to Hallock Hoffman, who had become president of the Pacifica Foundation, and to Chris Albertson, the new Manager of WBAI. They both replied that no matter what Schweitzer said, there never had been a "payola" rule in effect at Pacifica or WBAI, and that in any case WBAI was not subject to control by Schweitzer. Yet only a short time later, in the fall of 1965, almost half the staff of WBAI resigned in protest over what they deemed improper control by Schweitzer, its largest contributor.

In 1970, at the insistence of WBAI, I agreed to meet once more with officials of the station. Their main purpose turned out to be to ask me for a donation of $15,000. I declined the invitation, since I had no intention of walking into the "payola" trap again. Early in 1973, after further correspondence, Edwin A. Goodman, an able and amiable man who had just become the new President of Pacifica, wrote me that I would be "welcome to apply for air time on WBAI." This I did.

I went to the WBAI office and talked to Nick Egleson, the Public Affairs Director, about the matter, suggesting, among other things, that as Chairman of the National Emergency Civil Liberties Committee, I could make some pertinent comments about how the Bill of Rights was faring. Mr. Egleson said he would let me know about my broadcasting, but I never heard a word from him thereafter.

I believe that the ethics of history demands that I reveal the unethical way in which WBAI treated me. As I reflect on my exasperating negotiations with that station for more than twelve years, I am struck by how my attempt to be public-spirited and help the station stay on its feet boomeranged into gross injustice against me. It is evident that the officers of Pacifica and WBAI carried out a disingenuous policy toward me, to say the least. They refused to admit that any official "payola" rule was in effect, but were afraid to disregard the *unofficial* one that Schweitzer had improvised to bar me from WBAI—strange conduct from a supposedly liberal station.

To prevent such practices, I think that any radio or TV station supported by voluntary contributions should make public clearly defined regulations as to the rights and non-rights of donors to be heard over its facilities. I imagine that the Federal Communications Commission would also be interested in having such regulations put into effect.

Chapter XI   VICTORY OVER SENATOR JOSEPH McCARTHY

Just as lawless and menacing as the House Un-American Activities Committee was the Senate Permanent Subcommittee on Investigations, of which Senator Joseph McCarthy of Wisconsin was Chairman; it soon became known simply as the McCarthy Committee. In the early 1950's McCarthy and his staff exploded when they unearthed the fact that some United States Government departments were utilizing books that they regarded as "subversive," or were written or edited by a "Communist" or a so-called "fellow-traveler."

In 1953 the McCarthy sleuths reported that the Military Intelligence Section of the United States General Staff had published a brochure entitled *Psychological and Cultural Traits of Soviet Siberia*. McCarthy's agents then made the horrible discovery that the pamphlet included in its bibliography my book, *The Peoples of the Soviet Union*, a study of the 177 Soviet national and racial minorities, which made no attempt to analyze the Soviet political and economic system. It had been listed in the Army manual without my knowledge or consent. It was on the basis of this mere listing that McCarthy asserted that the Army pamphlet "quoted heavily" from me. Actually it printed no quotation whatever from my work.

On September 9, 1953, Senator McCarthy gave the press excerpts from this Army pamphlet and made the absurd claim that it was Communist propaganda. On September 11 the Army disclosed that McCarthy had failed to release passages hostile to the Soviet Union and to reveal that the purpose of the pamphlet was to develop among the United States armed forces "an understanding of the Soviet people which will be militarily useful in case of war." The Army stated that only one hundred copies of the manual had been printed, with some forty distributed to high Army officials; and that, since the document had a secrecy classification as "re-stricted," McCarthy's unauthorized release of much of it constituted a violation of the espionage law. The Army then proceeded to declassify the pamphlet from its restricted status "as a result of prior disclosures" by McCarthy.

About two weeks later McCarthy launched his attack on me. On the morning of Tuesday, September 22, I was at work in my study near Columbia University writing the first chapter of a long-planned book on civil liberties when the house phone rang and an unknown person announced that he had a subpoena for me from Senator McCarthy's investigating committee. I told him to wait and immediately called my lawyer, who said that I might as well accept it.

I went down to the lobby of the apartment house and accepted service of the subpoena, which summoned me to appear before the Committee the next day at 2:30 p.m. at the United States Courthouse in New York City. A witness should be given at least three or four days between the serving of a subpoena and his appearance at a Congressional hearing, and I was disturbed to realize that I had only a little more than 24 hours to prepare myself for the ordeal. It was typical of McCarthy's unscrupulous tactics to try to catch his victims off guard and to allow them no adequate opportunity to prepare.

I had realized, of course, that the McCarthy Committee might tap me, and had been thinking on and off about possible courses of action. I had been especially impressed by an article in *The Nation* in May of 1953 entitled "How to Stop the Demagogues," by the well-known attorney, Philip Wittenberg, and had talked briefly with him about the approach that he recommended. He had informally agreed to take my case if I were called before a Congressional committee.

I immediately phoned him, found he could see me, and took a taxi to his office. I had three long conferences with him before my Wednesday deadline. We settled the general principles on which I would stand and rehearsed a number of probable questions and the type of answer or refusal to answer I should make to them.

With these preparations in mind, I appeared before the McCarthy Committee at the Federal Courthouse with Mr. Wittenberg early Wednesday afternoon, September 23. Senator McCarthy himself was presiding, but it seemed odd that he was the only member of the committee present. Since he had announced this hearing as a closed executive session, which is supposed to be strictly private, I was surprised to see about a dozen spectators, men and women, sitting in one corner of the room. In another part, seated by himself, was the ever loquacious and pliant witness Louis Budenz, whom I recognized from his newspaper photographs. He had made a specialty of claiming that this or that person was or had been a member of the Communist Party or Communist fronts. He was present, I felt sure, for the primary purpose of intimidating me and trying to make me nervous.

At the very start I took my most decisive step when I asked permission to read a prepared statement objecting to the committee's jurisdiction. Since an objection to jurisdiction is absolutely basic, taking precedence over everything else, McCarthy had to allow my statement to be put into the record. In this three-page document, drawn up by Mr. Wittenberg in precise legal terminology rather than in eloquent language about the Bill of Rights, I challenged the legal and constitutional power of the McCarthy Committee to inquire into my political beliefs, my religious convictions, my associational activities, or any other personal and private affairs. I advanced four main grounds for this position.

In the first place, I cited the protections of the First Amendment and quoted the concurring opinion of Justice Douglas in the 1953 United States Supreme Court decision supporting the refusal of Edward Rumely, executive secretary of the right-wing Committee for Constitutional Government, to give testimony and produce materials before a committee of the House of Representatives. "The power of investigation," wrote Justice Douglas, "is also limited. Inquiry into personal and private affairs is precluded."

I also emphasized the First Amendment's guarantee of freedom of the press and urged that since Congress could not pass laws interfering with such freedom and since a Congressional committee can make inquiries relevant only to constitutional legislation, McCarthy had no right to ask me questions about the origin or content or purpose of my writings. Several of the Senator's questions were designed to disclose my sources of research as a scholar and the precise persons with whom I had discussed problems pertaining to my book. Such inquiries constituted attempted interference with freedom of research and of scholarship.

In the second place, I relied on the three-way separation of powers in the American Government by which the legislative, judicial and executive branches possess definite and limited functions. I claimed that McCarthy's committee would be trespassing upon the powers of the judiciary—from the Department of Justice through the courts and down to grand juries and trial juries—by inquiring into my personal beliefs and affairs. When in 1952 the Truman Administration instead of Congress decreed the government seizure of certain steel companies, the United States Supreme Court declared the action unconstitutional precisely because it violated the tripartite separation of powers. It did this although the Korean emergency was still acute.

In November, 1953, ex-President Truman, in his letter refusing to testify before the House Committee on Un-American Activities regarding the Harry Dexter White case, maintained that the committee was invading the rights of the executive branch of the government by subpoenaing him. In thus taking his stand on the doctrine of the separation of powers, Mr. Truman rendered valuable aid to the campaign to curb Congressional committees through the enforcement of this same general constitutional principle.

In the third place, I claimed that public law 601, establishing the Senate

Committee on Government Operations (parent committee of McCarthy's Subcommittee), so limited the scope of both the Committee and any Subcommittee as to debar the investigation of me as an author. For I was a private citizen who had never been employed by the Federal government, and the listing of my book in an Army publication took place without my prior knowledge or any consultation with me. No Congressional committee can be authorized to summon a writer and quiz him about his literary work merely because one of his books happens to be listed by a U.S. Government agency. If the author of any book copyrighted and then automatically placed in the Library of Congress were to be subject to Congressional investigation, the impact on freedom of opinion would be severe indeed.

In the fourth place and finally, I maintained that at the time of my hearing the McCarthy Committee was not a competent tribunal, because all of its Democratic members had resigned and had thus deprived the Committee of competency to act until properly reconstituted. The three Democratic Senators—Henry M. Jackson of Washington, John L. McClellan of Arkansas and Stuart Symington of Missouri—had formally withdrawn in July, 1953, as a protest against McCarthy's insistence that as Chairman of the Committee he had the exclusive power to hire or dismiss staff members.

In my opening statement I also volunteered the information that I was not and never had been a member of the Communist Party. This I did in order to throw McCarthy off balance and to spike his strategy of allegations to the press about an uncooperative witness being a secret, dangerous Communist. Realizing that a large part of McCarthy's effectiveness was in his voluminous newspaper publicity, I wished to set the stage so far as I could for favorable counter-publicity on my side and the side of civil liberties. I aimed, by disposing in advance of the ever-lurking Communist issue, to help clear the way for a calm and impartial court test in the event my case went to trial.

After receiving my statement in silence McCarthy launched into a long series of questions. I answered a few concerning recorded facts. Yes, I had published a book about the peoples of Soviet Russia, had written a chapter for *U.S.S.R., A Concise Handbook,*[1] edited by Professor Ernest J. Simmons, and had sent a letter to *The New York Times* criticising the decision of the United States Supreme Court in holding the Smith Act constitutional.

But most of McCarthy's inquiries I refused to answer, giving as my reason each time the objections expressed in my initial First Amendment challenge to the Committee's jurisdiction. Almost every question the Senator asked was loaded: for example, "Did you know that Mr. A, who wrote a chapter in this book used by the United States Army, was a member of the Communist Party?" "Did you know that Mr. B was a member of the Communist conspiracy?" and "Do you know any member of the Communist Party who to your knowledge engaged in either espionage or sabotage?" Instead of declining to answer, I should have preferred to say "No" to all such questions; but that would have undermined my legal position. There was always the possibility, too, that McCarthy was trying to trick me into a response that, through some slip of memory, would lay the basis for a perjury charge.

McCarthy continued his grilling for about an hour and then brought the hearing to a close. He said that I could not obtain a copy of the record because this session was "strictly executive," and ordered me to appear at a public hearing the following Monday, September 28, in Washington. At this point McCarthy, having said all along that my Wednesday hearing was an executive session and therefore "closed," suddenly announced that he was going to give a résumé to the press.

He called the reporters in and talked to them for some thirty minutes, informing them that I was guilty of contempt on at least two dozen counts. As he had made public his version of the hearing, I gave the newspapermen copies of my statement objecting to the jurisdiction of the committee, and discussed briefly the reasons for my stand. The press gave me excellent coverage; but usually McCarthy's tricky device of giving publicity to *his* version of a so-called private hearing from which reporters were barred was disadvantageous to the witness. Telford Taylor, reserve brigadier general and chief prosecutor at the trial of the Nazi war criminals, said: "It is an outrageous procedure, obviously designed for the sole purpose of publicity."

While questioning me, McCarthy paced up and down unsmiling, but he was not abusive. Of dark complexion and sinister mien, he looked to me like a Mafia-type scoundrel. And his unscrupulous conduct strengthened that impression. In my view he was the most dangerous demagogue in the history of American politics.

On Friday afternoon, September 25, a telegram came to my home from Senator McCarthy stating that my Monday hearing had been postponed. The wire added, "However, you are under continuing subpoena and both you and your counsel will be notified when your appearance is required." On Monday morning McCarthy went ahead with his public session and examined other witnesses. To my astonishment the transcript of this hearing showed that at the very beginning the "Honorable" Senator had asserted: "Mr. Lamont has not been subpoenaed. He was notified that he could come today and purge himself of the contempt of failure to answer last week. Is Mr. Lamont here?" "There was no answer," the transcript recorded.

Of course he had sent me no such message and had said in his telegram that I was still under subpoena. Apparently thinking that the cancellation of my hearing might be interpreted as a retreat on his part, he gave the false impression that the responsibility for my not appearing was mine.

The Senator used his two mis-statements and the calling of my name as excuses to make public the complete minutes of the "private" executive session at which I was examined on September 23. I protested to McCarthy against this whole procedure. On October 24 Francis B. Carr, Executive Director of the subcommittee and former head of the FBI in New York City, wrote me to say that the passages to which I had objected had been deleted from the record. This correction, however, did not offset the erroneous impression given originally to the press and the public by McCarthy's conduct.

Each person summoned by a Congressional committee must make his own decision, taking into consideration all the particular circumstances in his case, on the policy he will pursue. I believe, for instance, that reliance on the Fifth Amendment may be fully justified and that we must defend the right of witnesses to use it without any penalties being imposed upon them by either public or private authorities. However, in seeking a court test to halt the excesses of Congressional committees we cannot utilize the Fifth Amendment. We must stand upon the First Amendment and the separation of powers inherent in the American governmental system.

My reliance on the First Amendment in refusing to answer McCarthy's questions was the same in principle as that recommended in an historic letter written in 1953 by Albert Einstein in answering a letter from William Frauenglass, a teacher of English who, standing on the Fifth Amendment, had refused to answer questions by the Senate Internal Security Committee about political affiliations. Einstein's letter follows:

> Dear Mr. Frauenglass:
> The problem with which the intellectuals of this country are confronted is very serious. The reactionary politicians have managed to instill suspicion of all intellectual efforts into the public by dangling before their eyes a danger from without. Having succeeded so far they are now proceeding to suppress the freedom of teaching and to deprive of their positions all those who do not prove submissive, i.e., to starve them.
> What ought the minority of intellectuals to do against this evil? Frankly, I can see only the revolutionary way of non-cooperation in the sense of Gandhi's. Every intellectual who is called before one of the committees ought to refuse to testify, i.e., he must be prepared for jail and economic ruin, in short, for the sacrifice of his personal welfare in the interest of the cultural welfare of his country.
> However, this refusal to testify must not be based on the well-known subterfuge of invoking the Fifth Amendment against possible self-incrimination, but on the assertion that it is shameful for a blameless citizen to submit to such an inquisition and that this kind of inquisition violates the spirit of the Constitution.
> If enough people are ready to take this grave step they will be

successful. If not, then the intellectuals of this country deserve nothing better than the slavery which is intended for them.

Sincerely yours,
A. Einstein

What I and other recalcitrant witnesses before Congressional committees were trying to do through our cases was not to cripple the power of Congressional investigations, but to have them reasonably and specifically limited in scope and methods, according to the principles of the Constitution.

Editorial comment on my case was encouraging. *The New York Times* stated on September 25:[2] "The action of Corliss Lamont in defying the McCarthy committee on the ground that the latter is unconstitutionally violating the personal rights of private citizens raises again the interesting and important questions of how far Congressional committees can properly go. Many citizens who have no use for Communism are disturbed over the degree to which such committees threaten an incursion into the domain of private rights and constitutional guarantees. . . . The ultimate disposition of this case may help define the area in which privacy of the individual is still protected."

On September 29 *The Washington Post*[3] said in an editorial that I had "challenged the jurisdiction of Senator McCarthy's Government Operations Committee on substantial and significant grounds. . . . The basic issue, of course, is whether the courts, which have been understandably reluctant to impose broad, general checks upon the power of Congress to investigate, will be more willing to impose checks which Congress has not conferred upon them." On the same day a *St. Louis Post-Dispatch* editorial asserted that, "If the Senate should vote a contempt citation against Mr. Lamont, it would undoubtedly produce a test case that would go all the way to the United States Supreme Court where demagogues fare less well than they do in Congress. . . . Many Americans will applaud Corliss Lamont for having, in effect, spoken up for them and their right to be secure in their thoughts and their personal lives."

It was not until almost ten months later, July 16, 1954, that McCarthy initiated proceedings against me in the United States Senate for contempt of that body, on the ground that I had refused to answer a number of questions before the Senate Permanent Subcommittee on Investigations. On August 16 the Senate spent many hours considering the matter and debating McCarthy's treatment of me. It was an extremely interesting discussion. Senators Herbert Lehman, Democrat, of New York, William Langer, Republican, of North Dakota and Wayne Morse, Democrat, of Oregon, were my chief defenders. Lehman and Langer were both effective

and eloquent in my defense. A personal friend, Senator Leverett Salton-
stall, Republican, of Massachusetts, spoke favorably of my character, but
maintained that the courts should decide on the question of contempt.

McCarthy took the floor much of the time and at one point said of me:
"He was born with a silver spoon in his mouth. He has done more to
damage this nation than perhaps any other man in the country, with the
possible exception of Frederick Field." (A good friend of mine.—C. L.) I
interpreted McCarthy's remark as a tribute which meant in fact that
nobody had done more for his country than I.

The Senate finally voted to cite me for contempt, 71 to 3, with 22
Senators absent. Voting against the citation were Senators Lehman,
Langer, and Chavez, Democrat, of New Mexico. On October 14, 1954, the
Federal Grand Jury of the Southern District of New York indicted me for
contempt of Congress, carrying with it a fine of $1,000 and a possible year
in jail. I pleaded not guilty a day later and put up $1,000 as bail. On October
29 I moved that the indictment be dismissed. Attorney Philip Wittenberg
argued this motion on November 26 before Federal District Judge Edward
Weinfeld.

On July 27, 1955, Judge Weinfeld handed down his decision granting my
motion to dismiss the indictment, chiefly on the ground that McCarthy's
Committee had no legal or constitutional authority to investigate or question me at all. The indictment did not state at any point that the Permanent
Subcommittee on Investigations had actually been appointed by its parent
Committee on Government Operations, or that its inquiries were within
the scope of the parent committee. This left the McCarthy Committee
without any legal standing and made *all* of its many hearings and investigations lawless and beyond Congressional power.

My counsel Mr. Wittenberg developed the implications: "Had a Subcommittee been appointed it would have been necessary to assign to such
Subcommittee some authority. That authority would have served as a
limitation on its power to investigate. Senator McCarthy, pursuing a
lawless course, did not want any limitation on authority. Had he expressed
the authority that the Committee later assumed, that would have been
made in contravention of the representations made to the Senate. That
would have shown that he intended to exceed the limitation imposed by
Section 134 of Public Law 601, that the committees investigate but only
within their respective jurisdictions. That is why the so-called Permanent
Subcommittee on Investigations was never legally constituted."[4]

The Government carried Judge Weinfeld's dismissal of my indictment to
a Circuit Court of Appeals and filed its brief on February 23, 1956. I filed
my answering appeals brief shortly thereafter and the case was argued on
June 5, 1956. On August 14, almost three years after McCarthy haled me
before his Committee, Chief Judge Charles E. Clark and two associate
judges unanimously affirmed Judge Weinfeld's decision to dismiss my
indictment. The Court chided the Government for "attempting to hang

onto and retain for trial indictments for offenses which it cannot support in law." The Department of Justice heeded this opinion and did not appeal my case to the Supreme Court.

With my case, which McCarthy officially billed as "Communist Infiltration in the Army," the Senator foolishly renewed his wrangle with the military, a move which did much finally to discredit him. In October, 1953, he accused Secretary of the Army, Robert T. Stevens, and his aides of attempting to conceal evidence of espionage and sabotage at Fort Monmouth, New Jersey. This wild accusation was never sustained. Walter Millis wrote in *The New York Herald Tribune* of December 8, 1953, "This really vital and sensitive military installation has been wrecked—more thoroughly than any Soviet saboteur could have dreamed of doing it—by the kind of anti-Communism of which Senator McCarthy has made himself the leader and champion." Later in December the United States Senate passed a motion of censure against him, condemning him for offenses against the Senate. After this rebuke, McCarthy's influence steadily declined until his death in 1957 from whiskey and hepatitis. I was happy that by defeating this ruffian in the courts I had put a nail in his political coffin. It was no sorrow to me that a few years later he was deposited permanently in a real coffin.

I do not wish to give the impression that McCarthy was the sole Senator who bore moral guilt for my iniquitous treatment. To quote Mr. Wittenberg again: "The history in the courts of the citations for contempt of the McCarthy Committee indicates the shamelessness of the Senate in disavowing its own responsibility. Of eight indictments which have been brought none has ultimately been sustained. Apart from the unnecessary expense and the creation of a false public attitude there must be set the agony and fear of the individuals prosecuted under these indictments which followed the recommendations of the Senate. The blame must rest where the situations arose, in the Senate's extraordinary use of investigation for indictment and in its inability or unwillingness to set reasonable curbs on its members individually and on itself as a body."

To Philip Wittenberg's searing comment, I would add that our Senators and Representatives, all of whom are pledged to uphold the Constitution of this country, had become—with few exceptions—leaders or participants in a movement which could subvert and destroy the Bill of Rights. And so far as investigative procedures are concerned, our Congressional committees truly transformed representative government into government by misrepresentation.

The governmental and Congressional figures crusading so fanatically against the alleged danger of Communism in the United States do more than anybody else to make the predictions of the Communists come true. It has always been the claim of Marxists and Communists that capitalist countries are insincere about democracy and civil liberties, and are likely to throw them overboard in a time of crisis. Now this is precisely what has

been happening in America, where the triumphs of reactionary demagogues paradoxically become triumphs of Communist prophets.

As we have seen, my book *The Peoples of the Soviet Union* was a primary
reason why McCarthy came after me; and it is significant that the FBI, in its
heroic attempt to protect America, went to my publisher, Harcourt Brace,
and asked, "Was this book financed by Moscow?"—a foolish question to put
to one of the most successful publishers in the United States. The FBI
agent knew perfectly well the answer would be negative, but he wanted to
indicate to the publisher that the FBI did not approve of the book and did
not approve of me. Now what publisher after a visit from the FBI is going to
be enthusiastic about publishing another book by that author? Isn't he
going to think, "I don't want to get in trouble with the FBI again?" The FBI
did the same thing with another publishing firm, Philosophical Library,
which issued a volume of mine called *Soviet Civilization*.

In 1955, while my McCarthy case was still in the courts, the Teachers
Union of New York City honored me with its Annual Award for "valiant and
unswerving defense of intellectual freedom." Some people regarded me as
a hero because I risked a jail sentence when I defied the McCarthy
Committee, but actually I did not at any time belong in the hero category.
The fact is that my father and mother had set me up with an independent
income, so that I never had to worry about whether fines were imposed
upon me or about losing a job. The real heroes in the battle for freedom
after World War II were those thousands of Americans who defied Congressional Committees knowing that when they did so they would probably
be dismissed from positions that were their sole source of livelihood. Even
if they defeated a government committee in the courts, which happened
quite often, they frequently lost their jobs because of the committee's
having smeared them unmercifully as Communists. It is real heroism to
sacrifice your job in the middle of your career by standing firm for your
principles.

Above: Florence C. Lamont, mother of the author, in her Maine garden. Below: Thomas W. Lamont, the author's father, on an ocean voyage.

Above: The author, about four. Below: the author, on the Phillips Exeter Hockey Team, 1920

Corliss Lamont with his family, 1954. Left to right: Mrs. Lamont, Florence, the author. Standing: Margaret, Anne, Hayes.

Above: John Dewey. Below: George Santayana.

Above: John Masefield, with Mickey. Below: Bertrand Russell.

Helen and Corliss Lamont on picnic in Maine.

The author and his niece, Priscilla Cunningham.

The author at a dinner of the Emergency Civil Liberties Committee.

Chapter XII   THE AMERICAN CIVIL
                LIBERTIES UNION

The state of civil liberties after the conclusion of World War I was so precarious that more than fifty national groups were founded to defend the Bill of Rights. Many of them concentrated on some special aspect of the struggle for freedom, such as the National Association for the Advancement of Colored People, the Association on American Indian Affairs, the American Jewish Committee, the American Committee for Protection of the Foreign Born, the American Association of University Professors, the Central Committee for Conscientious Objectors, the National Committee Against Repressive Legislation and the Bill of Rights Fund. The leading organizations with an overall function are the American Civil Liberties Union (ACLU), founded in 1920, and the Emergency Civil Liberties Committee (ECLC)* founded in 1951 to take prompt action to fill gaps left by the then faltering ACLU.

Roger N. Baldwin, the first Director of the American Civil Liberties Union, remained in that position until 1950; working with him as Chairman was Harry F. Ward, Professor of Christian Ethics at Union Theological Seminary. Lucille Milner, an experienced social worker, became the first Secretary and held that post until 1945. In its first year the ACLU defended victims of the anti-Communist hysteria following World War I. Supporting the constitutional liberties of liberals and radicals who had been thrown summarily into jail as "Reds", it became itself the target of virulent attacks by public officials, newspapers and a whole wolf-pack of reactionaries. Even so rock-ribbed an institution as the *Atlantic Monthly* refused an ACLU advertisement soliciting members.

In this early period the ACLU took on free speech battles on behalf of Communists, Socialists, members of the IWW (The Industrial Workers of the World), birth control advocates and many others. It defended Margaret

---

*Later re-named the National Emergency Civil Liberties Committee.

Sanger, the courageous exponent of planned parenthood; Sacco and Van-
zetti, who were finally executed in a famous frame-up case with international implications; and John T. Scopes, science instructor who violated
Tennessee's law against the teaching of evolution. The Civil Liberties
Union grew steadily in prestige and influence. At the end of its first decade
it was generally recognized as the foremost organization for the defense of
the American Bill of Rights.

The Board of Directors elected me as a member in 1932 and I served in
that capacity for twenty-three years. Outstanding on the Board were the
able attorney, Arthur Garfield Hays, usually uncompromising in his support of civil liberties; the Reverend John Haynes Holmes, liberal minister
and founder of the Community Church in New York City; Norman
Thomas, the vociferous Socialist leader who constantly put partisan politics
above civil liberties; Dorothy Kenyon, a keen lawyer and an early suffrag-
ette; Osmond K. Fraenkel, author and the best civil liberties attorney on
the Board; and Morris L. Ernst, a lawyer who became personal attorney for
J. Edgar Hoover and a wavering supporter of the Bill of Rights because of
his paranoid anti-Communism.

Except during holiday seasons, the Board met regularly for luncheon
once a week until 1944, and then every other week. We decided upon the
fundamental civil liberties issues and cases that crowded our agenda; and
we were active in opposing both legislation and Congressional committees
that clearly violated the Bill of Rights. I found our meetings always interesting and often exciting with sincere disagreements developing among the
members and motions not infrequently passed by a majority of one or two.
We talked a lot, fought a lot at these Board meetings, yet from week to week
put through an enormous amount of business. I remember those meetings
as among the most stimulating experiences of my life.

However, as the years went by, and the Communist issue in the country
at large and in Congress became more acute, debates on the ACLU Board
tended at times to become acrimonious. A small minority led by Morris
Ernst and Norman Thomas pressed the Board to abandon its traditional
policy of confining itself to the American Bill of Rights and to take a stand
against anti-democratic governments abroad, especially those of the Soviet
Union and Nazi Germany. The same minority wished to limit the rights of
Communists in the United States, which would have been an obvious
betrayal of our principles.

In April, 1939, the Board clarified its position beyond all doubt, issuing a
leaflet, *Why We Defend Free Speech for Nazis, Fascists and Communists*,
which declared: "The Union does not engage in political controversy. It
takes up no position on any political or economic issue or system. It defends
without favorites the rights of all comers, whatever their political or
economic views. It is wholly unconcerned with movements abroad or with
foreign governments."

Meanwhile, irresponsible witnesses at public sessions of the House

Un-American Activities Committee, the Chairman of which was the notorious Martin Dies of Texas, branded the ACLU as a Communist front. The Committee stated: "We strongly urge that this organization be investigated." The Directors of the ACLU became increasingly nervous, and finally two of them, attorneys Ernst and Hays, went in October, 1939 to Washington to confer with Representative Dies. At the meeting in the Hay-Adams House Adolph A. Berle, Jr., an Assistant Secretary of State, was also present to represent the Administration.

At this conference Dies urged that the ACLU and liberals in general should cooperate with him and his Committee in investigating and exposing Communists in the United States. Later, in a letter to me, Representative Dies said: "I felt that we were seriously handicapped in exposing the Communists through a lack of cooperation from the liberals. At the meeting I suggested that if we worked together, we could destroy the Communist apparatus and influence within a few months, and that the liberals would share in the credit." A week or two later Ernst and Hays reported on the conference to the ACLU Board, but did not mention Dies's cardinal suggestion about liberals helping to track down Communists.

Soon after, however, the Ernst-Thomas group on the Civil Liberties Union Board started a high-powered anti-Communist "cleansing" operation that raised havoc in the ACLU for the next fifteen years. This drive was intensified by the rapid growth of anti-Communist sentiment in the United States in the fall of 1939, following the Nazi-Soviet Non-Aggression Pact, the outbreak of World War II and the Soviet invasion of Finland.

In an article in *The Call*, the official organ of the Socialist Party, Norman Thomas attacked Dr. Harry F. Ward, the stalwart Chairman of the ACLU as pro-Communist, accused alleged "Communists" and "fellow-travelers" on the Board of hypocrisy and called for their expulsion. It was the first time in the history of the organization that a Board member had discussed internal controversies and attacked fellow-directors in the public prints. The Board took no action except to appoint a subcommittee which reported that the Thomas article was "highly improper." Thomas, who had courageously run for President on the Socialist ticket four times, was something of a hero for many liberals and radicals. But I considered him a non-hero who, despite some positive achievements, was as double-faced as a Tammany politician; he betrayed the cause of civil liberties again and again. And he was perhaps the most egotistical man I ever encountered, always loudly shouting down his opponents in a discussion.

Now came one of the most unscrupulous maneuvers I have ever known. New elections were coming up on the ACLU early in 1940 and the special Nominating Committee made its report. But instead of sticking to its function of nominating officers, it also adopted a Resolution declaring it inappropriate for those who sympathized with totalitarian dictatorships abroad to serve on the Union's governing committees and staff. The Nominating Committee, with the full cooperation of Director Baldwin, suddenly a convert to enemies of civil liberties, mailed this Resolution to the National Committee of the ACLU for approval, in gross violation of the By-Laws which provided that the National Committee could pass only on matters first acted upon by the Board. Furthermore, when controversial issues were involved, it was the recognized custom to send out to the National Committee the arguments on both sides of the question.

On January 18 the Board voted that the Nominating Committee had exceeded its authority and that its action violated our By-Laws. Nonetheless, the National Committee went ahead and voted in favor of the Nominating Committee's illegal Resolution, 30 to 10, calling it an "advisory" expression of opinion. Meanwhile, the purge group and Baldwin canvassed votes behind the scene and came to the Annual Meeting of the ACLU on February 5, 1940, able to cite with considerable effect the National Committee's "advisory opinion." Relatively few members of the Board and National Committee were present at the meeting. I spoke vigorously against the Resolution and its illegality, but received little support. After only a brief discussion this civil liberties monstrosity initiated by the Nominating Committee was formally adopted. The final text read:

"While the American Civil Liberties Union does not make any test of opinion on political or economic questions a condition of membership, and makes no distinction in defending the right to hold and utter any opinions, the personnel of its governing committees and staff is properly subject to the test of consistency in the defense of civil liberties in all aspects and all places.

"That consistency is inevitably compromised by persons who champion civil liberties in the United States and yet who justify or tolerate the denial of civil liberties by dictatorships abroad. Such a dual position in these days, when issues are far sharper and more profound, makes it desirable that the Civil Liberties Union make its position unmistakably clear.

"The Board of Directors and the National Committee of the American Civil Liberties Union therefore hold it inappropriate for any person to serve on the governing committees of the Union or on its staff, who is a member of any political organization which supports totalitarian dictatorship in any country, or who by his public declarations indicates his support of such a principle.

"Within this category we include organizations in the United States supporting the totalitarian governments of the Soviet Union and of the Fascist and Nazi countries (such as the Communist Party, the German American Bund and others); as well as native organizations with obvious anti-democratic objectives or practices."

The purge group on the Board of the ACLU had carried on a whispering campaign to the effect that this 1940 Resolution was necessary in order to put an end to the Communist machinations of a minority bloc of Directors. This charge of a Communist plot was, of course, complete nonsense. What really happened was that a minority steadily resisted, as contrary to the principles of the organization, repeated efforts to institute a purge in the ACLU and to drive it into taking a position on political systems and foreign governments. Then the majority, partly to help put across the Resolution and partly to justify its own surrender to the anti-Communist furor, accused the minority of a Communist conspiracy.

To explain the Resolution to the public, Director Baldwin drew up and issued a press release that stated, contrary to the facts, that the Resolution did not "change the fundamental policy of the Union" and that "no member of the Communist Party . . . was ever elected or appointed to any position of responsibility in the Union." The fact is that William Z. Foster was on the National Committee from the time of the ACLU's founding in 1920 until 1930, and was re-elected three times after he had become an open member of the Communist Party in 1921; Anna Rochester was elected to the Board of Directors in 1928 when she was known to be a member of the Communist Party; and Elizabeth Gurley Flynn was re-elected as a Director in 1937 after she had formally notified the Board that she had joined the Party.

The press release, then, was a tissue of lies for which Roger N. Baldwin was directly responsible. He had founded the ACLU in 1920 and had many fine civil liberties achievements to his credit for twenty years. But in 1940 he was the prime architect, aided by Ernst, Thomas and others, in causing the organization to founder on the rocks of anti-Communism. The lasting harm that the 1940 Resolution did to civil liberties and democracy throughout the United States canceled out Baldwin's many affirmative actions. In the closing years of his long life he was lauded as the great leader in the struggle to maintain the Bill of Rights; but the truth is that he was a prime mover in undermining it. For many years, I was a good friend of Roger Baldwin, who had an attractive and genial personality. I do not like to hurt him or harm his reputation and it saddens me to have to do so. However, the ethics of history demands that we set the record straight about Baldwin and the Civil Liberties Union.

The 1940 Resolution was undoubtedly successful from a public relations standpoint. It received a great deal of newspaper publicity, almost all of it favorable at that time of hysteria to the Union's new policy. There was no question that the move gained "respectability" for the organization in influential business and political circles, including the gentlemen who composed the House Committee on Un-American Activities. Among civil libertarians in general, however, and among members, officers and locals of the ACLU the Resolution aroused intense opposition. Opposing it on the National Committee were such defenders of civil liberties as Henry T. Hunt of the U.S. Department of the Interior, Professor Robert Morss Lovett and Professor Alexander Meiklejohn. The most effective protest of all came from 17 prominent liberals who wrote an open letter to the ACLU. They stated:

"We believe that by the purge Resolution the American Civil Liberties Union encourages the very tendencies it was intended to fight. It sets an example less liberal organizations will not be slow to imitate. . . . The phrasing of the purge Resolution is so wide as to make the Civil Liberties Union seem a fellow-traveler of the Dies Committee. . . . The Civil Liberties Union has often found it necessary to mobilize public sentiment in order to defend civil liberties. Never before has it been necessary to mobilize public sentiment in order to defend civil liberties within the Civil Liberties Union."

The Board and the office staff of the ACLU had carefully prevented any adequate presentation of the minority position from being sent out to the members of the National Committee and of the organization in general. Hence six Board dissenters finally felt impelled to issue a pamphlet entitled *Crisis in the Civil Liberties Union*. Those who signed it were Robert W. Dunn, Nathan Greene, A. J. Isserman, William B. Spofford, Mary Van Kleeck and myself. I was in charge of the publication of this pamphlet and wrote the final draft after receiving the suggestions of the other signatories.

In our statement we stressed, first, that the 1940 Resolution threw overboard the traditional policy of the ACLU by forcing the organization to pass judgment on foreign governments and on the twists and turns of foreign politics; second, that the phrase "totalitarian dictatorship" was vague and ambiguous and might well apply to American Catholics as well as to Communists; and third, that the Resolution compromised the work of the ACLU by instituting censorship of opinion, adopting the fatal principle of guilt by association and encouraging government agencies and private organizations to put through similar purges based on the ideas and associations of suspect individuals.

In fact, the Resolution set up an anti-Communist loyalty oath of the sort the Union had long opposed, and it soon became almost the standard formula for the factional splitting of organizations over the Communist issue. Members of Congress cited the Resolution in speaking on behalf of suppressive legislation. In my judgment the ACLU's action at that time was a major turning point in the retrogression of civil liberties in America. Had the Union, with its great prestige in the battle for the Bill of Rights, stood firm for its fundamental principles in those hectic pre-war days, I feel sure that the post-war witch-hunt, with its emphasis above all on *guilt by association*, would never have gone so far. What the Civil Liberties Union did, in a time of crisis that everywhere tested men's moral calibre, was to sound retreat and surrender a central bastion of freedom. Its action laid the foundations for the assault on American liberties by Senator Joseph McCarthy ten years later.

Looking back now on that eventful year of 1940, I believe that I and other opponents of the 1940 Resolution should have brought suit to have the Resolution legally declared null and void because its adoption was put through by trickery and by constant violation of the By-Laws of the ACLU.

It might well have been possible to persuade a judge to issue an injunction to this effect.

The only member of the Board of Directors who was also a member of the Communist Party was Elizabeth Gurley Flynn, who had been a founding member of the Union. Miss Flynn was an outspoken fighter for the Bill of Rights, international peace and a Socialist America. Dorothy Dunbar Bromley, a columnist on the Scripps-Howard newspapers, to her lasting shame filed a formal charge for Miss Flynn's expulsion for belonging to the Party. Miss Flynn's hearing before the Board took place on the evening of May 7, 1940, at the City Club of New York.

It was a heresy trial, pure and simple: an inquisition into an individual's unorthodox opinions, as distinct from overt acts, and conducted by the American Civil Liberties Union, the last organization on earth which should have had anything to do with such a business.

During the long, heated debate not even the most bitter adversaries of Miss Flynn were able to cite a single instance in which she had written, spoken or acted in violation of the Bill of Rights or the civil liberties principles of the ACLU. The argument against Miss Flynn proceeded solely on the basis that she could no longer serve as a Union officer because of her left-wing views and her guilt by association in being a member of the Communist Party. The final vote on the Bromley charge was nine in the affirmative and nine in the negative. Dr. John Haynes Holmes as Chairman of the Board broke this tie in favor of the motion that Miss Flynn was ineligible to be a Director because of her political beliefs. He did not have to vote, but had the legal right to do so and vent his anti-Communist spleen on Elizabeth Flynn. The Reverend Holmes's action could not help but remind me of the leading role played by Bishop Pierre Cochin some 500 years previously in the heresy trial of Joan of Arc and her final burning at the stake.

Besides Dr. Holmes, those voting for the expulsion of Miss Flynn on this historic occasion were: Mrs. Bromley, Carl Carmer, Morris Ernst, Ben W. Huebsch, Florina Lasker, William L. Nunn, Elmer Rice, Roger William Riis and Whitney North Seymour. Those who cast their ballots against expulsion were: Robert W. Dunn, John F. Finerty, Osmond K. Fraenkel, Nathan Greene, Arthur Garfield Hays, A. J. Isserman, Dorothy Kenyon, Corliss Lamont and William B. Spofford. Alfred Bingham, Editor of *Common Sense* magazine, and Walter Frank, an attorney, both seasoned liberals, abstained from voting on the Resolution. Either one could have turned the tide in favor of Miss Flynn. Roger Baldwin did not vote, since he was never a member of the Board.

The Flynn trial ended at 2:30 A.M. I count the six hours of that meeting as one of the most severe ordeals I have ever experienced. And although I spoke up frequently in defense of Miss Flynn, I carelessly let slip an important point, as did her other defenders, that would have changed the result. When the vote was about to be taken, Miss Flynn acquiesced in Dr. Holmes's request that she leave the room. We should not have let her do so, because as a member of the Board she had the right to stay and vote. And her vote would have meant a 10 to 9 majority against expulsion.

Nineteen-forty was one of the most important years in my life. I had joined the Board of Directors of the American Civil Liberties Union in 1932 when I was thirty years old, to uphold the ideals of American democracy in the belief that I would be working with a group of idealists dedicated to the same cause. But when the crisis regarding Communists and Communism occurred, a majority of those individuals whom I had so admired compromised their civil liberties principles and utilized unscrupulous tactics to put across their purge program. It proved the greatest disillusionment to me and at the same time taught me that I had to be continually on my guard in the debased world of politics against the hypocrisy of some so-called liberals. I had been far too naive in my participation in public affairs. That is what the year 1940 taught me.

The 1940 Resolution and the Flynn ouster set the tone for ACLU policies during the next fifteen years. These actions made anti-Communist militancy and purity the main qualifications for nomination and election of individuals to the Board of Directors and to the National Committee. It is hardly surprising that the quality of Directors and national committeemen at the time steadily declined. Experience has demonstrated that a person's deep-seated animosity toward the Soviet Union and Communism is no assurance of his devotion to civil liberties in America.

From 1940 to 1955 the Civil Liberties Union compromised on many basic issues and often took an apologetic attitude in defending the Bill of Rights. It watered down its criticism of the House Committee on Un-American Activities, adopted a weak position on the Government's "loy-alty-security" program, boasted of its close and friendly relations with the FBI, approved the Internal Security Act's exclusion of Communists and Fascists as immigrants to the United States and, worst of all, refused at any time to denounce the compilation and use of the U.S. Attorney General's list of subversive organizations.

In 1950 Patrick Murphy Malin, a Professor of Economics at Swarthmore College, replaced as Executive Director of the ACLU Roger Baldwin, who had passed the usual retirement age of sixty-five. Mr. Malin did not have wide experience in the field of civil liberties, was overwhelmed by the complexity of the job and lacked the fighting spirit which had characterized Baldwin. Instead of assuming independent leadership and trying to re-cover lost territory for the ACLU, Malin weakly went along with the right-wing Directors and cooperated with them in taking the Civil Liber-ties Union further toward compromise and political partisanship.

It must be added that the Affiliates of the ACLU were in general doubtful of, if not opposed to, the compromise policies of the national Board of

Directors, with its headquarters in New York City. The Affiliates in Boston, New Haven, Northern California and Southern California were especially critical of the national Board.

Several Directors who had been opposed originally to the 1940 Resolution and Flynn expulsion dropped out in disgust; but I remained on the Board and upheld fundamental civil liberties principles as long as I could. This was not an easy task. I was fighting a losing battle; my views were constantly voted down. Several of the right-wing Directors continually baited me and reveled in making gratuitous personal attacks. Frequently, trying to win votes on a controversial issue, they would attempt to engage me in verbal brawls, hoping to create a tense emotional atmosphere helpful to their side.

Meantime, the group I had come to consider the Cold War bloc grew increasingly annoyed over my frequent opposition to Board policies and had become fearful that my defiance of the McCarthy Committee in September, 1953 would detract from the ACLU's "respectability." The upshot was that after I had been renominated in November, 1953 for a new three-year term on the Board, several Directors, including Morris Ernst, Norman Thomas and Ernest Angell, Chairman of the Board, threatened to resign if my name was retained on the ballot. At the next meeting of the Board the majority yielded to these bludgeoning tactics and rescinded my nomination.

I had come to the end of my more than twenty years' association with the Civil Liberties Union. Although a number of rank-and-file members of the ACLU in New York City urged that I permit my nomination as a Director through the special section of the By-Laws providing for such nomination by twenty-five regular members, I declined the suggestion. I told my friends that the situation had become too confused and unpleasant for me to continue as a Director, and that I was unwilling to go on working with a group which had forgotten the meaning of fair play.

After I was dropped from the Board of Directors of the ACLU I joined the Executive Committee of the National Emergency Civil Liberties Committee and in 1955 became Vice-Chairman of this organization. Its Chairman was Harvey O'Connor, the writer who had refused to answer the questions of the McCarthy Committee. The able Director was Dr. Clark Foreman, a Southerner by birth who had been a prominent official in the Roosevelt Administration. He was succeeded in 1970 by Edith Tiger, a tireless worker who did much to increase the influence and scope of the Emergency Committee. Our General Counsel was Leonard Boudin, one of the most experienced lawyers in the civil liberties field. In 1963 I became Chairman of the organization.

The Emergency Committee and its legal staff concentrated on supporting civil liberties cases in the courts and won many important victories, including several in the U.S. Supreme Court, such as the Rockwell Kent passport case and my own censorship suit against the Postmaster General.

NECLC, as the Committee came to be called, held a dinner every December to celebrate the ratification of the Bill of Rights on December 15, 1791. At that banquet we gave our annual Tom Paine Award to honor outstanding champions of civil liberties, among them I. F. Stone, Bertrand Russell, Carey McWilliams, Dr. Benjamin Spock, Tom Wicker and Jane Fonda.

I was not able to put out of mind the American Civil Liberties Union and my unhappy experience with that organization. I had kept in touch with Lucille Milner, Secretary of the ACLU, and occasionally had lunch with her. She had been sympathetic to my civil liberties positions. One day about five years after I had been pushed off the Board Mrs. Milner handed me a bulky black notebook, saying "This is the original stenographic transcript of the trial of Elizabeth Gurley Flynn." I was quite surprised, since I had not asked Mrs. Milner or anyone else to obtain a copy for me. "Keep it in your library," she said. I accepted the gift rather haltingly and when I arrived home, stowed it away in a special library shelf reserved for important documents.

Now I made another serious mistake. Instead of arranging for the publication of this precious and unique document while Elizabeth Flynn was still alive (she died in 1964), I more or less forgot about it for ten years. Then I offered the transcript of the trial hesitatingly to Ben Raeburn, Editor of Horizon Press. He was eager for Horizon to publish it as a book and they brought it out, with an introduction by me, during the summer of 1968. It received a few good reviews in the left and liberal press, but none of the big reviews, such as *The New York Times Book Review*, even mentioned it. The author Maxwell Geismar wrote a perceptive review for *Monthly Review*, and it was used as a preface to the paperback edition published in 1969.

In February, 1969, I sent a letter, with a copy of *The Trial of Elizabeth Gurley Flynn*,[1] to the Board of Directors of the ACLU petitioning it to rescind the 1940 expulsion of Miss Flynn from the Board and to reinstate her posthumously for the duration of her elected term. I cited especially a review of the book by George Slaff, President of the Southern California Affiliate of the Civil Liberties Union, in which he called upon the national Board of Directors to "reverse the action taken in 1940" regarding Miss Flynn. In supporting his appeal Mr. Slaff reminded the Board of a bit of history:

"The Catholic Church reversed the trial of Joan of Arc and canonized her. A governor of California granted a full pardon to Tom Mooney. Every decent unprejudiced human being who has studied the Sacco-Vanzetti case has reversed their conviction and sentence. The trials of the Salem 'witches' who were crushed under mounds of stones or hanged at the gallows have been reversed by history."

Nothing came of my letter to the ACLU Board or of Slaff's suggestion. Ernest Angell, Chairman of the Board, brushed me off with a brief note: "I acknowledge your letter of February 18 addressed to the Board of Directors of the American Civil Liberties Union. I have confirmed with Mr. George Slaff, whose book review you quote, that he has no intention of reopening the issue about which you wrote. As far as we have been able to ascertain, it is not the sentiment of the membership of the Board to reopen this issue."

George Slaff, however, is a man of principle and determination. A few years later he bought more than a hundred copies of *The Trial of Elizabeth Gurley Flynn* and sent them out to Board members of the ACLU. As a result of his continued agitation on the issue, the final outcome was that at its meeting in April, 1976 the ACLU Board voted 32 to 18 to rescind posthumously the purging of Miss Flynn in 1940. It was appropriate that Slaff himself presented the resolution, the decisive part of which read:

"1.   That there was no evidence of any nature whatsoever adduced before the May 7, 1940 Board meeting that Ms. Flynn had ever committed any act which in any way violated or transgressed any of the basic principles for which the ACLU has stood from its inception.

"2.   That Ms. Flynn was expelled from membership on the Board because she was a member of the Communist Party of the U.S.A.

"3.   That Ms. Flynn, a member in good standing of the Board of Directors, was not permitted to vote on the motion to expel her while three members of the Board who had brought formal expulsion charges against her were permitted to vote on the motion.

"4.   That the expulsion of Ms. Flynn was not consonant with the basic principles on which the ACLU was founded and has acted for fifty-four years.

"Therefore, it is the sense of this Board that Ms. Flynn should not have been expelled and should have been permitted to complete the term as a member of the Board for which she had been elected.

"This Board recognizes the great service rendered by Elizabeth Gurley Flynn to American labor and reiterates the recognition by an earlier Board of the American Civil Liberties Union of Elizabeth Gurley Flynn's 'long service to the cause of civil liberty.' "

Although it took thirty-six years to right the wrong, I considered the posthumous reinstatement of Miss Flynn a significant victory both for the honor and integrity of the Civil Liberties Union and for civil liberties in general. The prime credit for the ACLU's action must go to George Slaff, and I take pride and pleasure that my book played a decisive role in his statesmanlike campaign. I feel happy that my support of "heretic" Flynn from the start was in the end officially vindicated by the ACLU.

Carey McWilliams in *The Nation*[2] summed up the meaning of the Flynn affair: "By acknowledging that the ouster of Elizabeth Gurley Flynn was improper and that she should have been permitted to complete the term to which she had been elected, the ACLU has in effect met the test of consistency—that is, it has affirmed the proposition that the members, officers and staff of an organization should be judged on the basis of their commitments, as individuals, to its publicly stated objectives and not be prejudiced or tested by other affiliations or associations. And thanks should go to Corliss Lamont who more than any other person has kept the issue alive these last thirty-six years, and to the other eight members of the Board who during that hectic night session of May 7, 1940, joined with him in voting against the ouster of Elizabeth Gurley Flynn."

In August, 1977, *The New York Times* broke a story by Anthony Marro about the American Civil Liberties Union that astonished and bewildered civil libertarians and the general public throughout the United States. "For about seven years in the 1950's," Mr. Marro's report began, "a number of officials of the American Civil Liberties Union gave the Federal Bureau of Investigation on a continuing basis information about the organization, its activities and some of its members, according to materials obtained from the Bureau's files. In addition, the materials suggest that several of the officials asked the Bureau to help them identify Communist Party members who might be trying to gain seats on the boards of the ACLU's state affiliates. . . ."

Mr. Marro's story was based on a careful sifting of over 10,000 documents out of some 20,000 in the FBI files on the ACLU which obtained them under the Freedom of Information Act. The documents showed that during the great anti-Communist witch-hunt the collaboration was so intimate that top officers of the two organizations actually acted as informers for one another. It also revealed that members of ACLU governing committees handed over to the FBI confidential documents, including correspondence between ACLU officials, drafts of position papers and even Minutes of meetings. I was profoundly shocked by these revelations.

An official news release on the situation by the Civil Liberties Union stated: "The files show that on a number of occasions, almost entirely during the McCarthy era, certain persons who were then ACLU officials were in contact with the FBI to provide or obtain information about the political beliefs or affiliations of other ACLU members and officials, particularly those who were thought to be Communists. Whatever their motive, such contacts with the FBI were wrong, inexcusable and destructive of civil liberties principles. These incidents took place in a different era and are contrary to the way the ACLU operates today."

As a member of the Board of Directors of the Civil Liberties Union, I myself was caught in the web of ACLU-FBI intrigue. During those years certain Directors of the Union became worried over a ridiculous rumor that I was a member of the Communist Party. So it was that in the early 1950's Patrick Malin, then Executive Director of the ACLU, made a surprise report to a full meeting of the Board: "I was down in Washington a few days ago and dropped in on J. Edgar Hoover at the FBI. I asked him whether Corliss Lamont was a member of the Communist Party and he said, 'No'." I protested strongly against Malin's little interview on the grounds that it violated our principle of functioning on an independent basis and, in effect, gave the FBI clearance power in the selection of ACLU officers and staff. No other member of the Board present raised the slightest objection, but it did agree that the incident should not be mentioned in the Minutes of the meeting.

It turned out that during the same period Malin had sought the help of the FBI in trying to keep Communists off the Boards of affiliates in Detroit, Los Angeles, Denver and Seattle. When Malin first revealed his *tête-à-tête* with Hoover, I did not realize that he was carrying on such improper relations with the FBI. And so I unfortunately let the matter drop after my verbal protest.

Morris L. Ernst, who for twenty-five years shared the general counselship of the Civil Liberties Union with Arthur Garfield Hays, played a special role in the relations of the organization with the FBI. He became J. Edgar Hoover's personal attorney and referred to him as a "treasured friend." Ernst was not only a prime mover in the general ACLU-FBI collaboration, but independently started to pass information to the FBI as early as 1942.

In my opinion the collaboration between the ACLU leadership and the FBI was a scandalous betrayal of American civil liberties. It stemmed directly from the fanatical anti-Communism of the times, typified by the rantings of Senator Joseph McCarthy. Many ACLU personnel swallowed McCarthy's moonshine about a terrible Communist threat and became more concerned with exposing and crushing Communists than with preserving civil liberties. This was a crass violation of the trust that had been placed in the leadership of the Civil Liberties Union by the general membership of the organization and the American people.

We can be thankful that the present leaders of the Civil Liberties Union had no part in the ACLU-FBI collaboration and are completely opposed to any such compromise of principle. For many years now the ACLU has been doing a most creditable job. It is also to be remembered that all through the McCarthy era and down to the present, organizations such as the National Emergency Civil Liberties Committee, the National Lawyers Guild and the American Committee for the Protection of the Foreign Born have stood firm for civil liberties and against FBI influence and infiltration. All true civil libertarians, in light of the ACLU-FBI revelations, need to remain alert to see that such a disaster never occurs again.

Chapter XIII   DEMOCRATIC SOCIALISM

I became a convinced believer in democratic Socialism as the best way for the future of America and the world back in the early 1930's. National and international developments since that time have strengthened my Socialist convictions.

The Great Depression that started in 1929 provided the immediate stimulus for my skepticism regarding capitalism and caused me to explore systematically the possibilities of the Socialist alternative. My upbringing in a prominent banking family certainly had not instilled in me any bias in favor of Socialism. But I became early convinced that consideration for others is a high ethical value; it gave me a liberal slant on many questions. The Phillips Exeter Academy imbued in me a strong feeling for the American tradition of democracy and equality of opportunity; and Harvard and Columbia taught me that reliance on reason is the best method of solving human problems. As I have explained in previous chapters, I developed in my late twenties an affirmative Humanist philosophy that holds as its chief ethical aim this-earthly happiness, freedom and progress for all humanity. If we are serious about achieving this end, I think that intelligence leads us to strive for a planned, democratic Socialism on a world scale.

My own path to Socialism, therefore, was that of analysis through reason, combined with belief in a Humanist ethics and attachment to democracy in its broadest sense. I like the old phrase "public service." I am not implying that only radicals are public-spirited; many honest liberals and conservatives have worked hard to serve the public interest. What I am saying is that the ideal of public service in this era ought to bring more and more people over to the cause of Socialism.

A charge I have had to contend with is insincerity, because—while proclaiming the goal of a Socialist society—I do not at once reduce my standard of living to that of poverty-stricken groups in the United States.

Many years ago I had an encounter with that picturesque blusterer, banker and general, Vice-President Charles C. Dawes, who leapt up from an excellent Sunday dinner at the home of the Dwight W. Morrows, and paced round the table chewing angrily on his pipe, charging that I had no right to believe in Socialism until I gave away my last penny. I reminded the Christian multi-millionaire that it was not Marx but Jesus who had advised selling all one's goods and giving the proceeds to the poor. Mr. Morrow, ordinarily an understanding person, remarked that I still seemed to enjoy heartily the facilities of my father's country estate on the Palisades. I replied that I liked my parents very much and would continue to visit them whether they lived in a palace or a hovel.

There are more significant things to do for the achievement of Socialism than to make such dramatic gestures as giving away all one's money or breaking off family relations. It takes all kinds of people from different walks of life to create a successful radical movement. Workers for Socialism like myself do not pretend to be either angels or martyrs; it is unfriendly critics who concoct that myth and then accuse us of hypocrisy because we do not conform to their preconceptions. It would be folly for us to act as if full-fledged Socialism already existed here. It is more important for us to be effective on behalf of the Socialist goal than to satisfy the whims and criticisms of those dedicated to the eternal preservation of capitalism.

I have said enough to indicate that in the particular environment in which I grew up and with which I still have close connections there were pressures against my becoming a Socialist. I first gave some attention to the merits of Socialism when I was a Senior at Harvard in 1924. As I have recounted, at that time I fought, unsuccessfully, for the right of a student organization to invite Eugene V. Debs and other radicals to speak at the Harvard Union. But I rejected Socialism as undesirable and impracticable. That some years later I reversed my opinion was primarily due to a more profound study of economics, to a greater realization of the disaster of capitalist crises, and to a better grasp of the advantages of nationwide Socialist planning.

My capitalist friends are always accusing me of being biased, but in truth I overcame the anti-Socialist bias natural to my upbringing and have resisted the unremitting pressures to return to the fold of the capitalist faithful. While emotions have an important place in the life of a radical, as in everyone's life, the deciding factor in my being won to Socialism was not some emotional urge, but the uncompromising use of intelligence. Ultimately, the Socialist case rests on objective consideration of the relevant facts and theories. I find at least seven reasons why the Socialist solution is the best answer to the pressing contemporary social-economic problems in the United States and the world at large.

First, while I concede that capitalism has enormously increased the productive capacities of mankind, especially through the development of science and the machine, it has not been able, and never will be able, to

overcome its inherent difficulties and contradictions. Reforms in the struc-
ture of the capitalist system can result in genuine amelioration, but I do not
think that they can resolve its recurrent dilemmas of overproduction,
economic depression, mass unemployment and ruinous inflation. The
basic cause of these cycles is an economy in which profit is the main motive
and regulator of business; capitalists strive to make as much money as they
can and to reinvest the greater part of it to expand profit-yielding enterprises. The inescapable result is that the capacity to produce grows faster
than the ability to consume, which is determined by the people's purchasing power; and it has happened again and again that the disproportion has
been "solved" only by crisis and depression. The crisis of overproduction is
a crisis of underconsumption; both reflect the accumulation of wealth at
one end of the scale and of low income or poverty at the other.

Various superficial devices, fancy currency schemes and share-the-
wealth measures, have been tried as cures for this central contradiction of
capitalism. The most common and substantial remedy attempted has been
government spending on public works, as under President Roosevelt's
New Deal, or on colossal armaments, which since the end of World War II
now include the proliferation of nuclear weapons. War preparations and
warfare constitute a "cure" worse than the disease. Experience has
confirmed that so long as capitalism exists, no program of large-scale public
works will be permitted to transcend temporary emergency programs, to
be discarded as soon as the economy shows signs of returning to what
appears on the surface as normal.

Second, I find a tremendous waste inherent in the capitalist system and
its inevitable exploitation of people and of natural resources. The drive for
quick profits has brought about the irredeemable spoilage of billions of
dollars worth of oil and gas, coal and timber, and pollution of air and water.
Reckless deforestation has led to chronic floods, life-devouring dust bowls
and the ruin of huge tracts of fertile land. Throughout the capitalist world,
money-minded businessmen, heedless of the consequences to future generations, have been speedily exhausting the natural abundance of our good
earth, creating a situation aptly described as *Our Plundered Planet*,[1] to cite
the title of Fairfield Osborn's excellent book. Consider also the untold loss
of wealth through the enforced idleness of millions upon millions of men
and women and machines in depression after depression since the Industrial Revolution; through the deprivation of potential production in "normal" times owing to the chaotic, unplanned nature of competitive capitalism; and above all, through the colossal squandering of human beings and
goods in capitalism-caused wars.

My third point is that a planned Socialist society, operating for use
instead of profit, can put an end to most of the economic waste caused by
capitalism and can prevent the tragic paradox of poverty amid potential
plenty. Socialism does not automatically solve all economic problems,
particularly in agriculture, but it will do away with the crises and mass
unemployment characteristic of the capitalist era. And it can unlock to the

fullest extent the economic potentialities of the machine age with its scientific techniques. Because it has no fear of overproduction and technological unemployment, a Socialist economy welcomes new industrial inventions and labor-saving devices. Today we know that in industrially developed nations there is enough goods-producing machinery to ensure a high standard of living for all the people.

Fourth, it seems to me that if we follow through the logical implications of the idea of public planning, which has been gaining increasing weight in present-day society, we arrive at the key concept of *Socialist planning* functioning in conjunction with public ownership of the main means of production and distribution. I would not have a government agency take over any private business enterprise with a small number of employees. Socialist planning for abundance, democratically administered, permanently overcomes the contradictions of capitalism. Government planning organizations, with control over output, prices, wages, hours of work and finance, are able to keep the purchasing power of the population in close equilibrium with the production of goods. Under capitalism, countless fine individual intelligences and abilities continually work in competition with or against one another. Socialist planning would release and coordinate frustrated talents, bringing into action a concert of community minds operating on behalf of the common good and embodying the life of reason in social-economic affairs.

Fifth, I see in the successful functioning of the various Socialist states concrete examples of the achievements of Socialist planning, often under adverse conditons. The Soviet Five-Year Plans, for example, transformed an economically backward, chiefly agricultural country, whose people were seventy percent illiterate under the Tsars into a super-power rivaling the United States. Socialist planning in the U.S.S.R. turned that nation into a dynamic, forward-moving economy with highly developed industry and collectivized agriculture, with illiteracy almost totally abolished and workers excellently trained in modern machine techniques. All the world has recognized that the fundamental test came during World War II in which the Soviet planned economy was a major factor in the nation's repelling the Nazi invasion and sweeping back Hitler's armies all the way to Berlin. In its supreme ordeal the Soviet Union had the trained manpower to handle efficiently the most up-to-date engines of war, some of it provided by British and American Lend-Lease.

During the thirty-six years since the end of World War II with its death toll of more than twenty million, new Soviet Five-Year Plans performed a herculean job of economic reconstruction and brought about a steady increase in the standard of living, which had been interrupted by the Nazi onslaught. Soviet scientists learned the nature of nuclear power and became able to produce weapons that could match those of the United States. Unfortunately, and through no wish of the Soviet Union, a nuclear arms race has resulted.

If Socialist planning could be so successful in such a formerly backward country it would be far more successful in the United States with its highly developed industries and technology.

Sixth, I believe that Socialism not only lays the basis for a rational and just economic system but also gives promise of far-reaching cultural advances. By creating an economy of abundance, Socialist planning is able to multiply the production of cultural goods—books, school and college buildings, radio and TV sets, musical instruments, theatres and the like. It increases the number of teachers and pays them decent salaries. By replacing production for profit with production for use, Socialism ends the outworn method of judging artistic and cultural achievements primarily in terms of the money they may make and fosters their evaluation in terms of merit. Socialist economy and teaching effect a transformation of human motives, coordinating altruistic and egotistic impulses so that people find fulfillment in working for the good of the community instead of putting self-interest first. This entails a higher ethical philosophy than that of capitalism, and one more profoundly in harmony with the enlightened social ideals of Christianity.

Seventh and finally, I am convinced that Socialism offers the best way of fulfilling the promise of modern democracy, and of preventing the resurgence of Fascism. Since Fascism is basically capitalism stripped of democratic pretenses and other inessentials, its danger remains as long as the capitalist system is with us. A Socialist society builds the necessary foundations of a lasting democracy by establishing a stable economy and giving the people the economic and cultural prerequisites for democratic liberties. And it insists on full democratic rights for all racial groups and the approximately one-half of the population that is female.

Furthermore, I am of the opinion that in countries like the United States and Great Britain, which have long and strong traditions of democracy and civil liberties, we can accomplish the transition to Socialism through peaceful, democratic procedures. In nations like Russia and China, however, where under the old regimes democratic institutions were weak or nonexistent, violent revolution was in all probability the only recourse.

So far as the United States is concerned, in order to smooth the path to Socialism and maintain constitutional guarantees, I am in favor of the government's buying out the capitalists when it receives the voters' mandate to socialize natural resources, factories, banks, transportation and communication facilities. This would be in accordance with the Fifth Amendment of the Bill of Rights which reads in part: ". . . nor shall private property be taken for public use without just compensation." America is wealthy enough to adopt this procedure, and it would go far in staving off counter-revolutionary violence on the part of the capitalist class.

The reader will note that in my exposition of Socialism, I have not mentioned the Marxist view of the class struggle between capitalists and workers as the prime factor in establishing a Socialist society. I consider it *a* factor only; and sometimes not even that. In twentieth-century America labor has on the whole been pretty conservative and as a movement has never adopted the slogan of the class struggle or pronounced Socialism as its goal. Middle-class intellectuals in the United States have been the most articulate in defense of Socialism or Communism.

The most effective leaders of Socialist or Communist revolution, such as Lenin and Mao Zedung, were of middle-class origin. The same is true of most of the leaders in the Communist parties and governments in Europe. I do not think of myself as a member of the capitalist class who ought to be opposed to the working class, but simply as an American citizen doing his best to help build a better America and a better world. And I conceive of Socialism as improving not only the condition of the working class, but also of the middle class and indeed of everybody except a tiny upper-class minority.

One of the influences in my becoming deeply concerned with Socialism was a fellow Harvard graduate, John Reed of the Class of 1910 and from a middle-class family, who had espoused that cause and had published *Ten Days That Shook the World* (1919),[2] the classic eyewitness report on the great October Russian Revolution of 1917. Reed wrote this volume after he came back to the United States, but soon returned to Soviet Russia where he became a delegate to the Second Congress of the Communist International. He then went as a high-ranking delegate to the First Congress of Peoples of the East in Baku on the Caspian Sea. At that conference it seems probable that he contracted typhus; he returned to Moscow and died there in October, 1920, just two days short of his 33rd birthday. His ashes are interred in the Kremlin wall. Reed was a dynamo of a man, full of promise of literary achievement and valuable work on behalf of Socialism.

Harvard men had never appreciated the genius of John Reed and I undertook to do something about it. I was able to organize a Harvard Alumni John Reed Committee, with the purposes of encouraging the writing of a biography of Reed, and of having a portrait painted of him to be given to Harvard. Granville Hicks, Harvard 1923, wrote an excellent biography titled *John Reed—The Making of a Revolutionary* (1936).[3] And the artist Robert Hallowell, who was a Harvard classmate of John Reed and knew him well, painted a fine oil portrait of him on the unusual medium of glass.

It was presented to Harvard University by the Alumni Committee in 1935 with an accompanying letter to President James B. Conant, stating that John Reed's "qualities of courage, idealism and independent mind merit some recognition on the part of Harvard men. . . . It is not the object of this Committee to endorse the particular political beliefs of John Reed. Our aim is to honor the memory of an outstanding Harvard man of whom all Harvard men should be proud." The portrait hangs in Adams House at Harvard.

Chapter XIV   MARRIAGE WITH VARIETY

I believe in monogamous marriage: Despite all criticism of that institution, it continues to be indispensable throughout the world, and I cannot believe that human beings would lead happier lives without the possibility of marriage. The family remains the basic social unit in most civilized countries. But as the high incidence of divorce shows, matrimony needs to be radically reformed.

Marriage has been a prime subject for criticism and derision throughout history. However, in the United States during the second half of the twentieth century, attacks on it have been perhaps more drastic and widespread than ever. The mass media—books, magazines, newspapers, radio, television—have frequently voiced strictures. A growing number of men and women are living together without bothering with the wedding ceremony; the divorce rate steadily increases; premarital and extramarital sex relations are commonplace and more socially acceptable. It is reliably estimated that some 70 percent of American marriages are unhappy in a sexual sense. As Sir Julian Huxley has said, "Marriage poses as many problems as it solves."[1]

Many critics do not give sufficient attention to the welfare of children, who need a stable, permanent home with loving parents. I wish it were possible for all men and women to experience the joys of having children and, indeed, grandchildren. Divorce in a family usually has harmful effects on children even if they are fully grown. They are almost always sad over a permanent rupture between their parents, and feel harassed and pressed for time in trying to maintain a close relationship with each of them. Frequently the discarded partner in a divorce becomes lonely and unhappy for life. Because I divorced my first wife I unfortunately have firsthand experience in this sort of situation. I am convinced that certain changes in the attitude and behavior of married couples could make them happier and reduce the number of divorces.

The human being is a functioning unity of body, mind and emotion. To refer to my previous discussion in the chapter "The Myth of Immortality," the traditional concept of Christian dualism, which regards man as divided into two parts, body and soul (including the mind), is unacceptable. In this dualistic theory the soul possesses all the finer attributes of a person and after death goes marching on into the realm of immortality. The body, on the other hand, is steeped in sin and corrupted by base physical desires, the worst of which is sexual passion. In the mainstream of Christian thought until recently, sexual intercourse was regarded as evil because through it Adam's "original sin" is transmitted to every human being.

It seems incredible that in the year 1980 Pope John Paul II should declare that if a man looked lustfully even "at the woman who is his wife, he could likewise commit adultery in his heart." The notion that thoughts of making love with one's wife are obscene raised a furor throughout Italy. Italian feminists accused Pope Paul of male chauvinism because he did not mention that wives might lust after husbands. The entire episode was absurd and beneath the dignity of a Pope. It showed how deep and widespread are the puritanical attitudes that still mar the beauty of sex relations.

Man's sexuality is natural and no more sinful than his need for food and drink. There is no definite separation between the physical and the spiritual; love at its best represents a pervasive intermingling of the two. George Santayana expresses this beautifully: "Love would never take so high a flight unless it sprung from something profound and elementary."[2] Enduring romantic love between a man and a woman is, I believe, the greatest of all sexual experiences. True wisdom confirms sexual activity, rationally controlled, as a unique combination of joy and beauty that can enhance the life of every human being; and contributes mightily to the supreme goal of happiness for all mankind. We can rejoice wholeheartedly that we live in this exciting world of male and female. Let us be grateful that Nature has given us the power of preserving life on earth through the marvel of making love. Despite all this, we are faced with the bitter paradox that sexual activity and love, which can bring to humans the greatest pleasure, often result in unhappiness and misery.

Increasingly reliable methods of contraception have made possible a freer, more joyous sex life for a large proportion of the human race and have enabled husbands and wives to adopt careful and intelligent planning for the birth of children. I believe that abortion should ordinarily be lawful, as the United States Supreme Court has ruled, during the first three months of pregnancy; that every state should legally allow either party in a marriage to obtain a speedy, no-fault divorce on grounds of incompatibility alone; that the double standard in sex relations must be eliminated, with women to have complete equality with men, while maintaining their femininity; that men and women should rely on intelligence as well as emotion in choosing a marriage partner and in the conduct of their marriage; and that people differ so much in character, philosophy, sexuality and traditions that it is impossible to set up a code of sex ethics and conduct that will be acceptable to all Americans, let alone all mankind.

With these propositions as background, I shall go on to other and more controversial questions on how to achieve a happy marriage.

The guarantee of a decent living standard to everyone will alleviate marriage problems that are related to poor economic conditions. But such developments can never solve all the difficulties of marriage or bring assured happiness to wedded couples. Affluent husbands and wives are likely to have as much marital trouble as those with lower incomes. I suspect that in the Socialist society of the Soviet Union, despite economic progress since the Revolution of 1917, the percentage of married couples dissatisfied with their sex lives is close to the percentage in the United States. The divorce rate in the U.S.S.R. is almost as high as in the U.S.A. No revolution can be considered adequate or complete with a large proportion of the people unhappy in their sexual relations.

Many men and women who take wedding vows do so without knowing each other well enough for a lasting relationship and without being certain that they are sufficiently compatible sexually and in other ways. I am of the opinion that an experimental period of living together for at least six months, with strict birth control in effect, would be desirable for all who are engaged or contemplating matrimony.

Such a "practice marriage" should enable a man and woman to find out whether they are deeply in love or merely assuaging each other's sexual hunger. As Bertrand Russell states in his *Marriage and Morals:* "If the girl is expected to be a virgin when she marries, it will very often happen that she is trapped by a transient and trivial sex attraction, which a woman with sexual experience could easily distinguish from love. This has undoubtedly been a frequent cause of unhappy marriages,"[3] And men, of course, can be trapped in the same way. We have it on the authority of both Chaucer and Shakespeare that "Love is blind," and it is the blindness that we need to recognize.

In a premarital stage of living together, a couple will learn that sex for the sake of sex alone lacks the higher values of love and leads into mere sensuality. This sort of dead-end relationship between men and women is widely encouraged by our culture. Cheap pornography assails us from every side, and much of the mass media has been transformed into a voyeur spectacle that affronts one's sense of decency. This perversion of sex, in my view, debases the relations between male and female and treats the physical aspect, especially intercourse, as if it were the sole *raison d'être*.

Such pressures are likely to result in the denigration of sexual union as no more important than a handshake. "Instant sex"—the quick and casual orgasm between persons hardly acquainted—is a prime factor in the growing rate of venereal disease which can lead to the ruin of sex, love, health and life itself. The practitioners of instant sex miss most of the pleasure of love-making. They have no sense of the art of love, and bypass a range of emotions that with gentle tempo comes into play as a prelude to the sex act. The greatest joy in sex relations is experienced only when a man and a woman know each other well and share the full emotional quality of love.

In intimate sex relations, lovers are at their best when they combine a keen sense of beauty with a healthy eroticism. This quality of *eroto-aesthetic sensitivity* is fundamental to successful marriage. Of equal significance is the deep awareness of tenderness in sexual communion, the warm, wonderful sense of physical and spiritual oneness with the beloved, the feeling of simultaneous exultation and exaltation. When love is experienced in these ways, it becomes a powerful antidote to the loneliness that at times besets the human creature.

"There is, finally," as psychiatrist Rollo May says, "the form of consciousness which occurs ideally at the moment of climax in sexual intercourse. This is the point when the lovers are carried beyond their personal isolation, and when a shift in consciousness occurs which they experience as uniting them with nature itself. There is an accelerating experience of touch, contact, union to the point where, for a moment, the awareness of separateness is lost, blotted out in a cosmic feeling of oneness with nature."[4]

Of utmost importance for a happy marriage is the sharing by a couple, besides their romantic feelings, of other basic interests—art, music, politics, travel, sports, friends and possibly work. Such interests not only bring pleasure, but draw husband and wife more closely together in comradeship and make them more appreciative of each other's qualities. Walter Lippmann sums it up: "Love endures only when the lovers love many things together, and not merely each other."[5]

The most blessed element of all in a marriage is children. It is that which I tried to express in this poem from my book of verse, *Lover's Credo:*[6]

CREATION

They talk about the creative genius
Of artists, authors, scientists and statesmen;
But you and I together, beloved,
A man and woman average in talent,
Possess the precious power to create,
Through our ennobling love for one another,
An actual human being, a baby,
Who then will grow, mature, become an adult
And full-fledged member of the human race
With infinite potentialities
For happiness, achievement, service to man.
This gift sublime of creativity,
Bestowed by Nature on all living things,
Expands, enriches love's essential meaning,

Makes everyone in love a kind of god,
And blesses human sexuality
As the wonderful and happy way
To guarantee a future for mankind.

Now, I want to discuss what is bound to cause disagreement: the place of variety in marriage. A normal couple will of course find much variety in the pleasures they enjoy together. But there is a diversity that most marriage partners need in sex interplay beyond what they can give each other, and they should therefore have contacts with friends of the opposite sex. I am convinced that a grave danger to marital happiness is that wives and husbands see, hear and have too much of each other. I have seen this happen repeatedly in my family circle and among friends.

Shelley makes the point in his poem "Epipsychidion."

I never was attached to that great sect,
Whose doctrine is, that each one should select
Out of the crowd a mistress or a friend,
And all the rest, though fair and wise, commend
To cold oblivion, though it is in the code
Of modern morals, and the beaten road
Which those poor slaves with weary footsteps tread
Who travel to their home among the dead
By the broad highway of the world, and so
With one chained friend, perhaps a jealous foe,
The dreariest and the longest journey go.

My uncle, who was something of a wit, used to tell about a pair of newlyweds who chose to spend their honeymoon camping out on an island in Lake Sebago, Maine. A week after the wedding one of their friends remarked to my uncle, "I should think by this time they might be ready to see a friend." "Or," my uncle shot back, "even an enemy!"

The truth is that the variety principle applies not only to marriage, but to all sorts of personal relations. In family life, parents and children, inevitably in close contact much of the time, need periods of separation. Friends, too, must guard against seeing too much of one another.

The high rate of divorce may be primarily due, not to essential incompatibility between marriage partners, but simply to their getting bored with each other. "After thirty years we had nothing left to talk about," a college classmate told me when he was seeking a divorce. This sort of trouble is especially likely to occur when children go away to school or college, or leave home to pursue careers. Recently an old friend told me that the main reason for her divorce was that after her four children had flown the family nest, she could not endure the prospect of facing her husband, whom she still loved, alone at meals and trying to make conversation with him. And a relative of mine, after her husband retired at sixty-six and was at home most of the time, remarked to me in some alarm that in her marriage vows she had promised to take him for better or for worse, but not for lunch every day.

The question arises as to whether extramarital relations should go further than Platonic friendship, sharing dining, dancing, walking, going to the movies or the theatre. Naturally that depends on the temperaments of the individuals involved, their vitality, their sexuality, their life-style. There is often warm companionship between a man and a woman that involves little physical contact. But since it is clear that one can be sincerely in love with at least two persons at the same time, a husband or wife should feel free to go the whole way with someone whom he or she truly loves. Many married couples find a certain monotony in monogamy; what they may need, as a sort of safety valve, is some diversity in love-making. To limit the supreme sexual experience to one of the opposite sex for an entire lifetime represents unreasonable restraint and a kill-joy ethic.

The traditional one-and-perfect mate theory, always over-romantic and unrealistic, dissolves in the light of a little common sense. It assumes that the well-matched husband and wife are sufficient for each other for life and can minister to each other's every mood and need. But no woman can possibly combine the virtues of all women; no man has the excellences of all men. Every sensitive and completely alive person has something to give every other sensitive and completely alive person.

These considerations show how unreasonable it is to have the bride and groom, as in some of the traditional Christian wedding ceremonies, make the promise of "forsaking all others." The vow "until death do us part," always too absolute, made more sense in previous centuries when death was likely to part husband and wife sooner than now. As for the phrase "for better or for worse," that, too, ought to be eliminated from wedding services: how much "worse" is either of the partners expected to endure? What if—to consider just one possibility—one partner becomes an alcoholic?

One idea that rather appeals to me is a marriage contract limited to ten years, renewable for a chosen length of time if both parties agree; or, if one party insists, automatically dissolved without litigation or social stigma. Virginia Satir, a well-known family therapist, has suggested that the marriage contract be for five years, but that seems to me too short a time.

D. H. Lawrence, in lines written a full century after those I have quoted from Shelley, gives his version of the impulse toward variety:

> Since you are confined in the orbit of me
> do you not loathe the confinement?
> Is not even the beauty and peace of an orbit
> an intolerable prison to you,
> as it is to everybody?[7]

It is to be recognized that human beings are not instinctively monogamous. Most men and women possess polygamous tendencies; in many countries such tendencies find lawful or socially approved expression, at least for males. In the West one civilized example of the variety principle has been the traditional *ménage à trois*, in which what may be an unhappy triangle becomes a congenial trio.

The drive for sexual variety is discernible in today's increasing experimentation, in the communes, wife-swapping and the antics of "swingers"—dissatisfied couples who meet others with similar inclinations to exchange mates for sexual activity. The couples involved have usually had no previous acquaintance with one another. Swingers are concerned only with the physical aspects of sex; there is no real lovemaking because love is purposely ruled out. I find all this somewhat revolting. Curiously enough, swingers are likely to be rather conservative in politics and economics.

Within certain limits of physical and emotional capacity, the amount of love an individual can feel—be it for relatives, friends, lovers or fellow humans—is very great indeed. Sexual love outside marriage need not reduce the love within that relationship. Love is an unceasing fountain of tenderness, overflowing from inner springs of joy and growing more abundant with the giving. One involved in extramarital sex may well return to the spouse more loving than ever. Nena and George O'Neill state in their perceptive book *Open Marriage: A New Life-Style for Couples* (1972): "Despite our tradition of limited love, it is entirely possible to love your marital partner with an intensely rewarding and continually growing love and at the same time to love another or others with a deep and abiding affection. And this extra dimension of love feeds back into the love between the partners."[8]

One of the practices most helpful for a happy marriage is for the husband and wife to take occasional vacations from each other, through travel or otherwise, perhaps but not necessarily with a member of the opposite sex. Such vacations break into the marital routine and the "together forever" syndrome to keep the married couple fresh for each other. As everyone in love knows, there is a special joy in seeing your mate after an absence.

It is not only from each other that a husband and wife need vacations but from the family, especially when it includes several children. Such vacations are particularly needful for a housewife who is doing the cooking and taking care of the children. In fact, everybody ought to have periods of privacy in which to meditate on the course of his life.

Clearly, the extramarital relationships I have been discussing, whether or not they involve intercourse, demand that both husband and wife have no part of the sexual jealousy that has traditionally tormented humankind, even if the cause has only been an exchange of affectionate glances. Historically, a primary reason for the importance of physical faithfulness was the lack of reliable birth control. Now that control techniques, including abortion, are generally available, this importance has diminished.

Whether or not extramariatal sex occurs, either married partner is justified in objecting if the spouse is neglected in favor of some third person. Of course, in a successful marriage, regardless of the existence of outside sex relations, the husband and wife are likely to spend most of their non-working time with each other or with their family or friends.

Most divorced men and women tend to re-marry and thereby achieve variety. Yet they, too, in "serial marriage" may find the variety principle relevant. It is my position that recognition of this principle would considerably reduce the divorce rate. In any case we must regard divorce as the worst possible way of obtaining sexual variety and as a step to be taken only when everything else has failed.

Obviously, variety in love, always practiced to some extent, is more prevalent than ever in the present era. Until recently, however, extramarital sex has seldom been openly acknowledged and has for the most part been a male pastime. We raise it to a higher level by frankly acknowledging it as a legitimate, life-enhancing activity; and by abolishing the double standard, so that women are able to participate on an equal basis. Marriage with freedom, as I have described it, simply means taking the lock out of wedlock; and ethics demands complete honesty between husband and wife in acknowledging the variety principle.

If a married couple accepts it—and many happy couples never feel the need—it should be understood that the husband maintains primary allegiance to his wife as his true mate; the wife as well looks upon her husband as her true mate; any other relationship is secondary. Both seek to maintain marriage at its highest level, a union of two lovers devoted to the happiness of each other and their family.

Chapter XV   TRAVELS FAR AND WIDE

Like my parents, I have traveled extensively. In America my speaking tours took me to the South, the Middle West and the Pacific States, while during summer vacations, as I have written in a previous chapter, I drove with my wife and children through various National Parks in the West. For the beauty and drama of scenery those parks are unsurpassed.

I took my family also on trips to England and the European continent, chiefly France, Italy and Switzerland. I recall with special pleasure our visits to Mont St. Michel, the coast of Normandy, the fjords of Norway, the hill towns of northern Italy, and so many marvelous cities: London, Oxford, Paris, Rome, Florence, Venice, Dubrovnik, Athens, Madrid, Granada, Moscow, Hong Kong, Peking, Rio de Janeiro.

During my first trips abroad I always went by steamship, on a Cunarder, a Holland-America liner or the French *La Liberté*—a delicious way of crossing the Atlantic, with four or five days of complete relaxation away from the turmoil and pressures of city life, and practically no chance of being reached by phone. The ocean air was invigorating as one paced the full cirucit of the main deck; and there was plenty of time for leisurely reading, with the option of sleeping as late in the morning as one wanted. I found shuffleboard a fine game and learned to play chess. As the years went by, with regular air service across the oceans, I traveled more and more by air—a gain in time, to be sure, but a loss as well; and always some chance of a fatal accident. Yes, I have a haunting nostalgia for the big ocean ships.

For many years I had hoped to visit Mexico, a country more accessible to an American than any nation in Europe and one that offered wonderful opportunities for recreation and acquaintance with a foreign culture rich in political and social history, in archeological monuments, in artistic achievement and in colorful variety of population. The chance came in 1951 when, as I have written, the United States Department of State refused to renew my passport because of my publicly expressed dissenting views on U.S. domestic and foreign policy. But I did not need a passport to go to Mexico.

In the summer of that year I decided to make an extended trip to Mexico and flew to Mexico City, which I made my headquarters. My chief interest in Mexico soon became the work of the great triumvirate of Mexican painters: Jose Clemente Orozco, Diego Rivera and David Alfaro Siqueiros. I spent a week or more in Mexico City studying and admiring their work. It was a unique aesthetic experience for me. These three artists all did their main work in frescoes on the walls of public buildings, where the people could easily see them.

I also met Rivera while he was at work. I found him one morning at the new Mexico City waterworks on the outskirts of the city. There he was, a huge figure of a man, directing the workers on a large, symbolic mosaic on which he occasionally daubed some paint. He wore brown trousers and coat, a light brown sombrero and short rubber boots. Paint was spattered all over his clothing. When after twenty minutes or so Rivera seemed to be finished with his immediate job, I went up to him casually, explained that I was a correspondent for *The Daily Compass* of New York, a liberal newspaper, and asked whether he would mind answering some questions. He gave me an illuminating interview, later published in *The Compass*.

Rivera explained that five dominant themes ran through his murals: first, his burning antagonism toward the role of supernatural religion and the part played in Mexican history by the Catholic Church, including its responsibility for the horrors of the Inquisition in Mexico. Second, there was his hatred of the Spanish Conquest and the brutality of the Spanish invaders led by Cortés. Third, there was his unceasing ridicule of the upper classes, of the close tie-up between political power and economic privilege, and of money-mad capitalist civilization in general. Fourth, there was his emphasis on the successive revolutions which resulted in increased freedom for the Mexican people, and his additional sympathy toward the international Communist movement and Marxism. And, fifth, there was his sympathetic portrayal of the common people of Mexico, of the workers and peasants laboring in mine, field or factory, and of the native Indians in their fiestas and simple family life.

The United States also profited from Rivera's genius, since he painted outstanding murals for the San Francisco Stock Exchange, the Detroit Institute of Arts and Rockefeller Center in New York City. In my interview with Rivera, he recalled that in the painting at Rockefeller Center he had included a portrait of Lenin and that the sponsors, especially John D. Rockefeller, Jr., were so offended that they demanded he erase it and substitute some other noted leader of the human race. Rivera said he refused to accede to this demand because it would have violated his artistic integrity, trampled on the American Bill of Rights and been a surrender to capitalist power. "Let them destroy my mural," he had declared, "and the whole world will know about it within twenty-four hours. This will be very bad for Rockefeller and capitalism." Despite Rivera's protests, they destroyed the mural.

Fortunately, on my trip to Mexico in 1951, I saw Rivera's successful reconstruction of it in the Palace of Fine Arts in Mexico City. It is a remarkable mural, titled "Mankind at the Crossroads." Rivera informed me that in redoing the mural he took revenge on Rockefeller, who was a teetotaler, by painting in a half-length portrait of him at a sumptuous party sipping a glass of champagne and holding hands with a glamorous lady.

In one of my talks with Rivera, he suggested that I might like to have him paint my portrait. I was astonished that he would be willing to take the time to do such a job. However, I had never had my portrait painted before, and what an opportunity! I sat for it about six or seven times at his studio in Mexico City. It was a large picture in oil and unfortunately during my sittings Rivera's wife died. I thought he would want to postpone finishing my portrait, but he insisted on going right ahead after his wife's funeral. In the lower right-hand corner of the painting he included the large white lilies that were displayed at the funeral. I agreed with my relatives and friends that the portrait was a fine piece of work, but that it did not look much like me. I eventually presented it to the Phillips Exeter Academy.

On my first visit to the Palace of Fine Arts I noticed a man high up on a wooden scaffold working on a fresco. From an attendant I learned that this was none other than Siqueiros himself painting away on a mural that showed the invading Spaniards torturing an Indian chief named Cuauhtémoc. The Spaniards, representing Christian civilization of the sixteenth century, had kindled a fire near the chief's feet. I waited for an hour or so when a pretty, dark-haired woman in a black dress appeared. When the attendant told me it was Mrs. Siqueiros, I approached her and said I represented New York's great liberal newspaper, *The Daily Compass*. She freely answered my questions about her husband and finally invited me to have lunch with them the next day. Accordingly, I met them the following afternoon at a restaurant near the museum and talked with Siqueiros at length. He told me that the Mexican muralists are a product of revolution and therefore necessarily social-minded.

Nine years later in 1960 Siqueiros, who was an open member of the Communist Party, was arrested and jailed for various activities and speeches which in the United States would have been protected by the Bill of Rights. One of his crimes was to attack bitterly President Lopez of Mexico, who then vowed not to free the painter during his term of office, which still had some three years to run. In November of 1961 I was one of an American delegation of three who went to Mexico City to protest Siqueiros's imprisonment and demand his release. We had a fine interview with him through a wire grille at the prison. Although sixty-four years old and seriously ill with a liver disorder, he seemed as vigorous and militant as ever. Our mission, however, while stirring up sympathy for Siqueiros, did not succeed, and he was not released until 1965.

Since I had never been to South America, I decided in the summer of 1971 to make a tour there and to start with Chile where, the previous Fall, Socialist Salvador Allende had been elected President and was starting to put into effect a Socialist program. Using Santiago, the capital, as my base I drove to key places in the country and became impressed by the progress the Allende Administration was making. I managed to obtain an hour's interview with President Allende who expressed himself as very pleased with the recent nationalizaton of the Chilean copper mines.

Chile's winter comes in the months of June, July and August so I was able to have four days of first-rate skiing at the big ski center of Portillo, 9,500 feet high in the Andes mountains. The scenery was, of course, magnificent, with jagged, snow-capped peaks visible in every direction and the beautiful Lake of the Incas nestling in the valley in front of the main hotel.

Unhappily, the Allende regime did not last long. Although it succeeded in nationalizing several industries, it could not contend with the still powerful reactionary elements, especially the Army. In the fall of 1973 Chilean armed forces, surreptitiously backed by the CIA, led a military coup that overthrew the Allende government and resulted in Allende's murder; and imprisonment, exiling or execution of thousands of liberals, leftists and trade unionists. General Augustino Pinochet became head of an anti-Socialist dictatorship and reversed most of Allende's policies.

From Chile I flew over the Andes to Argentina and Brazil. I was particularly impressed by Rio de Janeiro. With its backdrop of small mountains, its lovely islands in the bay and miles of sandy beaches, Rio is of surpassing beauty among the cities of the world. While I despised the military dictatorship of Brazil, I yielded to temptation and spent four days in Rio where I enjoyed surf-bathing in the Atlantic, just a scant distance from my hotel, the Leme Palace, on Copacabana Beach.

When, as I recounted in Chapter X, I was granted a passport after the favorable Supreme Court decision in the Rockwell Kent case, it was eight long years since I had been able to travel across the seas. Hence, I decided to make up for lost time and to circle the globe. As a Humanist philosopher I had taught that the supreme ethical goal in life ought to be the happiness, freedom and progress of all humanity, regardless of nation, race or religion; but there was a lot of humanity I had never seen. I viewed my six months' world tour as a chance to come into closer contact with the people of distant countries, especially in the Far East, where I had never been.

So on the first day of Spring, 1959—surely a day of happy omen—my wife and I set sail from New York on *La Liberté*. For me the seven-day voyage across the Atlantic was a rebirth into freedom. When at last I glimpsed once more the familiar coasts of England and France, I felt that I was rediscovering much that had become, in many journeys of the past, an essential part of my being.

It was a most profound pleasure to return to England, for me a land of happy memories where I have had many good friends. It was a delight to stroll along the streets of London and through its splendid parks. English voices are always music to my ears, and I loved to listen to the people talking as I passed them, or as they went by while I sat in the sun on a park bench, looking out upon places where in World War II Hitler's bombers had created havoc. Most of the war's debris had been cleared away, but even so a number of burnt-out squares remained as silent monuments to the determination that "it must not happen again."

Our hotel in Half Moon Street was less than a block from Green Park, which runs into Hyde Park, famous not only for its wide green lawns, but also as a free-speech center where radicals and dissenters and crackpots can talk their heads off with no interference from the authorities. There ought to be a Hyde Park of free speech in every city of the world. As I listened to these orators in London's Hyde Park, I couldn't help reflecting how much better Great Britain had preserved its civil liberties since the end of World War II than had America. To be sure, during that period occasional violations of free speech had taken place in Britain, but the British experienced nothing comparable to the far-reaching suppression of the McCarthy era, the consequences of which are still visible in almost every sector of American life.

While I was in London, Parliament was in session, and I went over to the House of Commons two or three times to lunch with some of my M.P. friends in the British Labor Party. It was especially pleasant drinking coffee with them on the spacious Commons Terrace overlooking the Thames with its fine view up and down the river. We discussed the political situation at length.

During our last weekend in England my wife and I made a pilgrimage to Oxford University where I had studied at New College in 1924-25, as I have recounted in Chapter II. It was a joy to wander again around the University visiting my old haunts. The New College garden, bounded on one side by the old city wall built many centuries ago, is as quiet and lovely a place as can be found anywhere. The gardens of the twenty-five or so colleges that make up the University are unexcelled in their beauty, and give one a rare sense of isolation from the outside world. As everyone knows the creation and care of gardens in England have long achieved the status of art.

A final comment about London is worth making, and that concerns the cleanliness of the London Underground and the absence of meaningless, ugly, anti-social graffiti that so deface New York subways. By comparison with this vandalism, London's subways are almost immaculate. This situation confirmed my sad realization that in America during my lifetime there has been an increased vulgarization of our culture, including the vulgarization of the English language through the pervasive use of scatological terms.

We went on from England to the continent, spent a few days in Paris, ever a joy to the traveler, and relaxed briefly at Nice on the French Riviera. Then, on one long, rugged day, we drove to Florence, with sensational views every few minutes along the Mediterranean Côte d'Azur, past the cliffs of Monaco, into northern Italy with its steep and mountainous roads, and finally down into the Florentine plain.

We stayed three weeks in Florence, which is, of course, one vast treasure-house of art. Our hotel room looked out over the River Arno to colorful hills where we could see the old city wall and towers that Michelangelo helped to construct back in the sixteenth century. Below us, along the river walk, strolled the people of Florence, buoyant and uninhibited, young couples with their arms around each other, old couples enjoying the sun and children skipping along. At our open window we had a grand balcony seat to watch that gracious world go by. And every so often a singer with a guitar would saunter past and serenade us.

From Florence we made expeditions in all directions to Italy's hill towns—Siena, San Gimignano, Volterra, Perugia and Assisi. On approaching these magic cities from a distance, we saw their graceful towers rising far away, then disappearing and reappearing with the curve of roads and the shapes of the Tuscan hills. We were living in a pervasive atmosphere of beauty, where the loveliness of Nature continually merged with that of human creation. The hills and valleys were lush and green; and as twilight approached, a golden glow suffused the entire landscape.

The history of this region is absorbing, but it often makes one sad. For the city-states of Italy, at the height of their artistic flowering during the Renaissance, were continually assaulting one another. Not only were irreplaceable works of art ravaged, but the prime of Italian manhood was killed off. In a much later era, stiff fighting took place in and around Florence during World War II when the American Army was driving out the Nazis. The retreating Germans shelled the bridges across the Arno and smashed all of them except the famed Ponte Vecchio. At this moment art lovers held their breath. Would the Germans bombard the rest of the city? It did not happen, but it was close.

Our next highlight was Greece. This historic land was a very special experience for me because as a philosopher I was fascinated to see the places where Socrates, Plato and Aristotle walked and talked. We stayed in Athens several weeks. Every other day or so we went up to the Acropolis, wandered through the half-ruined structures built in the Golden Age of Pericles, viewed from every angle the architectural miracle of the Parthenon, and looked out between its white marble columns designed by Phidias to the city lying below and to the shining sea in the distance. It was all the sheerest aesthetic ecstasy. And it continued even into the hours of darkness, for every so often the Parthenon was lighted up at night and we could see it from the streets of Athens.

We made many exciting explorations of cities such as Delphi, Corinth, Mycenae and Sunium, where on a headland an ancient and perfectly proportioned temple to Poseidon stands out dramatically. In *Don Juan*[1] Byron referred to "Sunium's marbled steep," and it was there that we saw the poet's signature carved into a marble pillar. Then came our five-day boat trip through the Greek Islands of the Aegean Sea, an adventure into the living past and the enthralling present, centering around legend-encrusted isles like Crete and Rhodes and Delos.

As in Italy, we constantly absorbed panoramas of history along with the sublime art and the natural beauty. I took particular satisfaction in going out to the battlefield of Marathon and reconstructing from maps how the Greeks drove back the Persians in 490 B.C. I held up a whole busload of hurrying American tourists when I insisted on stopping to see the swamp that protected the Athenian right wing against a Persian cavalry charge. One plump, angry lady in the bus demanded that a vote be taken on whether I should be permitted to look at the swamp. For once I did not wait upon the democratic process, but got out of the bus quickly. There was a plaque at the edge of the ancient swamp which I thought would tell about the battle. What it stated was that some years ago the area had been filled in as a mosquito-breeding hazard with funds from John D. Rockefeller, Jr.!

In Greece even more than in Italy the ravages of innumerable wars are apparent. Athens, Sparta, and other Greek city-states were at one another's throats most of the time. The Persians sacked much of the country; and later came the barbarian invasions from the north. There was a most hideous war episode in 1687 when the Turks placed a powder magazine inside the Parthenon, and the attacking Venetians scored a direct hit on the building with a mortar shell, transforming the larger part of the Parthenon into a shambles. War is the enemy of art, as of every human value.

Yet despite the fact that almost all the architectural splendors of Greece, and much of its ancient sculpture, have been badly battered by violence or neglect, what remains is so magnificent that this small country offers an unsurpassed concentration of artistic glories. When I saw American bombers from the U.S. military airfield nearby zooming over Athens and heard talk about setting up a base for long-range ballistic missiles in Greece, I felt almost sick to think that this unique land, the birthplace of Western culture and a veritable sanctuary of art, might yet again suffer the destructiveness of war.

From Athens we took a small but comfortable steamship to Istanbul, passing through the Dardanelles and sailing across the Sea of Marmora. At Istanbul we could look out from our hotel window across the Bosphorus to the green-clad hills of Asia Minor. What I remember chiefly about Istanbul is surely one of the wonders of the world—the great Mosque of St. Sophia, with its remarkable blue coloring, which was later transformed into a museum.

Circling the planet on our long trip we naturally took in the Soviet Union and after visiting briefly Leningrad and Moscow, cities which we already knew well, flew in a Soviet jet to the southernmost section of Soviet Central Asia whose architectural creations of the old Moslem culture we had long wished to see. We also wanted to study the functioning of the Soviet minorities policy in an enormous region where five major Turko-Tatar peoples intermingled with the Russians. We were able to fulfill our two main purposes during our fortnight's stay in Tashkent, capital of the Uzbek Republic, with side trips in a 200-mile radius to such places as fabulous Samarkand, ancient capital of Tamerlane's earth-shaking empire, and the Fergana Valley, in which a network of irrigation canals has transformed former desert into a most fertile agricultural area.

Wherever we went in Central Asia there seemed to be ample food, as in the Moscow area. In the towns and cities crowds of people were busily buying the abundant consumer goods in the stores. The general standard of living, education and health was fairly high in this vast region, where before the 1917 Revolution, a primarily nomadic and Moslem population maintained a precarious existence in poverty and squalor, ever facing depredations of drought, famine, epidemic disease and invading conquerors.

From everything we could observe, the different peoples in Uzbekistan all lived together on a plane of equality, with the old radical prejudices and discriminations almost completely eliminated. Among the 444 deputies chosen for the Supreme Soviet of the Uzbek Republic in the last election held early in 1959, thirteen separate nationalities were represented. The most important minority is the Russian, with sixty-two representatives.

Another significant development was that of the 444 elected deputies 129 were women. It confirmed our impression that in this huge territory the female sex, traditionally held in bondage there by the Moslem male, had made immense strides toward equality with men. Not only has polygamy been abolished by law, but also most of the women have discarded the heavy, long, black horsehair veil that for centuries the Mohammedan religion had demanded that all females wear outside the home.

In Uzbekistan we enjoyed mingling with the dark-skinned, half-Oriental Uzbeks who make up the great majority in this land. They are a delightful and handsome people, with mobile, expressive faces, and their children are a pleasure to watch. The girls wear their hair in two long braids down their backs, and their dresses are brilliantly colored. The youngsters were frolicking everywhere like kids in any other country. Since it was extremely hot, with temperatures ranging from 85 to 90 degrees, one of my favorite recreations was to go swimming in Lake Komsomol, in the city's biggest park, where I was able to relax with the young at play.

One of our most enjoyable times in Uzbekistan was an afternoon when we went to inspect the big Sverdlov Collective Farm (cotton), just outside Tashkent, highly mechanized and operating most efficiently. After we had walked for quite a while in the broiling sun, with the Chairman of the Collective as our guide, we retired to a shady veranda where we were served "tea" consisting of a small portion of green tea and very large portions of vodka, champagne and plov, a national Uzbek dish of meat and rice. The Chairman raised his small vodka glass and proposed a toast to American-Soviet friendship. "Bottoms up," he said. Since my wife and I had chosen champagne, it was a bit difficult for us to drain our larger glasses. Nevertheless, we did so and then went gaily on to the next glass as I offered a toast to world peace.

We drank a lot of other genial toasts and a final one to the continued success of the Sverdlov Farm. Each time the Chairman repeated, "Bottoms up," we maintained the pace as best we could. At the end of the "tea" my wife and I and an American newspaperwoman who was present had consumed two whole bottles of Soviet champagne! It is testimony to the quality of that wine that it gave none of us a headache or a hangover.

On another afternoon we went to the most important mosque in Tashkent and witnessed an outdoor Moslem prayer service, at which, according to custom, the men and women are segregated. On this occasion all the women were out of sight in the back somewhere. So we walked through the midst of some 1,000 silent, bearded Mohammedan males to the chairs reserved for our small party. Almost all the men were native Uzbeks, many of them very handsome, and some, with their shaven or bald heads, resembling Yul Brynner. It was thrilling to hear the Muezzin call out repeatedly in a high-pitched voice, "Allah is great," and to see each worshipper, kneeling on his little prayer rug, bow his dead down to the ground. I was never so close to Allah before.

After the service, the Mufti, head of the Moslem religion throughout Soviet Central Asia, gave us tea, fruit and lamb stew at a beautifully set table. He was a dignified, charming man, with seven children and five grandchildren. We asked him many questions. He said that the Moslems had complete freedom of worship in Soviet Russia and that they trained young men to be mullahs in special seminaries and freely distributed the Koran at the mosques. He was very sincerely concerned about world peace.

The Mufti explained that according to the Koran, the Moslem religion, wherever it is functioning, should cooperate with the established government. He and his associates, he told us, are cooperating with the Soviet Government and are on good terms with it. This is also the attitude of the Eastern Orthodox Church, by far the most powerful religious body in the U.S.S.R. The patriotic services of this Church during World War II led to greatly improved relations between religion and state in Soviet Russia. The Orthodox Church now actually supports the Socialist economic system, which it does not find inconsistent with Christianity. The Soviet Government on its part has eliminated most of the crude anti-religious propaganda that had been carried on until the Nazi invasion in 1941.

I felt warmly toward all the people we saw in Uzbekistan and should like to have remained among them indefinitely. But we had set out to circumnavigate the globe and had to move on. On our last afternoon we signed our names in the Tashkent guest book of Intourist, the official Soviet travel agency. By coincidence on the opposite page there was a statement signed by seven American governors, who had left the day before, July 13. What they said is significant:

> On this day the undersigned have concluded a three-day stay in Tashkent, vital and inspiring capital of the Uzbek Republic. The warm friendship which has been extended to us by the people at every hand, the exemplary courtesy of all public officials, make us feel that our stay has been constructive. It will always remain in our memories as one of the most enjoyable experiences of our lifetime. We leave Uzbek and Tashkent with every wish for the protection of the ancient charm which has been so manifest and at the same time the continued business progress which has also been most conspicuous.

> [Signed] LeRoy Collins, Governor of Florida
> George D. Clyde, Governor of Utah
> John E. Davis, Governor of North Dakota
> Stephen McNichols, Governor of Colorado
> Robert E. Smylie, Governor of Idaho
> Robert B. Meyner, Governor of New Jersey
> Luther H. Hodges, Governor of North Carolina

Before breakfast the following morning we drove out to the Tashkent airport and took another Soviet jet, this time bound for India. Reflecting on my trip through the U.S.S.R., I felt more convinced than ever that this Socialist country run by Communists—with all its defects past and present—is a nation with which the United States can and should cooperate in normal international trade, intercultural exchange, the banning of nuclear weapons, general disarmament and the establishment of enduring world peace. The U.S.A. and the U.S.S.R. will continue to disagree fundamentally on issues of economics and politics; but such disagreements need not stand in the way of peaceful, though competitive, coexistence between the capitalist and Communist blocs.

The Soviet jet flew us over the towering Tien Shan ("Celestial Mountains"), over a part of Communist China's Sinkiang Province that juts out between the U.S.S.R. and India, then over the Himalayas with their soaring, snow-covered peaks stretching away for hundreds of miles on either side, and finally down to our destination on India's wide northern plain. It was the most exciting trip by air that we had ever made.

To reach Delhi took only about three hours. As we struggled through the Indian customs and out to a taxi, no less than six porters insisted on helping us carry our seven bags—a sign of the immense poverty that burdens India—and I felt obliged to tip each one. This situation was in striking contrast to our experience in Soviet Russia where tipping is now definitely frowned upon and where, having been rebuffed on several occasions, I finally gave up this pernicious custom altogether for the remainder of my stay in the U.S.S.R.

Delhi became the capital of India in 1931, and the section that functions as the seat of government is known as New Delhi. It is a spacious, well-planned city, with fine government buildings, parks and apartment houses. The older section of the city, Old Delhi, where we spent much of our time, is more picturesque than the new part but also contains the most depressed slums in the metropolitan area. The appalling poverty of the Indian people was readily apparent to us as we walked or drove through the streets and alleys of Old Delhi. On every hand there were wretched beggars, both young and old, some of them disfigured. It is a horrible fact that beggar parents in this country sometimes mutilate their children in order to make their begging more effective.

In Old Delhi we saw at first-hand the meaning of cow worship in India. Often a cow would saunter across a main street along which we were driving in a taxi; the driver would then have to make a detour, especially if the cow decided to lie down. When we were walking on the sidewalk, a cow would frequently be directly in our path; we watched cows calmly munching vegetables from stalls along the streets; the owners could not interfere because the cow is a sacred animal and must be fed. Over all of India literally millions of cows wander, a large proportion of them diseased, with the right of way over both human beings and vehicles.

There are also many bulls on the loose. A professor who had taught at the University of Calcutta told me that one day a big bull wandered onto the campus. No one was pleased, but no one dared to prevent the sacred animal from munching on the grass. A week or so later the bull charged and gored a student who was riding a bicycle through the campus. It was only when the young man almost died that somebody gently ushered the bull off the University grounds, still free to roam and gore at will. There have been many instances of bulls killing Indian men and women.

When we had tea with Malcolm MacDonald, British High Commissioner to India and son of Ramsay MacDonald, England's first Labor Prime Minister, he told us that the cow situation had become worse since the establishment of Indian Independence in 1947. While the British were still in control, they did not interfere with cow-worship, but neither did they encourage it. Shortly after Independence, however, the right wing of the Congress Party forced through a law prohibiting the killing of cattle throughout India. Monkeys, too, are sacred and constitute a destructive nuisance in many parts of the country.

Cow-worship is of course closely tied up with the belief in reincarnation, which is a fundamental doctrine in the Hindu religion. The Hindus—there are approximately 560 million of them among India's 667 million people— are reluctant to take the life of any animal. They think that if you kill a cow, you may in effect be killing your grandmother or some other deceased relative. Cow-worship and the law against the slaughter of cattle prevent the utilization of what could be a very substantial source of fresh meat. This is a major reason why the vast majority of Indians are undernourished. Furthermore, the cows and monkeys eat tons and tons of food that ought to be going to human beings. I know of no other nation where the dominant religion has such a deleterious effect on nutrition and health as in India.

On my visit to Calcutta I witnessed aspects of Hinduism that clearly belong in the category of primitive religion. One Saturday morning I went to the temple of the Goddess Kali, an important Hindu deity who has three eyes—one each for the past, the present and the future. In the stone courtyard of the temple, fire worship and animal sacrifice were going on. One Hindu family after another came in leading a little bleating goat and turned it over to the burly executioner. He pinioned the struggling animal in a sort of guillotine and quickly cut off its head with a large, sharp knife. The head and the body fell to the pavement and blood gushed out over the stones. Then a priest stepped forward, dipped his forefinger into the goat's blood and put a red mark on the middle of the forehead of each worshipper, including the small children.

An old woman squatting nearby took over the head of each goat and cut away the edible parts for the priests of the temple. Dogs lapped up the pools of blood, and the sacrificer carried home the body of the goat to eat. For the Hindus the goat represents animal passion. Sacrificing it symbolizes winning control over human passions, killing them, as it were.

After I had watched five or six goats being sacrificed, I felt I had had enough. I walked out of the temple grounds and down the street outside. It was lined with beggars, some of them naked, seeking alms from the crowds who had come to worship Kali. When four or five of these beggars spotted me as a foreigner and literally surrounded me, I had to break into a run in order to escape.

Of course there is much that is splendid about India, including its magnificent art and historic buildings; the beauty of the Taj Mahal can scarcely be exaggerated. Among the most admirable aspects of this nation has been its firm stand throughout the post-war period for world peace and disarmament, the intellectual alertness of its educated class, and the economic aspirations embodied in the Five-Year Plans that the Government has been carrying through in order to raise the standard of living and advance toward Socialism.

But the economic and social problems are so formidable that I could not see how Prime Minister Nehru—whom I admired as one of the leading statesmen of this century—and his Congress Party would be able to solve them. At the time of my visit in 1959 the population of this sub-continent was increasing at the rate of at least seven million a year, and birth control was making only slight progress. One of Nehru's Cabinet ministers was quoted as saying that during the next decade probably some 15 million Indians would starve to death—one well-known way in which economic problems are "solved."

Although Prime Minister Nehru and the Congress Party were formally committed to establishing democratic Socialism, the Indians I talked with told me that to a considerable degree only lip service was being paid to this aim. The Congress Party had not been militant in pushing through its economic and social programs, and many of its members were noted for their apathy and indolence. While my Indian friends did not look upon the Communist Party as the solution, they thought that the best hope for the ultimate success of Nehru and his associates was to acquire some of the militancy characteristic of the Communists.

As Walter Lippmann* put it, India needed above all "the organized pressures of a popular movement under government leadership so dynamic and so purposeful that it can inspire people to do voluntarily the kinds of things that in Communist China are done by compulsion."[2]

A first priority for a truly militant policy on the part of the Congress Party would be the elimination of the graft that is widespread throughout governmental administration, both at the federal and the state level. Another priority would be the general institution of elementary efficiency. As Arthur Bonner, a CBS correspondent who lived in India for more than five years, stated in his informative article, "India's Masses," "entering a government office is like stepping back 50 years or more. There are few filing cabinets and paper clips; papers are attached by a string threaded through a hole in one corner and then wrapped in a folder tied together by another string. A code letter is pinned to the cover; and the name of the file is registered in a ledger. The file is then tossed on a shelf along with mounds of others. The registers are tossed somewhere else and how any file is ever found again is a wonder."[3]

Looking back on my globe-circling tour, I feel that my experiences in India were the most significant of the whole trip. In no major country had I ever seen such dreadful poverty, disease-ridden people, backward religion, and abysmal and wide-spread ignorance. To me as an American the whole situation was a great shock—and a valuable shock. It made me understand more fully the 1917 Communist Revolution in Russia and the 1949 Communist Revolution in China, since in those two countries the living conditions of the masses of the people had been similar to those current in India.

When the Chinese Communists won power in 1949, living standards there were even worse than in India. A United Nations Statistical Bulletin,

---

*Walter Lippmann (1889-1974) was in my view the dean of American newspaper columnists and a journalist whose intelligent liberalism was a constant source of inspiration and wisdom. As a writer his lucid style was unsurpassed and as a personality he combined intellectual acumen with marked congeniality. I once proposed him for U.S. Secretary of State.

The best biography of him is *Walter Lippmann and the American Century* by Ronald Steel, published in 1980.[3]

National and per Capita Incomes, 70 Countries, 1949, estimated the per capita annual income in India, in dollar equivalents, as $57, as compared with China's $27. These estimates do not of course tell the whole story about the comparative standards of living, but there is no doubt that the Chinese level had been declining, owing to disastrous floods, widespread famine, civil and international war.

When a people numbering hundreds of millions lives generation after generation in misery and semi-starvation, it is not difficult to comprehend why they may eventually explode into revolutionary violence in hopes that a new socio-economic system will provide for their basic needs and give them a better chance to enjoy life. News of the dramatic economic upsurge in mainland China was not only reaching the Indian intellectuals, but also seeping through to the masses of the population. And unless India's Five-Year Plans bring about more rapid progress than at present, the example of Communist China will steadily grow more persuasive among the Indians and other peoples of the East.

Another point that India brought into focus was the relation between a country's economic system and the functioning of democracy. Political democracy in India today is weak and faltering. In this situation I want to stress the effects of the economic base on the educational prerequisites for democracy. While I was in India I kept thinking of John Dewey's insistence that there cannot be properly functioning democratic institutions unless the people are sufficiently educated to possess the information for voting intelligently on public issues. Nobody can pretend that this is the case in India. In this huge country there do not exist even the *material* necessities—schoolhouses, college buildings, pencils, paper, book publishing, funds for teachers' salaries—adequately to educate the electorate.

From Calcutta I flew on to Bangkok, Singapore and Hong Kong—all fascinating cities, but I shall discuss only Hong Kong. On a bay studded with numerous enchanting islands, ringed with small mountains, it is the most beautiful and dramatic harbor I have ever seen. It surpasses even San Francisco. Hong Kong boasts a long waterfront where you can watch Chinese junks and other boats being loaded and unloaded. Since there is a lively trade with Communist China, you can see many Communist boats flying their five-star flag at the docks. On the myriad junks and sampans—"floating communities," as they are called—live thousands of families in cramped and squalid, though picturesque, quarters.

Since the Communist take-over on the Chinese mainland, more than a million refugees had fled over the border to Hong Kong, creating an enormous problem for the municipal authorities. Naturally, these refugees are bitterly anti-Communist; but among the city's original Chinese population pro-Communist sentiment ran strong, even among some of the wealthier businessmen, who were proud to see China no longer subject to imperialist aggression and exploitation—finally a free nation standing on its own feet. Hong Kong in British hands serves as a valuable trade outlet and transshipment center for mainland China.

This British Crown Colony offers tourists a fine opportunity to buy a vast assortment of intriguing Oriental goods at low prices, and I started to purchase a few presents for my family and friends. Then I was stopped short by the discovery that the United States Government had put into effect a regulation that all articles, within at least thirty broad classifications, bought by Americans in Hong Kong would be confiscated by the U.S. Customs unless the buyer could obtain from the seller a Certificate of Origin certifying that the merchandise in question did not originate in Communist China or North Korea.

I was much incensed by this regulation through which the American Government pushed its unrealistic and out-of-date Far Eastern policy to a ridiculous extreme, interfering with the right of Americans to buy what they want abroad. I also felt surprised that the British Government, which had reluctantly agreed to the U.S. procedures, would allow such an infringement of its sovereignty. I bought very little in Hong Kong. I remained only five days in that city, but it is a place where I would like to have spent five months or indeed five years.

From Kowloon, on the mainland side of the bay, I drove toward the small Sham Chun River which denotes the border with the People's Republic of China, and was able to climb a little hill that gave me a view of two Communist towns a mile or so distant. That was the nearest I got to Communist China on my world trip of 1959. But I completed the circle by a visit to that country in 1976, which I describe in Chapter XVI.

Early in August I left Hong Kong for Tokyo on a Pan American Stratocruiser. The weather was clear as we flew over the Tokyo airport in the late afternoon, but instead of landing the plane started to circle and I quickly became aware that something was wrong. When I happened to hear the captain talking with the airport about his left landing gear, I realized that we might be in for real trouble, and finally, the hostess told the passengers to prepare for a crash landing because the left landing gear might not hold.

Some passengers were ushered toward the rear, where I was sitting. A Chinese mother and her two young children crouched between me and the back of the seat. The children were frightened and crying, but I was able to quiet them somewhat by singing a couple of American dance tunes. I remained outwardly calm, but felt terribly nervous. Then the plane came in. On the first bump the landing gear held firm, and I said aloud, "It held!" The flight officer opposite me said, "Wait for the second bump!" A moment later the second bump came, and everything was all right. We had made a perfect landing. As we descended from the Stratocruiser, I noticed six or seven fire engines drawn up on the airfield.

In Japan I made Tokyo my headquarters, staying at the Imperial Hotel— and frequenting especially the spacious and exotic old wing—which had been built by the architect Frank Lloyd Wright in the early 1920's. I went on all-day trips through beautiful Nikko National Park and Hakone National Park, and then on a four-day tour of the lovely temple cities of Kyoto and Nara and the atom-bombed city of Hiroshima.

Surprisingly for me, Hiroshima turned out to be one of the most splendid harbors I have visited—surrounded by jagged mountains and looking off to the colorful islands of Japan's big Inland Sea. Since I had taken an active part in the campaign against nuclear weapons, I was particularly interested in Hiroshima and explored it thoroughly in order to obtain as clear an idea as possible of what happened when a plane of the U.S. Air Force dropped the first atom bomb in history upon this city on August 6, 1945.

A party of four Japanese took me around. My official guide and interpreter had been a soldier in the Japanese Army, stationed near Hiroshima when the bomb struck. The following day his unit was sent into the city to render aid. He gave me innumerable grisly, ghastly details. Most helpful also was Dr. Ichito Moritaki, Professor of Philosophy at Hiroshima University and Chairman of the Hiroshima Council Against A- and H-Bombs. He had lost his right eye on A-bomb day. Of the two girl students who spoke English and also accompanied us, one was injured when the bomb fell.

I went through three Hiroshima hospitals. The first was the Atom Bomb Hospital, which administers only to patients suffering from the effects of the original explosion. Fourteen years later, scores of people were still coming to this hospital for treatment every day; I saw many of them in the waiting room. The director told me that in the first eight months of 1959, twenty-seven Japanese A-bomb victims had died.

The second hospital, run by the Atomic Bomb Casualty Commission and partly supported by American funds, concentrated on research into the effects on human beings of the A-bomb explosion. It did not try to cure anyone, but its work was bound to be very important in the long run.

The third hospital I visited was a small private institution run by Dr. Shima and built on the ruins of the old Shima Hospital, which happened to be in the exact center of the atom bomb strike. The fifty patients and ten staff members that day were obliterated in one minute or less. The hospital was completely destroyed. I talked at length with Dr. Shima, who was operating at a hospital out in the country when the bomb fell. He told me he came back quickly to Hiroshima to help his patients, but all he could find in the ruins of his hospital was the charred body of the head nurse. The fact that the very center of the bomb's destructive power was a hospital ministering to the sick for the preservation of life seemed to me symbolic of the horror of nuclear weapons. It is a remarkable coincidence that at Nagasaki, too, the direct center of the American A-bomb attack proved to be a medical institution, the Nagasaki Medical School.

What I saw and learned at Hiroshima was all very grueling to me. I came away more convinced than ever that the United States had made a terrible mistake in letting loose the A-bombs on Hiroshima and Nagasaki. In terms of dead, injured, suffering, and of long-range effects on health, these bombings were the most frightful military actions perpetrated against civilian populations in the entire history of warfare.

Since the Japanese Government was already prepared to negotiate terms of surrender with the United States, the use of the A-bombs was unnecessary to terminate the war. In my opinion, the primary reason for dropping the bombs was twofold: first to keep the Soviet Union, which was due to enter the war against Japan on August 8, from participating in the peace negotiations; and, second, to stage the mightiest military demonstration in history in order to alarm the Soviet Union and make it more amenable to U.S. pressures.

President Harry Truman's resort to the A-bomb was inexcusable; it marked a new low in international morality. He went ahead with the bombings in spite of the fact that all the Joint Chiefs of Staff were opposed to the action on the grounds that Japan would very probably surrender anyway and without the pressures of an American invasion. As recounted in the diary of Secretary of War Stimson, General Eisenhower told Stimson he was against the A-bombings on two counts: "First, the Japanese were ready to surrender and it wasn't necessary to hit them with that awful thing. Second, I hated to see our country be the first to use such a weapon. . . ."

During my three weeks in Japan, I came to like its people very much. I have never known a people so polite, thoughtful and smiling—so pleasant in general. To everyone, including hotel personnel and taxi drivers, I returned the bows and smiles with equally deep bows and broad smiles of my own. I found this sort of give-and-take an amiable and heartwarming custom.

The Japanese traits I have described have often been ridiculed in the United States, but they are sincere expressions of the national character. They represent an example of how a deeply civilized country can be misled into nationalist aggression and eventual disaster by an autocratic and ruthless military clique. How could it happen? I have no pat answer to this paradox. Important factors were undoubtedly the long tradition of strict feudalism, the fanatical Emperor worship and the tendency of the ruling class in recent times to imitate the most hardboiled features of German militarism and its Prussian code.

I did not want to leave Japan just as I had not wanted to leave Hong Kong, India, Soviet Russia, England and Greece. Indeed, wherever I went on my six months' trip, I always wanted to remain much longer than I could. Every country, every city had something unique to offer in the way of natural beauty or artistic achievement. Above all I liked the people, of every nationality, of every race and color. The warm feeling I had always had for humanity throughout the earth was constantly reinforced by my day-to-day experiences. Brotherhood extending over the globe is no mere dream. The Humanist aim of working for the welfare of the family of Man is the greatest and most worthwhile of all ideals.

In August, 1961 I returned briefly to Japan as a member of the American Delegation to the Seventh World Congress Against A- and H-Bombs, spending a week or so in Tokyo and again visiting Hiroshima. The country was as attractive to me as ever. At the opening session of the Conference in Tokyo I made the official speech on behalf of the American Delegation. I said in part:

"Horrible and inexcusable as was the first atom bomb attack on Hiroshima, we must remember that a hydrogen bomb possesses at least 50 times the explosive power of the original A-bomb. One H-bomb could devastate the whole of New York City or Moscow or London or Tokyo; and the radioactive fallout from the explosion would extend for hundreds of miles. These terrible nuclear weapons threaten to annihilate the whole human race. . . .

"I believe that the U.S. Government, backed in a bi-partisan manner by both the Democratic and Republican Parties, has adopted a dangerous and aggressive attitude in foreign relations. Already in April of 1961 that attitude took an ugly, concrete form in the criminal, and unsuccessful, invasion of Cuba—an invasion supported, planned and financed by the Kennedy Administration through the hateful Central Intelligence Agency.

"This adventure in international immorality was typical of the American Government's position that it has a right to intervene directly or indirectly in various countries throughout the earth in order to crush anti-imperialist and Socialist movements. And we all know that the U.S. Government maintains more than 400 military bases in foreign lands. . . .

"Mankind's struggle for peace has been going on for thousands of years. We of this twentieth century are at last going to win this long and arduous fight—you and I and hundreds of millions of our fellow human beings throughout this planet. We march forward with them, with the whole great family of humanity, dedicated to a final victory for a happy world of international peace, disarmament and security."

Yet already the bomb-happy United States Government was making a mockery of my address by preparing for a massive war in Vietnam which would last fourteen years, cost some $150 billion, cause more than 50,000 in American dead, and devastate from end to end a country that had never performed any act of hostility toward the American people.

My last major trip to Europe was in 1977 when I spent about a month in Spain. I had not wished to visit that country so long as General Francisco Franco and his reactionary Fascist regime were in power. During the Civil War, 1936-39, I was one of those Americans who supported the democratic government against the Fascist revolt. Franco died in 1975 and was succeeded as chief of state by the liberal Prince Juan Carlos, who assumed the title of king. Under Carlos and his Prime Minister, Adolfo Suárez, most of the Fascist institutions were soon dissolved and free elections established for the Cortes, the Spanish parliament. Spain thus became a political democracy in the form of a constitutional monarchy. There were still, however, many scars left from the ferocious Civil War; and ever the problem of the ethnic minorities such as the Basques and Catalans struggling for more autonomy. Complete democracy in Spain will not be fulfilled for many a year.

My friends and I entered Spain at the city of Santiago de Compostela near the northwest coast and stayed at a remarkable hotel that had been built as a fortress-castle in the fifteenth century and transformed into a vast, museum-like hospice with many courtyards and fountains. It was a so-called *parador* hotel. The food was good and the accommodations comfortable, as they were in the other hotels where we stayed. An unusual thing in Spain is that the Government owns and runs many of the best hotels and restaurants *(paradores)*.

Next day we drove the short distance to Corunna, the long and sheltered harbor where the Spanish Emperor Philip II's "Invincible Armada" assembled in 1588 before setting out on its disastrous attack against England. It was thrilling to stand on the high ground above the port and imagine the 130 ships of the Armada gaily riding at anchor there before they set sail for unsuspected doom.

We flew to Madrid and took up residence at the Palace Hotel, a short walk from the Prado Museum with its treasured masterpieces by Velasquez, Goya, El Greco and others. What I cherished most about this incomparable city was its many squares with fountains playing freely. In fact, throughout our Spanish excursion I was unexpectedly delighted by the numerous fountains playing in every city we visited. On the other hand, I was unexpectedly appalled by the amount of automobile and truck traffic, especially when it caused jams in narrow medieval streets. Every now and then Spain resembled only too much the United States.

My most significant side-trip from Madrid was to Avila, sacred to me as the place where George Santayana spent most of his youth. His father had moved the family from Madrid to Avila when Santayana was three and it became the center of his "deepest legal and affectionate ties," giving him "a most firm and distinctive station. For the freest spirit must have some birthplace, some *locus standi* from which to view the world and some innate passion by which to judge it."[4]

Avila was a lovely city with old defense walls of large crenelated stones and battlements jutting out every 200 or 300 yards. We were able to walk along the top of the broad walls and look off over green fields to low-lying mountains in the distance.

The high point of our Spanish trip for me was Granada, held by the Moors until 1492, and its famous Alhambra, a surpassingly beautiful group of buildings forming a citadel that overlooked the city. This architectural triumph was celebrated in *The Alhambra* by Washington Irving, whose memory was honored by a plaque hung on one of the walls.

From Granada we drove on to Valencia with its excellent sandy beaches and swimming. And finally we reached and explored Barcelona, the chief city of Catalonia, the center of Spanish radicalism, which had been the seat of the loyalist Government that had opposed Franco in the Civil War. It is undeniably one of the main cultural centers of Spain, and there again I was charmed by the many public squares and fountains.

Chapter XVI   AMERICAN AGGRESSION
              AGAINST VIETNAM

In working for international peace, I was for long unaware of the dangerous situation building up in the Far East and Southeast Asia. It was only in 1962, when I was sixty, that I became very much concerned about what the United States was doing in Southeast Asia and especially in Vietnam where President John F. Kennedy was continuing U.S. military intervention with troops and arms. In February of 1962 *The New York Times* printed my letter criticizing Kennedy's policy regarding Vietnam.

I decided, however, that it would be more effective to publish statements in the major press signed by a number of eminent citizens. Many liberal and radical newspapers and magazines opposed American intervention in Vietnam, but their subscribers overlapped to a large degree and their circulation was limited. Accordingly, in the spring of 1962 I drew up this Open Letter to President Kennedy, with sixteen signatories besides myself, and inserted it as an advertisement in *The New York Times* of Sunday, April 11:

Dear President Kennedy:
As individuals who believe that the only security for America lies in world peace, we wish to ask you why at present the United States is sending its Army, Navy, and Air Force to bring death and bloodshed to South Vietnam, a small Asian country approximately 10,000 miles from our Pacific Coast.

In other words, since you have the ultimate responsibility in this matter, we want to raise with you the question of the American Government's massive military intervention in South Vietnam to bolster the corrupt and reactionary dictatorship of Ngo Dinh Diem. According to reliable newspaper reports, the United States has sent nearly 5,000 troops to South Vietnam, together with enormous quantities of small arms, machine guns, artillery and helicopters to transport the soldiers of the Diem Government. In addition, Mr. President, you have set up a special U.S. Military Assistance Command for Vietnam.

All of these measures are calculated to thwart the will of the South Vietnamese people who have been fighting year after year in a broad, country-wide movement, made up primarily of peasants, to get rid of the tyrannical Diem Government. While a proportion of Communists are active in this movement, and there may be some support from North Vietnam, there is substantial participation in it by non-Communists. And considerable opposition to dictator Diem is anti-Communist, as witness three attempts by the military to overthrow his Government, and two exiled political groups, the Democratic Party and the Free Democratic Party, both with headquarters in Paris.

The United States intervention in Vietnam is in specific violation of the 1954 Geneva Agreements which marked the final defeat of France in Indochina and which established Cambodia, Laos and Vietnam as independent countries. These treaties prohibited foreign troops and foreign military bases in Vietnam, limited military advisers to 685, banned fresh military supplies except for replacements and provided for national elections in 1956 to establish a single, unified government for both North and South Vietnam. The American Government through its intervention has clearly violated all the military prohibitions of the Geneva pacts; and it supported President Diem in his illegal refusal to go through with the promised plebiscite.

United States troops have been definitely taking part in military operations in South Vietnam; and U.S. casualties are piling up, including the 93 Army men who lost their lives when a Super Constellation crashed on March 16 while flying them from San Francisco to Saigon. It is evident that the United States is involved in a real, though undeclared, war. Yet neither Congress, which under our Constitution alone has the power to declare war, nor the American people have had an adequate opportunity publicly to air and debate the present policy of your Administration in South Vietnam. And you yourself, Mr. President, have given out only the scantiest information about this dangerous situation. We must agree with the Republican National Committee, in its official publication *Battle Line*, that you have a "clear responsibility to make a full report to the people" as to the extent of American intervention in South Vietnam.

The most persuasive statement we have found about the need of more information in such a perilous situation as this nation confronts in South Vietnam was made by you, Mr. Presient, in a speech on the floor of the United States Senate, April 6, 1954, about the Vietnam crisis of that time. We are taking the liberty of quoting a few passages from your address as printed in the *Congressional Record* of that date:

The time has come for the American people to be told the blunt truth about Indochina. . . . But the speeches of President Eisenhower, Secretary Dulles and others have left too much unsaid in my opinion—and what has been left unsaid is the heart of the problem that should concern every citizen. For if the American people are, for the fourth time in this century, to travel the long and tortuous road of war—particularly a war which we now realize would threaten the survival of civilization—then I believe we have a right—a right which we should have hitherto exercised—to inquire in detail into the nature of the struggle in which we may become engaged, and the alternative to that struggle. Without such clarification, the general support and success of our policy is endangered. . . .

To pour money, matériel and men into the jungles of Indochina without at least a remote prospect of victory would be dangerously futile and self-destructive. . . . I am frankly of the belief that no amount of American military assistance in Indochina can conquer an enemy which is everywhere and at the same time nowhere, "an enemy of the people" which has the sympathy and covert support of the people. . . .

For the United States to intervene unilaterally and to send troops into the most difficult terrain in the world, with the Chinese able to pour in unlimited manpower, would mean that we would face a situation which would be far more difficult than even that which we encountered in Korea. . . .

The facts and alternatives before us are unpleasant. . . . But in a nation such as ours, it is only through the fullest and frankest appreciation of such facts and alternatives that any foreign policy can be effectively maintained. In an era of supersonic attack and atomic retaliation, extended public debate and education are of no avail, once such a policy must be implemented. The time to study, to doubt, to review and revise is now, for upon our decisions now may well rest the peace and security of the world and, indeed, the very continued existence of mankind. And if we cannot entrust this decision to the people, then, as Thomas Jefferson once said: "If we think them not enlightened enough to exercise their control with a wholesome discretion, the remedy is not to take it from them but to inform their discretion by education."

It seems to us, Mr. President, that all of your comments as Senator in 1954 apply to what your Administration is doing in 1962 in regard to South Vietnam. In 1954 you expressed the belief that "no amount of American military assistance" could bring victory for the United States in Vietnam where there exists "the most difficult terrain in the world." We must have the same doubts about American victory today; and some high Washington officials have themselves conceded that it might take years—perhaps as much as a decade—to defeat the guerrillas of South Vietnam.

Most important of all, as you said in 1954, "The time has come for the American people to be told the blunt truth. . . . We have a right . . . to inquire in detail into the nature of the struggle in which we may become engaged, and the alternative to that struggle." Both Communist China and the Soviet Union have warned the United States Government that its "undeclared war" in South Vietnam constitutes a peril to world peace. Are we running the risk of becoming embroiled in another large-scale conflict such as the Korean War, Mr. President, or even in a nuclear bomb war?

Frankly, we believe that the United States intervention in South Vietnam constitutes a violation of international law, of United Nations principles and of America's own highest ideals. We urge, Mr. President, that you bring this intervention to an immediate end and that you initiate a special international conference to work out a peaceful solution to the crisis in Vietnam, as you have endeavored to do in Laos.

The people of South Vietnam have suffered enough. Having fought eight long years to win independence from France, they have been compelled to fight seven more years, 1955–62, to achieve independence from dictator Diem and the United States, which has maintained him in power. It is time to end the ordeal of the South Vietnamese people and to permit them to enjoy the fruits of liberty and the pursuit of happiness.

Signatories
Roland H. Bainton, Professor of History, Yale Divinity School
Edmund C. Berkeley, Businessman, Newtonville, Massachusetts
Mrs. Elizabeth B. Boyden, Cambridge, Massachusetts
Professor Thomas I. Emerson, New Haven, Connecticut
Royal France, Attorney, New York City
Rev. Stephen H. Fritchman, Unitarian Minister, Los Angeles
Professor Fowler V. Harper, New Haven, Connecticut
James Higgins, Managing Editor, *York Gazette and Daily*
Corliss Lamont, Author and Educator
Rev. Donald G. Lothrop, Minister, Community Church, Boston
Linus Pauling, Physicist (Nobel Prize)
Harry R. Rudin, Professor of History, Yale University
Frederick L. Schuman, Author and Professor of Political Science
Dr. Erling R. Skorpen, Philosophy Department, Yale University
Professor Ralph E. Turner, History Department, Yale University

In April of 1963 my wife Helen and I collaborated in writing a second Open Letter to President Kennedy, for which we obtained sixty-two signatories. We urged him to let the Vietnamese settle their own affairs and bring home all American troops and other military personnel from Southeast Asia. It was published in *The New York Times* of April 3. My wife and I wrote six additional messages on the Vietnamese War that appeared as advertisements in *The Times*, including two Open Letters to President Richard M. Nixon. Here is the text of one of them printed in *The Times* of October 26, 1969:

Mr. Nixon:
The best way to stop inflation is to stop the War! Why not tell us the *whole* truth, Mr. President? The greatest single cause of the high cost of living today is the Vietnam War.

You didn't mention this in your speech about inflation. You didn't tell us that the Vietnam conflict is costing the U.S. taxpayers at least 30 billion dollars a year!

The cost of living has gone up 20 percent since Johnson began to escalate the war in 1965.

This runaway rise in prices parallels the steady rise in U.S. war casualties. From January 1, 1961 through October 18, 1969, the figures are:

Total dead (including non-combat.)   45,871

Total casualties   302,721

More and more businessmen think the war is crippling our economy. The Stock Market has the jitters, and the cost of food, clothing and services keeps on mounting! . . .

Insist on a coalition peace government in Saigon!

Act to stabilize our economy by a total, speedy withdrawal of all U.S. armed forces from Vietnam!

Stop inflation—by stopping the war!

I knew personally only one important American official directly involved in the United States aggression in Vietnam. That was my Harvard classmate, Henry Cabot Lodge, Ambassador to the South Vietnamese Government during both the Kennedy and Johnson Administrations, and a friend in the Harvard Class of 1924. I wrote two Open Letters to him about the situation in Vietnam, the first of which was dated November 1, 1965:

Ambassador Henry Cabot Lodge

U.S. Embassy

Saigon, South Vietnam

Dear Cabot:

You will recall that as classmates in the great Harvard Class of 1924 we both helped to found the Harvard Debating Union during our college days and that you and I had brisk exchanges of opinion at its meetings. Ever since that time, more than forty years ago, we have carried on a running debate concerning basic issues that have confronted our country and the world. You consistently maintained a conservative position, and before long became a prominent member of the Republican Party. I must say that in my judgment you were always one of the better Republicans.

Now our disagreement has become more far-reaching and fundamental than ever because of your active support, as American Ambassador to South Vietnam, of the Johnson Administration's cruel, illegal and immoral war of aggression in Vietnam. Furthermore, you were willing to become Ambassador a second time precisely when Marshal Ky, the new Premier of the South Vietnamese Government, had proclaimed that his great hero was Adolf Hitler.

Like Secretary Rusk and the U.S. State Department, you have pretended that South Vietnam was established as a permanent independent state in the Geneva Accords of 1954, whereas you well know that the division of Vietnam into South Vietnam and North Vietnam was designed as a temporary measure and that the Accords provided for all-Vietnam elections in 1956 to unify that country. You must be aware, too, that it was the United States and its puppet, President Diem of South Vietnam, that refused to permit these elections and thus clearly violated the Geneva treaty.

As Walter Lippmann has pointed out, "While our government endorsed the Geneva agreements, and especially the provision for free elections, it opposed free elections when it realized that Ho Chi Minh (President of North Vietnam) would win them. General Eisenhower states this frankly in his memoirs. Since that time we have insisted that South Vietnam is an independent nation." (*New York Herald Tribune*, April 20, 1965). What all of this adds up to is that in this matter the United States has been guilty of double-dealing and a failure to honor its pledged word.

The inscription on the seal of Harvard is *Veritas*, a motto that has deep meaning for Harvard men. Do you really think, Cabot, that you are serving Truth when you join in distorting the meaning and history of the Geneva Accords that are so basic to understanding the situation in Vietnam?

Again, every objective observer knows that the National Liberation Front in South Vietnam, with its military arm—the so-called Vietcong—is leading a nationalist uprising supported by the vast majority of the population. The fact that Communists strongly back this revolution and share in its leadership does not nullify its indigenous character. What we have here is the resolute and unyielding effort of a former colonial people to assert its freedom. Opposing this is a white Western nation, the U.S.A., determined to reimpose shackles such as France maintained for almost a century. As the noted British historian, Arnold Toynbee, tells us, the Vietcong struggle is part of a world-wide "revolt of the *native* majority of mankind against the domination of the Western minority."

The Vietcong guerrillas possess effective modern weapons in considerable quantity, but only a trickle of arms reached them from North Vietnam (at least up to February 1965). It is the United States that has been the main source of supply. For the guerrillas have obtained their guns chiefly from deserters bringing in American-made arms or by capturing such arms from the apathetic troops of the South Vietnamese Government.

In spite of these well-recognized facts, the U.S. Government last February, when it realized the Vietcong was winning the civil war, suddenly started intensive bombing of Communist North Vietnam on the specious ground that that country all along had been invading South Vietnam and bore the major responsibility for the trouble there. Johnson and his military advisers invented this line in order to justify their own savage aggression against North Vietnam.

This crass propaganda issuing from the White House you, Cabot Lodge, have supported all the way in public statements. In your heart of hearts, can you possibly think that this is *Veritas*? U Thant was right when he said in reference to Vietnam: "In times of war and of hostilities, the first casualty is truth."

You have also misled your fellow-Americans by claiming that the U.S. Government's purpose in Vietnam is to save freedom and establish democracy. In fact, starting with the brutal dictator Diem, the United States has bolstered up one puppet dictatorship after another in Saigon—nine different governments in the past two years—as successive military coups have taken place. These South Vietnamese governments rule through police-state methods of crude violence, terror and torture. None of them would have lasted a week without the military support of the United States. . . .

In all frankness, Cabot, how can you sleep nights when you sanction the horrible and wholesale slaughter by U. S. bombers of women, children and peasants—of noncombatant civilians in general—throughout Vietnam? In the past few months American planes have repeatedly dropped napalm and heavy-duty bombs indiscriminately on South Vietnam villages where a few Vietcong were "reported" to be. Here is what a U.S. Air Force officer recently told the Associated Press: "When we are in a bind, we unload on the whole area in order to save the situation. We usually kill more women and children than we do Vietcong." In North Vietnam, our bombers have destroyed hospitals and patients, schools and schoolchildren, residential houses and civilians. Owing to the terrific bombings in South Vietnam, more than 600,000 destitute refugees have fled to the coastal cities.

You are among those responsible, not only for the killing of scores of thousands of Vietnamese, but also for the death of more than 1,000 American soldiers who have resolutely given up their lives in this futile, useless war 10,000 miles from our Pacific Coast—a madcap adventure in which the United States has already wasted billions of dollars collected from American taxpayers. The probabilities are against our winning this conflict even if our trigger-happy President sends 1,000,000 troops to Vietnam. We cannot win because of the jungle terrain, because the overwhelming majority of the Vietnamese people is opposed to the U.S. intervention and because no stable, effective government can be established in Saigon.

Yet the United States build-up increases at a rapid rate. Some 150,000 U.S. ground troops are in South Vietnam, while thousands more Americans participate in the air from carriers, warships and planes located outside of the country. On June 30, 1964, a well-known U.S. diplomat was asked what he thought would be the consequences of massive involvement in Vietnam. His answer was: "Well, that means we become a colonial power and I think it's been pretty well established that colonialism is over. I believe that if you start doing that you will get all kinds of unfortunate results; you'll stir up anti-foreign feeling; there'll be a tendency to lie back and let the Americans do it and all that. I can't think it's a good thing to do."

My dear classmate, do you know who said that? Why, it was none other than the Honorable Henry Cabot Lodge, then serving his first term as

Ambassador to South Vietnam. So now that long-suffering country is, as implied by your own words, fast becoming a U.S. colony. Are you hoping soon to become governor of the fifty-first American state—South Vietnam?

Please consider carefully that if the President keeps on escalating this Vietnam conflict, and grabbing more and more Asian real estate, the Soviet Union and Communist China will surely react with far more effective countermeasures than they have used hitherto. Herein lies a terrible danger. For continuing escalation could finally erupt into the Great Nuclear War that would bring untold devastation to the U.S.A. and many other countries. Johnson and you, Cabot, are gambling with the survival of our nation and of the human race itself.

Addressing you now as a former Senator, there is a special point I want to make: As a member of the U.S. Senate for many years, you ought to be much concerned with the prerogatives and powers of that august body as set forth in the American Constitution. Today, President Johnson is usurping the functions of both the Senate and the House of Representatives by taking this country into a *de facto* war in Vietnam and thus bypassing the Constitution's pronouncement in Article 1, Section 8, that Congress alone has the power to declare and make war.

You, as an ex-Senator, should be one of the first to protest against the President's dictatorial flouting of the Constitution—an obvious illegality that is contributing toward the breakdown of democratic government in the United States. Another example of Johnson's dangerous misuse of the Executive function was his dispatching of 20,000 Marines to the Dominican Republic last spring to prevent a liberal regime from coming to power. (See Senator Fulbright's notable speech of September 15, 1965.)

I should think that you, Cabot, as a former U.S. Ambassador to the United Nations, pledged to uphold its Charter and international law in general, could not but suffer many qualms of conscience in supporting the President's current foreign policy. For the Administration's brutal course of action in Vietnam flagrantly violates the Charter of the United Nations, the Geneva Accords of 1954, the principles laid down at the Nuremberg Trials of Nazi war criminals and the 1949 Geneva Conventions of the International Red Cross dealing with the "rules of war."

As a member of the United States diplomatic corps, you cannot be unaware that President Johnson's Vietnam venture has seriously set back American influence and prestige virtually everywhere in the world. Johnson has been able, through judicious arm-twisting, to obtain token support here and there, but even America's own allies are really appalled at our Vietnamese policy. On the shelf for the duration are the pressing tasks of working out disarmament agreements regarding both nuclear and conventional weapons. And in general, to cite Walter Lippmann again, "the war in Vietnam is blocking the progress of the nations, including that of Red China itself, toward the peaceable coexistence and accommodation which is the predominant need of all the peoples."

The way out of the Vietnam mess is clear. There must be a cessation of U.S. bombings in all of Vietnam and a general cease-fire; a peace conference that includes the National Liberation Front as an independent authority, as well as the various nations directly involved; and a settlement that returns to the original Geneva Accords. This would mean the complete withdrawal of the United States Army and all other foreign troops from South Vietnam, a guarantee against any foreign military bases in that country, and elections to enable the Vietnamese people freely to choose their own government in accordance with the long-established principles of self-determination.

It is often said that America would lose face if it gets out of Vietnam without winning a clear-cut victory. But the United States has already lost so much face because of its barbaric conduct in Vietnam that this argument has little merit. In all truth, our country would gain great prestige by retiring from Vietnam, just as did France and President de Gaulle when they finally agreed to Algeria's independence.

Of course, a negotiated settlement in Vietnam would be helpful to the Communist countries as well as the capitalist. The self-interest of every nation is served by peace. Thus, the position I have presented is essentially pro-American and pro-humanity. It is a position shared in general by millions of American teachers, students, writers, clergymen and workers, as well as such eminent individuals as President de Gaulle, Senator Gruening, Senator Morse, Professor Linus C. Pauling, Bertrand Russell and Arnold Toynbee.

In conclusion, then, I urge you, Cabot Lodge, to stop abetting President Johnson's evil actions and designs in Vietnam. It would be an enormous pity at this advanced stage of your career for you to fatally tarnish your reputation by qualifying as a leading War Hawk. Resign your ambassadorship and rebuild your public image before it is too late! The highest patriotism is not militaristic; it is to strive for justice and peace and that international amity which is the best assurance for America's national security. Come home and help transform the Republican Party into the great American party of peace, opposed to U.S. military intervention in Asia, Latin America or anywhere else. On that platform you and the Republicans might well win another election.

Sincerely yours,

Corliss Lamont

P.S. Because of the pressing importance of the Vietnam issue, I am treating this communication as an Open Letter and am sending it to our fellow Harvard classmates.

In my Open Letters to President Kennedy and Ambassador Lodge I made no mention of Cambodia (Kampuchea), a nation of about seven million people that had a common border with Vietnam. President Nixon, on the advice of Secretary of State Henry Kissinger, was already bombing Cambodia when Prince Norodom Sihanouk, the peace-loving Chief of State, was ousted in a CIA supported coup in 1970. Thereafter, the air bombardments were stepped up, obliterating villages, ruining farms and crops, killing and maiming hundreds of thousands of peasants. The massive bombing went on for several years and well-nigh destroyed the agricultural and rice economy of Cambodia. Some two million Cambodians starved to death.

During the greater part of three years, President Nixon, while pretending that the U.S. was maintaining strict neutrality, had our Air Force carry out more than 3,500 bombing strikes in Cambodia. The secret was kept by means of the U.S. Air Force falsifying its combat records. The bombings constituted a criminal aggression against a peaceful and innocent population; an immoral, unconstitutional use of Presidential power; and a crass deception of Congress and the American people. The U.S. bombings left Cambodia in shambles and were the main factor in causing an entire decade of horror and suffering for the Cambodian people.

When I reflect on the record of the American Government in Vietnam and Cambodia, I say without hesitation that it represented the most evil series of events in the history of U.S. foreign policy. Some of our government leaders in Washington in those years rivaled the Fascist dictators in their unscrupulous, cruel and inhuman actions. And I feel fully justified in calling them war criminals.

When we add to the Vietnam-Cambodian invasions the 1945 atom bomb massacre of more than 200,000 civilians at Hiroshima and Nagasaki, the 1961 American-backed attempt to overthrow the Castro Government of Cuba through force of arms, and the initiation of the nuclear arms race, the actions of the United States Government—not the people—caused it to stand out as those of a ruthless and mindless giant in the annals of that era.

Chapter XVII   TRIP TO COMMUNIST CHINA

In my 1959 trip around the world I was not able to include mainland China, but made up for that omission in a three weeks' tour in the spring of 1976. My parents had made a similar trip back in 1920. I went to Communist China, with its population mounting steadily toward one billion, on a group tour with twenty-three other Americans from different parts of the United States. Selected as "political activists," they made a congenial and interesting company.

We traveled more than 2,000 miles in China, visiting six major cities—Peking, Anyang, Chengchow, Wuhan, Changsha, Shanghai—and two minor cities, Linshien and Shaoshan, the birthplace of Mao Zedung (for many years spelled Mao Tse Tung), Chairman of the Communist Party. The China Travel Agency was in charge of our trip and did an excellent job throughout. The hotel accommodations were all first-rate and the food quite good on the whole. Arriving at Peking, practically the first thing we learned was that no tips were permitted or received throughout China. This was good news; I have always despised the custom of tipping.

Of course, Peking is one of the most beautiful cities on earth and has many glorious sights. During our first morning we walked through the vast Tien An Men Square, the greatest public gathering place in all China, and then on through the monumental Tien An Men Gate to the Forbidden City, a huge compound where the emperors had lived and to which the ordinary Chinese had been forbidden entrance. Now the City is open to everyone. It is a stunning place with beautiful buildings and pagodas on every hand and interior decorations of high artistic quality. The Forbidden City as a whole is an architectural paradise; and it was for me a profound aesthetic experience equal to that of viewing India's Taj Mahal.

We made all our excursions by bus; the next day we drove to the Great Wall of China, about two hours north of Peking. That famous Great Wall, built to keep the "barbarians" out of China, is eighteen feet wide and extends over valley and mountain for more than 3,000 miles. We were able to walk and climb along it for a half-mile or so. American astronauts circling the earth said that the Great Wall was the only human construction they could see.

In my Peking hotel I enjoyed getting up before breakfast and watching the thousands of workers ride by on their bicycles. Travel by bike extends throughout China, Peking alone has two million bicycles and since there are comparatively few automobiles, buses or trucks, there is virtually no air pollution from machine exhausts in any Chinese city.

The few cars one sees are government owned, used for government business, or belong to foreign embassies. As the magazine *New China* observed: "Will China ever turn to private ownership? Probably not. The Chinese are well aware of the undesirable effects of dependence on private cars in many Western countries—high rates of traffic deaths and injuries, congestion, air and noise pollution, depletion of oil resources, and the high cost of individual upkeep. Producing cars on a large scale would also mean diverting vast resources from projects which have far higher priority for the Chinese, such as mechanizing agriculture and developing a modern industrial state."[1]

A fascinating place near Peking is the Summer Palace, situated on lovely Kun Ming Ho Lake, a retreat for the Chinese emperors and royal families as far back as 1000 A.D. We walked the length of the Long Corridor with its gorgeous Painted Gallery and thence to the fabled Marble Boat. After the British, in savage imperialist style, had burnt down most of the Palace in 1860, the Empress Dowager Tzu Hsi rebuilt it in 1888 with funds that had initially been assigned to the Chinese Navy. Would that we in America could appropriate funds from the Navy to build a splendid palace of art! After the fine luncheon in one of the Palace restaurants, we concluded our visit by going for a jaunt on the lake in a barge towed by a motor launch.

To turn to the Socialist economic system of China: Chairman Mao Zedung and the Communist leadership early decided that agriculture must be given priority in order to feed an enormous population that had often suffered from hunger and famine. There are now few Chinese who are ill fed. We drove out to the Nanyan People's Commune about thirty miles outside Peking, in which there were 10,000 families, 40,000 people and about 5,200 acres of land. A commune consists of villages and collective farms, and is supposed to grow enough food to feed itself and to send its surplus to the national government for distribution in the cities.

The government aims to hold to a minimum the need for transportation and wants each commune to be as self-sufficient as possible. The typical commune not only produces rice, corn and other foods, but also has construction facilities, factories for light industry, retail stores, medical units and a Home for Respect of the Aged. In the Nanyan Commune work is carried on by sixteen production brigades divided into 116 production teams; it possesses a few tractors and trucks, but mechanization is not crucial when so much manpower is available. Each peasant family may, if it so wishes, have a private plot where it can grow its own vegetables.

The Chinese commune is actually a large agricultural-industrial combine and represents the principle of decentralization that is a fundamental feature of the economy. The commune exercises local initiative and responsibility, but operates within the general framework of the governmental nationwide Five-Year Plans. The Soviet Union has been experimenting with a somewhat similar unit called an "obyedinenie" (combination), administered by a Council of Collective Farmers.

Decentralization is also the order of the day in Chinese cities where large living units called "neighborhoods" function efficiently. In Peking we visited the Temple of the Moon Neighborhood with a population of 150,000, four main streets, five hospitals, two clubs, two parks and several medical clinics. Self-sufficiency is the aim and the practice.

While the Communist regime is able to provide the necessities of life for the people, the leadership is fully aware of the magnitude of the population problem. For this reason the authorities recommend that women do not marry until they are twenty-five and men not until they are twenty-eight. Married couples are urged to have no more than two children. Birth control techniques are encouraged; full equality for women is guaranteed as a constitutional right. The Chinese frown upon premarital and extramarital sex. Such practices, the Government believes, take time and energy away from the building of Socialism. Communist China is, at least for the present, puritanical.

From Peking we took the four-hour train ride south to Anwang and the small city of Linshien. I expected to catch up on my reading and managed to get a window seat, but as soon as the train moved out of the city, I noticed a line of small, recently planted trees about fifteen feet beyond the tracks. The light, flickering through the trees, made reading impossible. This experience confirmed the fact that the Chinese have put across a tremendous tree-planting program since the Revolution in 1949 as part of the agricultural upsurge. Trees retain moisture and preserve the soil. The trees that prevented my reading were very likely designed also to screen the passing trains.

Linshien before the Liberation, as the Chinese call the successful Communist Revolution, had been in the center of a vast valley continuously afflicted by drought. There was a fine river, the Changho, on the other side of the mountains, not large but dependable for plenty of water, and the Communists decided to bring that water to the drought-stricken valley by constructing a tunnel right through one of the mountains. The youth in the area were especially important in hewing the "Red Flag Canal" out of solid rock for half a mile and with rather elementary tools. We stood at the exit of the canal from the mountain and watched the water sweep forward to three other main canals connecting with it and thence to a thousand sub-canals that irrigated the whole valley. Inside of two years it became one of the most productive agricultural regions in China. To manage the tons of available water many reservoirs were built, as well as 300 pumping stations and 50 hydro-electric plants.

The Linshien achievement is one of similar irrigation projects that have been completed throughout China. In the old days the two largest rivers, the Yangtze and the Yellow, would overflow their banks every couple of years, with floods that ruined huge portions of farming land and killed millions of peasants. But now the big rivers have been tamed and harnessed for agricultural production. The lands that were formerly flooded are to a large extent being cultivated by the peasants, with vast increases in rice, wheat, corn and other crops, and with agricultural production at least doubled since 1949. I think that the flood control and irrigation throughout China are the most impressive accomplishments of the Communist regime. And I was moved by the sheer drama of it all.

At Linshien we also visited a middle school. There the children, about ten to seventeen, staged a marvelous ballet with singing. The dances were intricate and most professionally performed, and the youngsters were beautiful. This was their program:

1. Welcome Americans
2. Barefoot Doctors are Like Sunflowers
3. Picking Cotton on the Other Side of the Red Flag Canal
4. War Situation Prevails at Red Flag Canal
5. Deliver Grain to the State
6. Singing of a Hundred Birds
7. People of All Nationalities Love our Great Leader, Chairman Mao

I must comment on two of the ballet numbers, and first on the reference in the second event to "Barefoot Doctors." Not long after Liberation the Communist leadership decided that the peasant population was receiving inadequate medical care. Accordingly, Chairman Mao issued a call for medically trained personnel to volunteer for work in the countryside. Thousands of young people responded, especially in the south of China where it tends to be warm, so that the young paramedics, who had had three to six months' training in a hospital, frequently went barefoot. They soon became known as "Barefoot Doctors" and when the movement moved north, though the doctors on the farms and communes wore shoes, the term stuck.

"All Nationalities" in the title of the final ballet refers to the fifty-four national minorities in China, comprising about five percent of the population. Each nationality has a considerable measure of autonomy, with the right to speak its own language, have it taught in the schools and used in newspapers and books. But it is obligatory to learn Chinese. In Peking we spent an entire afternoon at the Institute of Nationalities located in a large complex of buildings.

From Linshien we went by train to Chengchow and Wuhan, cities far in the interior of China, five or six hundred miles from the ocean. At Cheng-chow we stood on the banks of the Yellow River (Huang Ho) and saw the great dike system, and at Wuhan we drove back and forth over the big Yangtze Bridge which the Communists had constructed to connect north China with south China. For thousands of years a ferry was the only way to cross the river.

This was the place where Chairman Mao took his famous swim across the Yangtze in 1966. He later wrote a little poem about it:

> Now I am swimming across the great Yangtze,
> Looking afar to the open sky of Chu.
> Let the wind blow and the waves beat,
> Better far than idly strolling in a courtyard.

Chairman Mao also said, "Swimming is an exercise in struggling with the forces of nature, and you should toughen yourselves in big rivers and seas." The nation has taken up swimming in a big way, and many other sports as well; tens of millions play ping-pong; and the Chinese stress physical exercise programs and setting-up exercises that can be done to the beat of radio music at fixed times during the day.

We made a special visit to the University of Wuhan overlooking a beautiful lake, and received a briefing from a professor of microbiology, Dr. Gow, who spoke perfect English and was most congenial. He had taken his Ph.D. at Yale University in 1935 and also studied at the Rockefeller Institute. On all of our excursions—to schools, factories, neighborhoods, communes and so on—the first thing was tea for all, with a briefing by the head person, translated by one of our interpreters. A member of the group acted as chairman; we asked questions; after they were answered we would go on a tour of the place.

As a teacher, I was selected as chairman at the Wuhan University briefing, and said at the start to Professor Gow: "I bring you greetings from Columbia University where I taught and Harvard University where I graduated." Professor Gow told us that there were 500,000 college students in China. Progress in education has been spectacular under the Communist regime, despite serious setbacks during the Great Cultural Revolution. Illiteracy, which had run to about eighty percent in the old China, had been almost eliminated. Education through the college and graduate school levels was free for all qualified individuals, and university, middle and primary school students made up more than one-fifth of the total population.

At Wuhan we also went through a mammoth factory, an iron-steel combine with six coal mines, four blast furnaces and 70,000 workers, of whom more than 10,000 were women. The lowest wage was 40 yuan per month and the highest was 320 for engineers. From interviews at communes, neighborhoods, factories and educational institutions, we learned that the average wage in China was about 65 yuan a month; with the yuan worth 56 cents, that's about $37.00. Some skilled workers received more than 100 a month.

At the present stage of Chinese Socialism, wages are paid according to the individual's ability and skill, with seniority also a factor. Men and women are paid equally for the same work. Prices are cheap. The average person pays two yuan monthly for full medical care, though it is provided free to trade union members. Rent for a city apartment with four rooms, including kitchen, toilet and running water, costs five yuan a month.

The train we took from Wuhan to Changsha arrived in time for a late supper and as we were entering the dining room at the hotel one of the interpreters appeared, waving a one-yuan note. The interpreter said someone had left the yuan on the train in compartment 18 and would the occupant of No. 18 please claim the note; the person spoke up and recovered his yuan—a nice example of the strict Chinese honesty.

I must add a word about medicine. In the twenty-seven years since the Revolution, the new regime has gone far toward eliminating the main epidemic diseases of China, such as malaria, smallpox, tuberculosis and venereal disease; sanitation too has made enormous strides. It is a healthy country. One morning in Changsha I woke up with a mild cold. It didn't amount to much, but I called in a doctor just to see what it would be like. A pretty young lady of about twenty-five came to my room with an interpreter around 9:30 A.M. I told her I did not feel that the cold was serious, but perhaps she could give me some pills to knock it out. At once she presented me with Vitamin C and Tetracycline, the very pills my New York doctor recommended to stop a cold.

The weather on our trip was mild and sunny, much like New York in the spring. However, there was one day of rain at Changsha, on the afternoon we were supposed to take an airplane for Shanghai. The Chinese are careful about air travel in bad weather and I was happy when they canceled the flight for I was always nervous about flying in a rainstorm. We stayed the day at Changsha and flew to Shanghai the next morning.

Shanghai is the largest city in China, with a population of more than ten million. Our hotel was close to the harbor and it was easy to walk to the edge and see the multitudinous ships go by. It was fascinating, too, to wander out before breakfast to the park strip along the waterfront and watch the Chinese doing their complex setting-up exercises. We visited another school and a recreational center for children called Children's Palace. When I stepped off our bus at the Palace, a lovely little girl of about ten came forward and took me by the hand. Her name was Happy Ting. I found her guidance very touching. She led me to the central room, sat beside me during the briefing, led me to other rooms where various activities were going on, and then led me back to the bus and we said goodbye. The schoolchildren seemed alert, intelligent and hard-working. It was clear from the ballets and other shows they put on for us that they were being well trained in the arts and in aesthetic appreciation.

Though China remains a dictatorship, they rarely shoot dissenters; they "re-educate" them—a procedure that applies as well to the highest officials: Teng Hsiao-ping, dismissed just as everyone thought he would succeed the deceased Chou En-lai (later spelled Zhouenlai) as Premier, was not in jail, but thinking things over and being re-educated. (Mr. Teng made a comeback after Chairman Mao's death, becoming Deputy Prime Minister of the Chinese Government, with his name re-spelled as Deng Xiaoping.) The spirit of re-education and rehabilitation governs the treatment of crimes and disputes. A local Council of Conciliation carries out the main investigation and hearing, attempting to solve through conciliation the problem or controversy in question.

The re-education process applied also to the tens of thousands of prostitutes of the old regime, so that after a period of retraining they became functioning workers in the Socialist system. The regime of Chiang Kaishek, President of China before Liberation, had been notorious for the graft among government officials at all levels; and now it was not only prostitution that had been eliminated, but also opium, harmful drugs, graft and corruption.

In present-day China economic progress will in all probability continue, including more highly developed industry, but the Communists are determined not to tolerate harmful by-products of modern technology, such as pollution of water, air and soil. Experts have been working on these problems. Complete Socialism remains the goal. The spirit of the workers and peasants is summed up by the widely distributed pins reading "Serve the People"—a slogan enlarged on a big streamer in the Shanghai Airport with the quotation from Chairman Mao: "Serve the People of China and the World."

Since Liberation, the standard of living has gone up dramatically in terms of food production, health, housing, clothing, education, employment opportunity, wages and cultural amenities. Everywhere we went the people seemed dynamic, dedicated and fairly happy, but admittedly they were only a tiny segment of the population. At the local level, in commune or factory, there is a good deal of "participatory" democracy; people speak up, criticize and put up large posters with messges. They have a long way to go, however, before achieving complete Socialism.

My most severe criticism is of Communist China's foreign policy, particularly its enmity toward the Soviet Union. Both countries must share some blame for the bad relations between them, but Chinese hostility toward the U.S.S.R. exceeds the bounds of reason and constitutes a sort of compulsive, automatic anti-Sovietism.

The Chinese decry détente between the United States and the Soviet Union and urge America to put an end to it, which would mean a revival of the Cold War. I have worked for American-Soviet cooperation and détente for more than forty years, and find the Chinese position here quite unreasonable and dangerous to peace. I cannot accept their leadership's premise that war between the U.S.A. and the U.S.S.R. is virtually inevitable.

The sound attitude for Americans is to maintain critical sympathy towards both China and the U.S.S.R. and to counsel cooperation in place of hostility between those two great countries. Perhaps we need an American Association for Chinese-Soviet Friendship.

On September 9, 1976, after a long illness, Chairman Mao Zedung died. He was one of the great revolutionary leaders in all history and one of the major statesmen of the modern era. With such able associates as Chou En-lai and Chu Teh, he led the Communist Party against fearful odds to victory in the Revolution of 1949; and despite some crucial mistakes, guided the people toward the new life of Socialism. He was the chief architect of the Cultural Revolution commencing in 1960 which in some ways seriously interfered with the over-all progress China was making, and he also bore primary responsibility for initiating China's bitter anti-Soviet attitude.

Since Mao's death the Government has reversed some of his policies, especially in emphasizing the development of industry and restoring some of the traditional principles and methods in education. But unfortunately this post-Mao regime shows no signs of altering Chinese hostility toward the Soviet Union, which has made repeated overtures to improve the situation.

Even worse than its attitude toward the U.S.S.R. was the Chinese Government's unprovoked invasion of North Vietnam in February, 1979, "to teach the Vietnamese a lesson." Though the Vietnamese Army and civilians resisted heroically, the Chinese penetrated far into the country and left a heavy trail of devastation before withdrawing. In my opinion China's cruel aggression against Vietnam goes far in canceling out the values inherent in the domestic achievements I have described. And the invasion undermines the revered Marxist doctrine that because Socialism cuts away the economic roots of war, therefore Socialist and Communist countries will never initiate military conflict.

In the United States and other Western nations reformers and radicals have been in search of the ideal society where all the basic human values would hold sway. At first they thought that the Russian Revolution and Soviet Socialism would fulfill their dream. But when in the U.S.S.R. the Stalinist regime and continuing Communist dictatorship thwarted the establishment of democracy, social idealists became disillusioned and transferred their hopes to Communist China, under the leadership of Chairman Mao, to bring about the great society. However, Mao is now discredited to a considerable degree and China, still ruled by a dictatorship, is far from being the ideal state. Utopia-seekers must exercise more restraint in this complex and turbulent modern world.

Chapter XVIII   EPILOGUE

In these Memoirs I have told of the things that meant most to me during a crowded and often controversial life, the causes for which I have fought, the ideals I have upheld, the individuals I have admired and the scoundrels I have encountered.

I am using as a departing point for comparisons the election in 1932 of Franklin D. Roosevelt as President of the United States. He assumed office at the depth of the Great Depression, and his New Deal measures bolstered the stricken economy and strengthened it sufficiently for the country to participate successfully in World War II. During three Administrations Roosevelt renewed the morale of the American people, becoming an inspiring leader during the crises of war and peace. I rank F.D.R. as one of the greatest American Presidents.

A terrible setback to political progress in the United States occurred with the assassinations of President John F. Kennedy in November, 1963, and some five years later of his younger brother Robert F. Kennedy in June, 1968, when he was seeking the Democratic Presidential nomination. As leaders of the Democratic Party both Kennedy brothers supported a broad spectrum of liberal policies. I had admired them and their tragic deaths were among the most upsetting events of my life.

It remains to ask whether the causes I have supported made any progress during my lifetime. In the realm of civil liberties there can be no doubt that through the vigorous action of innumerable liberals and leftists we have on the whole registered considerable progress. During the Roosevelt Administrations the American working class made notable gains in the founding of trade unions. In another sector of civil liberties, that of public discussion of sex relations in the written and spoken word, the liberty to disseminate information on birth control and planned parenthood, important gains were won during the Roosevelt years. However, it was not until the Sixties and Seventies that the nationwide and usually successful push for equal rights for women took place, including the right of abortion. Yet in the early Eighties we were still fighting for the adoption of ERA, the Equal Rights Amendment to the United States Constitution.

In the general reaction after World War I and World War II, especially during the McCarthy era, civil liberties lost ground. But the cause of freedom, with substantial aid from the judiciary all the way to the United States Supreme Court, surmounted many of these crises, and forged ahead in the Seventies with special assistance from the Freedom of Information Act. I myself won four important civil liberties cases in the United States courts, while the National Emergency Civil Liberties Committee, of which I was the Chairperson, chalked up many court victories on significant issues. Progress in the actualization of the Bill of Rights has demanded at every juncture a dedicated struggle by concerned Americans.

Even more clearly, noteworthy progress has taken place in civil rights for racial minorities. Early on, I had stated: "Race prejudice, particularly, I have always felt was one of the great abominations of modern society. I can think of nothing more unjust, more cruel, more truly uncivilized than discrimination against individuals or groups because of their color, racial characteristics or ethnic origin." I have long helped support the National Association for the Advancement of Colored People (NAACP) and the National Urban League. And I thought that Hitler's campaign of genocide against the Jews, with the cold-blooded slaughter of at least six million Jews in the European holocaust during World War II, was one of the most horrible happenings in all history.

In America the gravest problem of racial injustice has been suffered by the black minority of some twenty-five million, although Jews, Indians, Orientals, Mexicans, Hispanics and others have suffered severe intolerance. In their long march forward, the blacks received a great impetus in 1954 when the United States Supreme Court, in a unanimous decision, declared that racial segregation in America's public school system was unconstitutional. However, it has been a most difficult task to see that this decision is actually put into effect throughout the country.

In April of 1968 the senseless assassination of the Reverend Martin Luther King, Jr., champion of civil rights and charismatic orator, who in 1964 had won the Nobel Peace Award, was an irretrievable blow to black-white collaboration and black advancement in general.

A serious problem that remains on the agenda for blacks is freedom of housing, the right to live in any neighborhood whatsoever. I was shocked to read in *The New York Times* (August 9, 1979) that the house into which a black family of six had just moved, located in a predominantly white community in Yonkers, New York, had been destroyed in the middle of the night by arsonists. Five members of the family were injured and narrowly escaped with their lives. The County Executive of Westchester, Alfred D.

Del Bello, stated, "This was not an attempt to scare, this was an attempt to kill."

A week later the *Times* reported the burning of a three-foot wooden cross on the front lawn of a Long Island house a few days after a black family had moved into it. In the same issue the *Times* summarized a study by the Regional Plan Association for the New York metropolitan area, which stated that blacks, who represent 12 percent of the region's total population, are confined by racial discrimination to about 1.35 percent of the region's residential land.

Meantime, there has been a resurgence of the vicious Ku Klux Klan throughout the country; and every state now has its Klan chief, known as the Grand Wizard. These various Klan and anti-black happenings show that strong racist feelings continue to exist among the whites of the United States and that in the year 1980 blacks and other ethnic minorities still face a hard struggle for full equality.

Another sector in which freedom has been seriously threatened over the last decade is in what *Time* magazine calls "The Growing Battle of the Books." Private citizens, often parents, and private organizations have increasingly pressured public and school libraries to eliminate and ban books that discuss frankly radical opinions and sex relations. The censors have concentrated on such works of literature as J. D. Salinger's *Catcher in the Rye,* John Steinbeck's *The Grapes of Wrath,* Aldous Huxley's *Brave New World,* Kurt Vonnegut's *Slaughterhouse Five,* Joseph Heller's *Catch-22* and William Shakespeare's *The Merchant of Venice.*

As *Time* puts it, the book vigilantes have been ". . . eager to protect everybody from hazards like ugly words, sedition, blasphemy, unwelcome ideas and, perhaps worst of all, reality. . . ." The chilling effect of censorship, says *Time,* "whether intellectual, political, moral or artistic, is invariably hazardous to the open traffic in ideas that not only nourishes a free society but defines its essence."[1]

Turning to the turbulent arena of labor, we find that trade union organization forged ahead with the Labor Relations (Wagner) Act of 1935, but met many obstacles after World War II. The worst of these was the Labor-Management Relations (Taft-Hartley) Act of 1947 passed over President Truman's veto and bringing into effect unconstitutional restrictions. Some of the bad features of this Act were later repealed. Labor kept fighting and in October, 1980, won a landmark victory when after almost two decades of struggle it obtained a collective bargaining contract from the J.P. Stevens Company of North Carolina. This was not only an important victory in itself, but also proved a great organizing stimulus for labor throughout the South.

The American Federation of Labor and the Congress of Industrial Organizations had merged in 1955—a big stride forward. Yet despite ceaseless efforts, the AFL-CIO have succeeded in organizing only 26 per cent of Americans employed in industry and government.

Unhappily, the trade union movement as a whole, with conservative George Meany as its president for its first twenty-five years, took an anti-liberal course culminating in its support of the American war against Vietnam. A few individual unions, however, opposed Meany's policies. The New York City Teachers Union, of which I was a member, was one of these. There is reason to hope that the AFL-CIO will take a more progressive attitude under the leadership of its new President, Lane Kirkland.

When we ask whether the philosophy of naturalistic Humanism has made progress in general since the publication of *Humanist Manifesto I* in 1933, almost fifty years ago, a definite answer is difficult. Membership in official Humanist organizations such as The American Humanist Association or the Ethical Culture Societies has not notably increased. Pope Pius VI warned that Humanism is the main rival of organized Christianity, but it is a sign of progress that Humanism has become more widely known and that even high authorities of the Catholic and Protestant churches have admitted that it is a viable alternative.

Some Humanist beliefs have penetrated most churches and universities. Furthermore, as Paul H. Beattie, President of the Fellowship of Religious Humanists, states, "Buddhism and Confucianism, two of the great world religions, are both humanistic. They teach no concept of supernaturalism. They do teach an ethic of reason and compassion, each religion providing its unique 'enlightenment.' Buddhists find freedom from suffering, and Confucianists achieve the balance that grows out of a study of the Chinese classics. More than half the world's people today, those touched by Confucianism and Buddhism, come from a religious and cultural background that is non-theistic and, in effect, Humanist. This striking fact augurs well for the Humanist prospect."[2]

On the negative side there has been a widespread revival in the traditional religions and fundamentalism, with their spokesmen denouncing secular Humanism as the great enemy, a spiritually corrupting influence. In some quarters Humanism has replaced Communism as chief scapegoat. Also we have witnessed an alarming outburst of bizarre religious cults such as "Jesus freaks," Hare Krishna groups, devotees of astrology, Devil Worshippers, spiritualists, the followers of Sun Myung Moon ("Moonies"), and believers in one form or another of the paranormal. Throughout the Middle East a militant Islamism is on the rise; and the Soviet Union is worried about adverse effects on its Transcaucasian republics such as Azerbaijan where there is a large Moslem population.

Most menacing on the American scene is the so-called Moral Majority, which has played an active role in conservative politics and spent huge sums of money for radio and TV propaganda on behalf of fundamentalist religion. The Moral Majority calls for a "Christian Bill of Rights" and a "Christian America," thus threatening the separation of Church and State, and America's principle of religious pluralism. Members of this group are prominent among the complainants who are demanding the removal of books they disapprove from public libraries.

In the condemnation of secular Humanism, spokesmen for the Moral Majority have singled me out for attack on television, radio and in published media. In the onslaught on Humanism the Moral Majority relies heavily on a muddleheaded book, *The Battle for the Mind* (1980)[3] by Tim LaHaye, which quotes extensively from my volume, *The Philosophy of Humanism*. He prints no fewer than twenty-nine passages from my book. Showing his lack of objectivity and unfairness to Humanism, LaHaye at no point makes clear that this way of life incorporates many of the ethical principles of Christianity, such as certain tenets of the Ten Commandments and much of the teachings of Jesus.

We have also had frightful examples of fanatical religion on the loose in extremist death-dealing actions. The most shocking came in October of 1978 when the civilized world was aghast over the mass suicide of some 900 members of the People's Temple, a recently organized American religious cult, at Jonestown in the tiny country of Guyana in South America. The leader of this esoteric cult was the Reverend Jim Jones, who had extraordinary powers of eloquence and persuasion over his followers. He promised them a beautiful and happy immortality after death and told them that the time to die was at hand if they would join him in a delicious drink, which was actually a mixture of cyanide and purple Kool Aid. That hundreds of adult Americans, healthy of body but sick of mind, should literally carry out this directive shows to what dangerous extremes fanatical religion can go and the deep-felt lure of belief in blissful survival beyond the grave. A recent poll claimed that 69 percent of American adults had faith in an afterlife.

The Humanist movement itself has been weakened by a large amount of infighting, so that no effective unity has emerged among freethinkers, rationalists, atheists and Humanists. Strife has too often taken more of their energy and time than the exposure of religious myth and superstition. But there is an important exception in the cooperation of Humanists and the Ethical Culture Societies for half a century.

In environmental control, spectacular progress has been registered. The public has awakened to the necessity of curbing industrial assaults on forests, rivers and waterfronts; and of conserving the natural beauty and wildness that are such a magnificent part of the American heritage. City, state and national measures have been put into effect to offset pollution of air, earth and water. And the Federal Government has recognized these problems by establishing the Environmental Protection Agency.

As for democratic Socialism, it attained its greatest strength in the United States in the general election of 1912, when I was only ten years old and completely unaware of the meaning and management of a Socialist society. In that year Eugene V. Debs polled 901,000 votes as the candidate of the Socialist Party for President, and more than 340 cities and towns elected about 1,200 members of the Party to public office, including seventy-three as mayors. The Party's official weekly publication, *The Appeal to Reason*, attained a circulation of more than 700,000. The outlook was promising.

But World War I and the Russian Revolution of 1917 had immense effects upon all radical groups. The American Socialist Party split apart and an American Communist Party was established. By the time in the middle Thirties when I became a serious supporter of Socialism, the Socialist movement in the United States was at a low ebb.

That is only part of the story, however. For the U.S. Government has put into effect social welfare programs, such as unemployment insurance, Social Security and Medicare, that had been stressed in the political platforms of Socialist and Communist parties. In Europe the nationalization of railroads and some industries has taken place. But real nationwide Socialist planning exists only in Communist countries where dictatorships are still in power and where civil liberties and other democratic institutions are but slightly developed. I am unwilling to say that Socialism has arrived unless democracy is part of it.

During the twentieth century we find that the capitalist system has gone through repeated crises that have weakened it. First there was the big stock crash of 1929 with the resulting Great Depression, to which only the onset of World War II in 1939 brought an end. After World War II, capitalism was again afflicted by enormous unemployment and economic recession. Then in 1978 an energy crisis arose when the Arab countries in the Middle East suddenly raised the price of oil substantially. For several months in 1979 a gasoline shortage hit America; one could obtain gas only by waiting in long lines at service stations; the price of gas shot up and increased the general inflation that had been under way.

In a letter carried by *The New York Times* (October 2, 1979), I commented on the close relationship between inflation and armaments:

"The worst problem facing the nation is our severe and continuing inflation, which *Business Week* calls 'the worst, most prolonged and most pernicious' in our history. The primary cause is, as Professor Seymour Melman of Columbia University has stated, the colossal military expenditures of the U.S. Department of Defense. The 1979 military budget has risen to $137 billion, and the Pentagon is demanding $172.2 billion by 1982. President Carter has also given the go-ahead for the mad MX missile program which will cost at least $40 billion.

"Meanwhile, the Soviet Union, although also spending huge sums on armaments, has relatively little inflation because its planned socialist system includes strict, though flexible, wage and price controls.

"America's ever increasing military budgets, instead of strengthening our defenses, are steadily weakening our economy through inflation. Clearly, the cure is drastic reduction of our armaments budgets and cooling the arms race. The first steps are ratification of SALT II by the Senate, followed by the Administration starting an all-out drive for world-wide reduction in both conventional and nuclear weapons."

During the Seventies inflation steadily increased in the capitalist countries and in the United States in 1980 was 13.5 percent for the year. Early in 1979 the Chrysler automobile company had announced that it needed a government loan of $1 billion to keep afloat, and obtained it. Commenting on this situation, Professor John Kenneth Galbraith, the most able economist in the English-speaking world, said: "It is now amply established in all of the industrial countries that if a corporation is large enough it can no longer be allowed to fail and go out of business. So it was with Lockheed and the Eastern railroads in this country, Leyland and Rolls Royce in Britain and dozens of large French and Italian firms. Socialism in our times comes not from socialists but from the heads of a large corporation when they learn from their bankers that resort must be had to the government—and fast."[4] Corporate Socialism seems to be a real possibility.

Some of America's most eminent capitalists have seen the handwriting on the wall and believe that capitalism must be drastically reformed, if not discarded. Among them have been Cyrus Eaton, former Chairman of the Board of the Chesapeake and Ohio Railway; Edward Lamb, the remarkably successful Ohio business executive; and John D. Rockefeller 3rd, eldest of five Rockefeller brothers and noted for his wise and generous philanthropy. He was Chairman of the Rockefeller Foundation for nineteen years and instrumental in the creation of Lincoln Center for the Performing Arts.

Mr. Rockefeller was also the author in 1973 of a little-known book, *The Second American Revolution*.[5] This second revolution is taking place because of the enormous economic growth and technological development in the United States, containing within it the Black Revolution, the Youth Revolution and the Women's Revolution. Rockefeller calls for "Humanistic capitalism" and makes the radical suggestion that to defeat poverty, "The best prospect seems to lie in some form of the guaranteed annual income." Most significant of all, he adopts the prime Socialist aim, that of a planning society. Actually, he goes quite far in the direction of democratic Socialism.

The gist of all this is that Socialism may arrive in the United States, not through the formation of new political parties, but through recognition by the Establishment or the major parties that the economic situation demands it. Inflationary capitalism may lead into some sort of planned Socialism. In any event, the case for democratic Socialism in the United States is stronger than ever as capitalism staggers from crisis to crisis.

Whether or not progress has been made in the various fields I have analyzed in this chapter, the fearsome shadow of nuclear war hangs over all of them. During the twentieth century there have been two terrible world wars, and now the danger looms of a third World War far more terrible because of the possibility that nuclear weapons may be unleashed by the Great Powers. A nuclear conflict involving the United States and the Soviet Union would be so destructive, not alone for those two countries but for the entire world, that it would cancel out much of the progress made by the human race, wiping out whole civilizations.

It is not sufficiently realized that the fallout from the explosion of nuclear weapons will not only bring death over vast expanses of the earth, but will make it impossible for life to revive in those poisoned lands for thousands and thousands of years. A nuclear war would be a world doomsday. Even the wastes generated by nuclear power plants will, according to informed scientific opinion, remain toxic for thousands of years; and so far no viable plan has been developed to dispose safely of these wastes.

I am among those who favor the destruction of all nuclear weapons before they destroy us. Not much progress has been made toward that objective. American-Soviet negotiations for the control of nuclear weapons culminated in 1980 in the mild provisions of the Strategic Arms Limitation Treaty (SALT II). But U.S. Senate approval of that treaty was put off by the election of Ronald Reagan and a Republican Senate majority. Since the United States was the nation that first made atom bombs, and used them in 1945 in the hideous and unnecessary attacks on Japan, this country has a special moral obligation to help bring about the control and ultimate elimination of nuclear weapons. However, the United States had for several decades lagged in international efforts on behalf of that goal. The tentative rejection of SALT II, although the Soviet Government had ratified it, was another instance of U.S. non-cooperation for peace.

Professor Galbraith made a significant statement about those in America supporting the arms race: "It's a mistake to attribute everything to the corporate interest in arms expenditure. We have a big bureaucratic interest, too. The military-industrial complex—to use President Eisenhower's famous and very valuable reference—includes the public bureaucracy as well as the vast private bureaucracy, the vast private corporations. And there's a tendency among liberals—people who are concerned with this problem—to attribute everything to the private corporations. It is the juncture of power between the public and the private bureaucracies that is important here."[6]

Turning to another sector of international affairs, I find most heartening the progress made in the winning of independence by colonial peoples from imperialist rule. This has happened in practically all the colonial domains of Africa and Asia. In those two continents more than seventy former colonies have achieved freedom since World War II and are now self-ruled. But there is an underlying dilemma in the situation. The imperialist powers did not attempt to train the subject peoples in the art of self-government or to educate them in general. Hence the colonial countries have had a difficult time in establishing stable governments, and most of them have gone over to dictatorships.

In an interview with James Reston, Zbigniew Brzezinski, President Carter's National Security Adviser, with whom I have usually disagreed, made some relevant remarks about the new nation-states: "I think the most fundamental force of change in our time is the massive awakening of man politically and socially. This has happened within your lifetime and mine. Even a few decades ago, most of the world was organized on the basis of colonial empires that dominated much of Asia and Africa, or of political systems in which participation of the people was very limited. In our lifetimes, empires have crumbled, the number of nation-states has more than quadrupled, literacy has spread, people are more concentrated in cities, more susceptible to mass political mobilization and to mass communications. There is a new world-wide social and political consciousness which has never existed before." (*The New York Times Magazine*, December 31, 1978.)

I think that my life on the whole has been meaningful, worthwhile and reasonably happy. I have written some significant books, spoken widely on important subjects over radio and TV, and worked with institutions of value to the community. As a radical and civil libertarian I have taken part in many a fight for human rights and have usually enjoyed the fray.

The many warm responses to my activities have been a constant encouragement to me through the years, and I remember with particular gratitude two or three assessments. The first was a kind of epitaph on my efforts for civil liberties by Republican Senator William Langer on the floor of the Senate in 1957 in reference to the courts dismissing my McCarthy indictment for contempt of Congress: "I believe that Mr. Lamont rendered a great public service to the people of the United States in standing upon his rights as a private citizen and refusing to answer the questions involving his private life and private beliefs, and that he is to be congratulated upon his complete vindication by the court of appeals. Through the many years of his life, Mr. Lamont has demonstrated time and again that he is in the very forefront in the fight to concentrate his efforts to protect the rights of private individuals, and I feel that all liberty-loving men and women in this country, who believe in our Constitution and particularly the Bill of Rights, should feel indebted to him."

And I was also grateful for Edward Lamb's statement written for *Free Mind* (1976), a periodical published by the American Humanist Association: "When I think of Humanism, I think of my preceptor, Corliss Lamont. To even think of Corliss Lamont is to become attuned to controversy. Big controversy. Not low-brow, alley brawling, but the high level weighing of human values. The ideology of men and women trying to determine their own destiny.

"For more than five decades, ever since we were rebellious students—he at Harvard University and I at Dartmouth College—his identity with the cause of human freedoms and civil liberties constituted the torch by which many Americans found their paths to fuller, more enriching lives. He wrote *Issues of Immortality* in 1932. His magnificent work, *The Philosophy of Humanism* (1949 and revised in 1965), encouraged us to look beyond traditional dogma towards a rational coexistence with all of Nature. For we laymen, mired down with the limitations of formal ideologies, preferred to discover the path to the viable life where we could help, in a small way, the improvement in the lot of our fellow men.

"Professor of philosophy, author, builder of bridges of friendship among nations of differing social systems, Corliss Lamont descended into the market place of the activist life, not in chasing political honors for himself, but in progressive reforms for the betterment of the human condition. An unstable, irrational and shaky capitalist America screams out for quick correction. A more equitable sharing of our assets must take place in the United States and among all the peoples of the world—and those leaders of society like Corliss Lamont should feel honored to be labelled radicals, Communists or whatever as they point the way to the future. Oblivious to the witch-hunt, they exercise leadership and concentrate on the fundamental privileges of the human race."[7]

And lastly I feel privileged to quote from a heartwarming letter written me by a fellow Humanist, Gerald A. Larue, Professor of Biblical History and Archeology, which said in part: "I am proud to be associated, however tangentially, with persons like yourself. Your pioneering work in developing the A.H.A. [American Humanist Association], in defending civil liberties and in expressing humanistic philosophy are very impressive. What a role model! . . . Inspired by you and persons like you, I am determined to do my bit. Thank you for what you mean to so many of us."

Although I suffered greatly in the divorce of my first wife Margaret, and in the premature death of my second wife Helen, I have had beautiful and affectionate children and grandchildren, who are in a special and wonderful class by themselves. I have had a loving relationship with my many relatives, the Lamont Circle, as I call them; and have taken profound pleasure in my many friends from all sorts of walks of life. I tried to express my feelings toward them in a Christmas card I sent out in 1980:

> I am wishing you a very merry Christmas and a very happy New Year.
> But I want to say much more than that. I want to tell you how glad and grateful I am that you are my friend, that over the years I have had a chance to share with you personal warmth, intellectual excitement and the flow of joyous experience. These deep and enduring relationships are what count most in life. I wish that during these holidays of happiness and human brotherhood I could enjoy your company.

In the swift pace of modern life, with all its pressures, meetings, committees and other distractions, I have not seen you nearly so often as I should like. Yet I am sure you know that my feeling of friendship remains the same. If only somehow I had the power to reach out and embrace all of my friends and relatives at once wherever they may be throughout America and the world! If only I could tell each one of you face to face how much you have meant to me and drink a toast with each of you for a joyful 1981!

Those are my thoughts for this holiday season and I send them to you in all affection.

Looking back on my life during the writing of these Memoirs, I came to realize more fully the large extent to which I have been involved in battles of one kind or another. Starting with my exposé of baseball trickery in my school days and my endeavor to have radical speakers invited to Harvard, I went on to fiercer struggles in the larger world, especially court cases concerning civil liberties and the unconstitutional practices of Congressional investigating committees and government agencies. Now, as I conclude this volume, I am still fighting the FBI in the courts to obtain its complete file on me, and, as I said earlier, defending Humanism against the scurrilous attacks of the Moral Majority. Yes, in one sense my life has been a ceaseless series of battles and crusades.

Yet there has been time for plenty of recreation. I have immensely enjoyed a large variety of sports and visits to America's magnificent National Parks. And I have had the pleasure of traveling far and wide both in the United States and abroad. Truly my existence has been one of constant opportunities and precious experiences. And I am full of gratitude to those dear relatives, friends, co-workers, fellow teachers, secretaries and the many others who have made possible such an abundant life.

Delving into my past has evoked both happy and painful memories. I am now more aware of serious mistakes I have made, of opportunities lost and time wasted. If I have had my share of bad luck, I have experienced a large measure of good luck, and on the whole life has been fulfilling for me.

The time and place of one's birth and one's parentage are matters of chance. It was my good fortune to enter into life at the beginning of a century that has probably been the most eventful in history. It has been a remarkable spectacle. I have been witness to two frightful World Wars, two epoch-making Communist revolutions, the winning of freedom by virtually all the African and Asian peoples under imperialist rule, and the maturing of technological wonders—the electric light, the typewriter and the telephone, the automobile and the airplane, radio and television, nuclear energy and the exploration of space. The sheer excitement of living in the twentieth century has been like that of watching an absorbing drama unfold at the theatre—but here what has unfolded is living history.

I do not think that there is any lost cause among the causes for which I have worked. With life viable upon this planet for billions of years, we must consider that the human race is still in its early stages. A long future is open for the achievement of civil rights, democratic Socialism, the Humanist way of life and international peace at last. Nearing the age of eighty I am still actively participating in such causes. I do not intend ever to retire.

The extraordinary success of President Ronald Reagan and the Republican Party in the 1980 elections meant a setback for liberal and radical political aspirations in the United States, but in the long perspective of history it is likely to prove a temporary aberration. After all, Reagan received only twenty-six percent of the possible electoral vote. Many liberals and leftists were galvanized into more vigorous action because of the extent of the conservative victory. And they will make every effort to curb any illiberal measures at home or dangerous, provocative policies abroad. For instance, we must be on guard against the Senate Subcommittee on Security and Terrorism established in December, 1980 by the reactionary Republican Senator, Strom Thurmond, as Chairperson of the Senate Judiciary Committee.

My final word is that in the battles that confront us today for America's freedom and welfare, our chief aim as public-spirited citizens must be neither to avoid trouble, nor to stay out of jail, nor even to preserve our lives, but to *keep on fighting* for our fundamental principles and ideals. Our central purpose is not a ripe old age—although somehow I have achieved it—but the generous expenditures of our energies for the good of our fellow citizens and the well-being of humanity.

Fighters for freedom throughout history have had to face ordeals similar to ours. We should remember that American liberals and radicals in general have suffered comparatively little as compared with their opposite numbers in Europe and Asia during the twentieth century.

I think that as we grow older, we ought to grow more active rather than more timorous about the basic progressive issues. For we who have lived half a century or more have already enjoyed a very interesting and varied existence with probably a good deal of personal happiness. No dictator, no demagogue, no tyrannical government, can take away our past. True, they may interfere with our future, but the important thing is that we should continue to resist and combat misguided men and evil institutions as long as our hearts go on beating.

Our permanent rebellion is not a matter of force and violence; it is the daily rebellion of our spirits against the injustices perpetrated by the cruel, the uninformed, the selfish, and the short-sighted. In our struggle for a better world, we find a constant challenge to our intelligence, our ability, our perseverance in the face of heavy odds. And we march forward with sensitive and courageous men and women who are the salt of the earth. For my own part I must admit that nothing gives me greater pleasure than a good fight in a good cause. And if in my remaining years I can make a worthwhile contribution to society, I shall be happy indeed.

REFERENCE NOTES

Citations or quotations within the text which do not give full titles or dates are given in this section.

CHAPTER I—FAMILY BACKGROUND

1. *True Relation of Sir James Lamont of that Ilk, His Actings and Sufferings* (c. 1661).
2. Thomas W. Lamont, *My Boyhood in a Parsonage* (New York: Harper & Brothers, 1946).
3. Corliss Lamont, (ed.) *Man Answers Death* (New York: G. P. Putnam's Sons, 1936).
4. ———, *Lover's Credo* (Cranbury, N.J.: A. S. Barnes & Co., 1972).
5. Anatoli Vasilyevich Lunacharsky, Russian writer, quoted in Louise Bryant, *Mirrors of Moscow* (New York: Thomas Seltzer, 1923) p. 71.

CHAPTER II—SCHOOL, COLLEGE AND MARRIAGE

1. Anne M. Lindbergh, *Bring Me a Unicorn* (New York: Harcourt Brace Jovanovich, 1972).
2. ———, *Gift From the Sea* (New York: Pantheon Books, Inc., 1955) p. 115.
3. John H. Randall, *The Making of the Modern Mind* (Boston and New York: Houghton Mifflin, 1926).
4. Corliss Lamont, *Humanism as a Philosophy,* later retitled *The Philosophy of Humanism* (New York: Philosophical Library, 1952) and Fifth Ed. (New York: Frederick Ungar Publishing Co., 1965).
5. Helen B. Lamb, *Vietnam's Will to Live: Resistance to Foreign Aggression from Early Times Through the Twentieth Century* (New York: Monthly Review Press, 1972).
6. ———, *Studies on India and Vietnam* ed. Corliss Lamont (New York: Monthly Review Press, 1976).
7. Corliss Lamont, "Victory," *Lover's Credo,* p. 63.

CHAPTER III—FIRST TRIP TO THE SOVIET UNION

1. Corliss Lamont, co-author with Margaret I. Lamont, *Russia Day by Day* (New York: Covici-Friede, 1933).
2. ———, *The Peoples of the Soviet Union* (New York: Harcourt Brace & Co., 1946).
3. ———, *Soviet Civilization* (New York: Philosophical Library, 1952 and 1955.).

CHAPTER IV—BASIC BELIEFS

1. *New Leader,* Oct. 14, 1942.
2. Corliss Lamont, *Freedom of Choice Affirmed* (New York: Horizon Press, 1967 and 1981).
3. ———, *The Illusion of Immortality* (New York: G. P. Putnam's Sons, 1935) Walter J. Black, 1946) Bk. III, lines 448 ff.
4. ———, *The Independent Mind* (New York: Horizon Press, 1951).

CHAPTER V—SPORTS AND RECREATION

1. Norman Rosten, "The Ballad of Mount Snow" (unpublished).
2. John Masefield, "The Western Hudson Shore" in *The Thomas Lamonts in*

America, Corliss Lamont (ed.) (privately printed, 1962), also Folkways Records FL 9843, 1977.

3. Corliss Lamont, "Palisades Memoir," *Lover's Credo,* p. 21.
4. Albert Rhys Williams, *Through the Russian Revolution* (New York: Boni & Liveright, Inc., 1921).
5. ———, *Journey Into Revolution: Petrograd 1917-18* (New York: Quadrangle Press, 1969).

CHAPTER VI—THE MYTH OF IMMORTALITY

1. Homer, *The Odyssey,* xi, 489.
2. Richard Haitch, *The New York Times,* Feb. 8, 1981, p. 41.
3. Lucretius, *On the Nature of Things,* trans. Charles E. Bennett (New York: Walter J. Black, 1946) Dk. III, lines 448 ff.
4. H. L. Mencken, *Treatise on the Gods* (New York: Alfred A. Knopf, 1930).
5. Harlow Shapley, "We Are Not Alone," *The Christian Register,* July, 1956, p. 38.

CHAPTER VII—THE PHILOSOPHY OF HUMANISM

1. William James, *The Principles of Psychology* (New York: Holt, 1923) Vol. I, p. 348.
2. Corliss Lamont, *Freedom of Choice Affirmed,* op. cit.
3. Robert C. Johansen, *The Churchman,* Feb. 1981.
4. Morris B. Storer, (ed.) *Humanist Ethics* (Buffalo: Prometheus Books, 1980) pp. 1-2.
5. John Dewey, *Experience and Nature* (Chicago & London: Open Court Publishing Co., 1925).
6. ———, *How We Think* (Boston: D. C. Heath & Co., 1910).
7. ———, *Ethics* in *The Encyclopedia Americana* (New York: *Scientific American,* 1903-06, Vol. VII).
8. ———, *Reconstruction in Philosophy,* Enlarged Ed. (Boston: The Beacon Press, 1948).
9. ———, *Poems,* Jo Ann Boydston (ed.) (Carbondale, Ill.: Center for Dewey Studies, Southern Illinois University Press, 1977).
10. ———, *Democracy and Education* (New York: The Macmillan Co., 1916).
11. ———, *A Common Faith* (New Haven: Yale University Press, 1934).
12. Corliss Lamont (ed.) *Dialogue on John Dewey* (New York: Horizon Press, 1959 and 1981).
13. Frederick Matthias Alexander, *Man's Supreme Inheritance* (New York: E. P. Dutton & Co., 1918).
14. Bertrand Russell, *Marriage and Morals* (New York: Horace Liveright, 1929).
15. Corliss Lamont, *Freedom Is As Freedom Does: Civil Liberties in America,* Third Printing (New York: Horizon Press, 1956 and 1981).
16. Erich Fromm, "Prophets and Priests" in *Bertrand Russell, Philosopher of the Century,* Ralph Schoenman (ed.) (Boston: Atlantic Little Brown, 1967) p. 79.
17. George Santayana, *Soliloquies in England* (New York: Charles Scribner's Sons, 1923).
18. ———, *The Last Puritan* (New York: Charles Scribner's Sons, 1936).
19. ———, *The Life of Reason—Reason in Common Sense; Reason in Religion; Reason in Society; Reason in Art; Reason in Science* (New York: Charles Scribner's Sons, 1905 and 1906).
20. ———, *Interpretations of Poetry and Religion* (New York: Charles Scribner's Sons, 1905) p. 250.

21. ———, *Reason in Common Sense*, p. 21.
22. ———, ibid., p. 284.
23. ———, *Soliloquies in England*, p. 43.
24. Corliss Lamont (ed.) *Dialogue on George Santayana* (New York: Horizon Press, 1959 and 1981).

CHAPTER VIII—THE MASEFIELD SAGA

1. John Masefield, *The War and the Future* (New York: The Macmillan Co., 1918).
2. ———, *In The Mill* (New York: The Macmillan Co., 1941) p. 97.
3. ———, "The Western Hudson Shore," op. cit.
4. ———, *Salt-Water Ballads* (London: Grant Richards, 1902).
5. ———, *The Widow in the Bye Street* (London: Sidgwick and Jackson, 1912).
6. ———, *Reynard the Fox* (New York: The Macmillan Co., 1919).
7. ———, *Right Royal* (New York: The Macmillan Co., 1920).
8. ———, *Dauber* (London: William Heinemann, 1913).
9. ———, *The Everlasting Mercy* (New York: The Macmillan Co., 1912).
10. ———, *Gallipoli* (London: William Heinemann, 1916).
11. ———, *The Nine Days Wonder* (London: William Heinemann, 1941).
12. G. Wilson Knight in Geoffrey Handley-Taylor, *John Masefield, O. M., The Queen's Poet Laureate: A Bibliography and 81st Birthday Tribute* (London: Cranbrook Tower Press, 1960) p. 9.
13. John Masefield, *Collected Poems* (London: William Heinemann, 1924).
14. ———, *Lollingdon Downs* (New York: The Macmillan Co., 1917).
15. ———, "No Man Takes the Farm" in *Lollingdon Downs*, op. cit.
16. ———, "Sonnet V," ibid.
17. ———, *Good Friday* (New York: The Macmillan Co., 1916).
18. ———, "August, 1914" in *Philip the King and Other Poems* (London: William Heinemann, 1914).
19. ———, *The Trial of Jesus* (London: William Heinemann, 1925).
20. Corliss Lamont, *Remembering John Masefield* (Cranbury, N.J.: Fairleigh Dickinson University Press, 1971).
21. ——— and Lansing Lamont (eds.) *Letters of John Masefield to Florence Lamont* (New York: Columbia University Press, 1979).
22. John Masefield, *Wonderings (Between One and Six Years)* (New York: The Macmillan Co., 1943).

CHAPTER X—ADVENTURES IN CIVIL LIBERTIES

1. *St. Louis Star Journal*, Dec. 1932.
2. Henry Steele Commager in *New York Herald Tribune Book Review*, Dec. 9, 1951, p. 1.
3. *Toronto Globe and Mail*, May 10, 1956.
4. Justice Douglas in *Lamont* v. *Postmaster General*, Apr., 1965.
5. Judge Weinstein in *Lamont* v. *CIA*, Feb., 1978.
6. *Letters and Other Writings of James Madison* (Philadelphia: J. B. Lippincott & Co., 1865) Vol. II, p. 141.

CHAPTER XI—VICTORY OVER SENATOR McCARTHY

1. Ernest J. Simmons (ed.) *U.S.S.R., A Concise Handbook* (Ithaca: Cornell University Press, 1947).
2. *The New York Times*, Sept. 25, 1953.
3. *The Washington Post*, editorial, Sept. 29, 1953.

4. Philip Wittenberg (ed.) *The Lamont Case: History of a Congressional Investigation* (New York: Horizon Press, 1957) p. 73.

CHAPTER XII—THE AMERICAN CIVIL LIBERTIES UNION

1. Corliss Lamont (ed.) *The Trial of Elizabeth Gurley Flynn by the American Civil Liberties Union* (New York: Horizon Press, 1968).
2. Carey McWilliams, *The Nation,* July 3, 1976, p. 4.

CHAPTER XIII—DEMOCRATIC SOCIALISM

1. Fairfield Osborn, *Our Plundered Planet* (Boston: Little, Brown & Co., 1948).
2. John Reed, *Ten Days That Shook the World* (New York: Boni & Liveright, 1919, International Publishers, 1926, and Modern Library, 1935).
3. Granville Hicks, *John Reed—The Making of a Revolutionary* (New York: The Macmillan Co., 1936).

CHAPTER XIV—MARRIAGE WITH VARIETY

1. Sir Julian Huxley, *Memories II* (London: Allen and Unwin, 1973) p. 246.
2. George Santayana, *Reason in Society,* op. cit., p. 32.
3. Bertrand Russell, *Marriage and Morals,* op. cit., pp. 123-24.
4. Rollo May, *Love and Will* (New York: W. W. Norton & Co., 1969) p. 316.
5. Walter Lippmann, *A Preface to Morals* (New York: Macmillan, 1929) p. 309.
6. Corliss Lamont, *Lover's Credo,* op. cit. p. 62.
7. D. H. Lawrence, "Both Sides of the Medal" in *Look! We Have Come Through* (New York: B. W. Huebsch, 1918) pp. 87-88.
8. Nena and George O'Neill, *Open Marriage: A New Life-Style for Couples* (New York: M. Evans & Co., 1972) p. 250.

CHAPTER XV—TRAVELS FAR AND WIDE

1. George Gordon, Lord Byron, "The Isles of Greece" from *Don Juan,* Canto III.
2. Walter Lippmann, *New York Herald Tribune,* Dec. 11, 1959.
3. Arthur Bonner, "India's Masses," *The Atlantic Monthly,* Oct. 1959, p. 50.
4. George Santayana, *Persons and Places* (New York: Charles Scribner's Sons, 1944) pp. 96-97.

CHAPTER XVII—TRIP TO COMMUNIST CHINA

1. Chieu Chang, "Private Cars? Who Needs Them?" *New China,* Sept. 1976, pp. 11-13.

CHAPTER XVIII—EPILOGUE

1. Frank Trippett, "The Growing Battle of the Books," *Time,* Jan. 19, 1981, pp. 85-86.
2. Paul H. Beattie, "The Prospect for Humanism," *Religious Humanism,* Vol. XIII, No. 4, Autumn, 1979.
3. Tim LaHaye, *The Battle for the Mind* (Old Tappan, N.J.: Fleming H. Revell Co., 1980).
4. John Kenneth Galbraith, *Washington Post,* Oct. 3, 1979.
5. John D. Rockefeller, *The Second American Revolution* (New York: Harper & Row, 1973) p. 89.
6. John Kenneth Galbraith, *In The Public Interest,* Nov. 1980, Vol. 8, No. 7, p. 2.
7. Edward Lamb, "On a Great Leader," *Free Mind,* Jan.-Feb. 1976, p. 4.

Index